TRAVELERS' TALES BOOKS

Country and Regional Guides
America, Australia, Brazil, Central America, Cuba, France,
Greece, India, Ireland, Italy, Japan, Mexico, Nepal, Spain,
Thailand; American Southwest, Grand Canyon, Hawai'i,
Hong Kong, Paris, San Francisco, Tuscany

Women's Travel
Her Fork in the Road, A Woman's Path, A Woman's
Passion for Travel, A Woman's World, Women in the Wild,
A Mother's World, Safety and Security for Women
Who Travel, Gutsy Women, Gutsy Mamas

Body & Soul
The Spiritual Gifts of Travel, The Road Within,
Love & Romance, Food, The Fearless Diner, The Adventure
of Food, The Ultimate Journey, Pilgrimage

Special Interest
Not So Funny When It Happened,
The Gift of Rivers, Shitting Pretty, Testosterone Planet,
Danger!, The Fearless Shopper, The Penny Pincher's
Passport to Luxury Travel, The Gift of Birds, Family Travel,
A Dog's World, There's No Toilet Paper on the Road Less
Traveled, The Gift of Travel, 365 Travel, Adventures in Wine

Footsteps
Kite Strings of the Southern Cross, The Sword of Heaven,
Storm, Take Me With You, Last Trout in Venice, The Way of the
Wanderer, One Year Off, The Fire Never Dies

Classics
The Royal Road to Romance, Unbeaten Tracks in Japan,
The Rivers Ran East, Coast to Coast, Trader Horn

TRADER
HORN

TRADER HORN

A YOUNG MAN'S ASTOUNDING ADVENTURES
IN 19TH CENTURY EQUATORIAL AFRICA

Alfred Aloysius Horn

with Ethelreda Lewis

TRAVELERS' TALES
San Francisco

Travelers' Tales books are distributed by Publishers Group West, 1700 Fourth Street, Berkeley, California 94710.

Cover Art Direction: Michele Wetherbee/doubleu-gee
Cover Design: Stefan Gutermuth/doubleu-gee
Page layout: Cynthia Lamb, using the fonts Minion and Mrs Eaves

Library of Congress Cataloguing-in-Publication Data
Horn, Trader, 1861-1931.
    Trader Horn: a young man's astounding adventures in 19th century
  equatorial Africa / Alfred Aloysius Horn ; with Ethelreda Lewis.
    p. cm. — (Travelers' Tales classics)
  ISBN 1-885211-81-3
    1. Horn, Trader, 1861-1931. 2. Africa, West—Description and travel.
  3. Africa, West—Biography. 4. Adventure and adventurers—Africa,
  West—Biography. I Lewis, Ethelreda. II. Title. III. Series.

DT476.23.H67 A3 2002
916.604'23—dc 21
                                   2002276244

Printed in the United States
10 9 8 7 6 5 4 3 2 1

TO

A.A.H.

Forgive me, old friend and fellow craftsman, if our book is in many respects different from what you had expected it would be. Fine and simple as is your own narrative, it yet cannot paint your own portrait in such detail as your conversations. I have, therefore, reproduced these as accurately as lay in my power to do, believing that the Unknown Reader (that shadowy figure beckoning in the background of all our literary work together in the last six months) would wish to see you clearly, not only as the boy-pioneer in West Africa, but as the embodiment of that man, attractive to all humanity, who "in his time plays many parts."

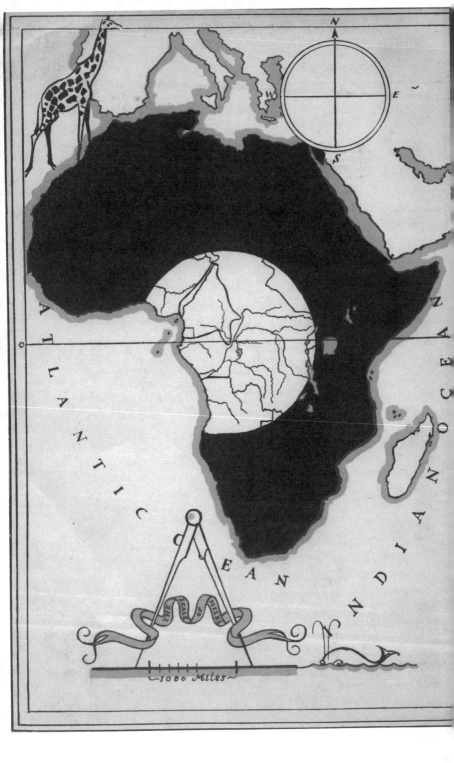

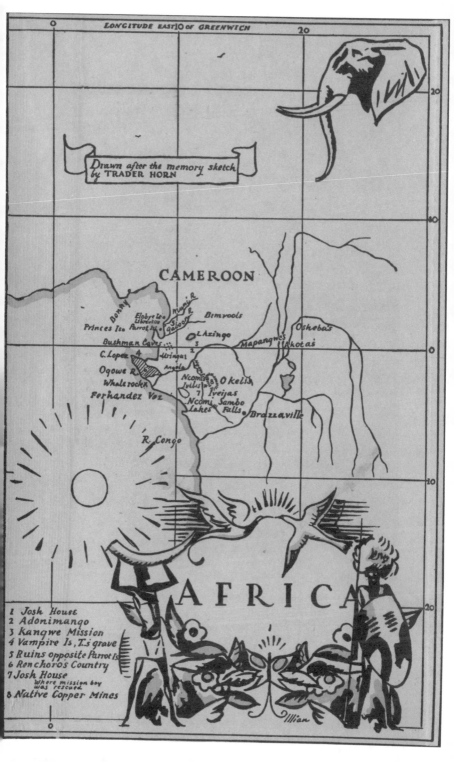

LONGITUDE EAST 10 OF GREENWICH 20

Drawn after the memory sketch
by TRADER HORN

CAMEROON

Bonny
Elobre Iso. Munii R.
Libreville Bimvools
Princes Iso. Parrot Iso. Gaboon
Bushman Caves   L. Azingo   Oshebas
                 Mapangwes Akotas
C. Lopez Uringui
Oqowe R. Angola
Whale rocks   Ncomi Okelis
Ferhandez Vez   Ivilis   Iveijas
                Ncomi Sambo
                Lakes Falls Brazzaville

R. Congo

AFRICA

1 Josh House
2 Adonimanqo
3 Kanqwe Mission
4 Vampire Is, T.s grave
5 Ruins opposite Parrot Is.
6 Renchoro's Country
7 Josh House
   Where mission boy
   was rescued
8 Native Copper Mines

Illian

Trader Horn and one of his griddle irons.

NEW INTRODUCTION

BY TIM CAHILL

This captivating book, full of unlikely adventures, was originally published in the United States in 1927. It was generally excoriated by critics worldwide and for reasons contemporary readers may find to be entirely beside the point. Was the book awash in racial stereotyping, ecological pillage, and abiding chauvinism of the masculine variety? Surely, but the critics of the day were troubled by other matters: the prose, they declared, did not seem sufficiently grounded in reality. In point of fact, reliable researchers have been able to situate many of the locations, and confirm (more or less) most of the stories told by the man whose pen name was Trader Horn.

Born in England in 1861, Aloysius Smith was expelled from a Catholic boarding school—in the English fashion he refers to the school as "college."—at the age of seventeen. He shipped off to West Africa, and worked for a British trading company, exchanging trade goods for ivory or rubber. Aloysius, called Wish, canoed and charted various rivers, fought mini-wars with his "boys," killed when he had to, and admired some of the "natives": people he felt were "almost as intelligent as us."

It was an eventful life. Smith returned to England for a time, where he worked as a reporter and then a policeman. Somehow he fell in with Buffalo Bill Cody and appeared in the famous Wild West show. He lived for a time in Mexico, Australia, and Madagascar. The present volume is about Smith's early adventures in West Africa.

For those who prefer to knock back their armchair adventure in large Indiana Jones-sized drafts, *Trader Horn* will deliver. It takes some time, but the reader will watch a man exchanging real jewels for fake ones in a shadowed temple of…well, a temple of doom. A maiden is imprisoned, or perhaps not. A rescue is attempted. An evil witch doctor dies in an act of cunning treachery.

These are the kind of tales (and attitudes) one might read about in Kipling, had that author concentrated on Africa. But Aloysius Smith was no Rudyard Kipling. Indeed, he first stumbles out of the doss house and onto the literary scene in 1925: a little old man with long white beard selling gridirons door to door in Johannesburg, South Africa.

The American reader will want to know that a "doss house" is London slang for a homeless shelter and that a "dosser" is a homeless individual of the type once called a bum or a tramp. Put it this way: in his later years, Aloysius Smith enjoyed an intemperate fondness for alcohol. The doss house was the Salvation Army Center in Johannesburg, and a gridiron is the grill one places over an open fire, though the appliance in this case, I think, was probably used to heat bread.

So, an old bum comes to the door selling toasters. He's got a gift of gab, this charming old reprobate, and his prospective customer is the nationally noted novelist, Ethelreda Lewis. Ah, but all that is in the story you are about to read, and perhaps the most beguiling part at that.

The foreword was written by John Galsworthy, who was one of the great literary lights of the day and the winner of the 1932 Nobel Prize for Literature. Some critics feel that Galsworthy's imprimatur sealed the book's success, but if one reads the end-of-chapter conversations between Smith and Lewis, it is the homeless man who continually advises the novelist about what Americans want in a book. He was right. Americans bought *Trader Horn* by the bushel. It was the number four non-fiction bestseller in 1927 and number three in 1928.

Wish Smith—this arrogant old stumblebum—also advised Etheleda Lewis on how to put together action sequences so their collaboration would be salable to the movies. And, in 1931, the film *Trader Horn*—the first non-documentary ever shot in Africa—was released. It was nominated for an Academy Award.

The old bum knew what he was talking about, and though his attitudes are those of a Victorian colonist (probably because he *was* a Victorian colonist) there are odd contemplative sections—sparely placed and almost hidden—where one may watch in a kind of hope-filled awe as Wish Smith seems to struggle toward the light. He never makes it, but one wants to feel that he came close in his heart.

The man, whatever his faults, told a fine tale. He was, it seems, consumed by his travel lust: what he called his "gift for roaming." Wish Smith died in England, a relatively wealthy man, and his last words are almost too perfect: "Where's me bloody passport? I'm off to Africa."

Tim Cahill is the best-selling author of nine books, most recently Hold the Enlightenment: More Travel, Less Bliss *from Villard. Other titles include* Jaguars Ripped My Flesh, Pecked to Death by Ducks, Dolphins, *and* Pass the Butterworms. *He is also the editor of* Not So Funny When It Happened: The Best of Travel Humor and Misadventure, *and the co-author of the IMAX film,* Everest, *as well two other Academy Award nominated films. He describes what he does for a living as "remote journeys, oddly rendered." He lives in Montana, and shares his life with Linnea Larson, two dogs, two cats, and a host of friends.*

FOREWORD

By John Galsworthy

THIS is a gorgeous book, more full of sheer stingo than any you are likely to come across in a day's march among the bookshops of wherever you may be. These untutored memories of youth adventuring long ago in a wild place, recorded with an untutored pen in a Johannesburg doss-house, are like the gold ore of the "so-called golden City," as Alfred Aloysius Horn would call it, except indeed that the proportion of gold in them is so very much greater. Nothing more racy and full of original wisdom than the conversations at the end of each chapter has come my way for an age. The spelling of this "Old Visitor"—who surely is his time has been a most notable adventurer in the raw world—is best described as lordly, and the mixture of jejune phrasing with sayings incomparably pithy makes for a dish that will tickle the appetite of the most jaded.

Let me serve up a few *hors d'oeuvres*:

"That elephant hunt makes a pretty splash of activity."
"What is poetry but the leavings of superstition."
"The Quakers, Ma'am, I've always held to be above par."
"A few schooner-rigged females—"
"The Americans—a moral people except when it comes to murder and so on."
"Big-game hunters—an equatorial gang of cut-throats, wasting wild life to make what they call a bag."

"Like a lad in a toy-shop—Rhodes."

"But the correctful thing in all literary books is to remember that even the truth may need suppressing if it appears out of tangent with the common man's notion of reality."

Don't we novelists know how true *that* is! Put a bit of life, just as it was, into a novel, and at once people will write to tell one that it's the only impossible incident.

"There's no softness about Nature. When you're driven from the herd, it's for good. I've seen a beaten old Chief weep like a child. No wounds, mind you. But his heart broke. Aye, he knows there's not redress in a state of Nature. No newspaper talk to prop him up again. None of this so-called diplomacy. He sees Finis written all over the sunlight—same as an old elephant."

But of *hors d'oeuvres* one so easily eats too much. Suffice it to say, then, that the pudding is stuffed with spice.

Mrs. Ethelreda Lewis, the South African novelist, to whose credit stands the discovery of this gold mine, has explained, in her remarkable introduction, how it came about, and the layout of what is apparently only the first volume of Alfred Aloysius Horn's reminiscences. With real inspiration she had adopted the only method which could have displayed the full value and flavour of this "Old Visitor's" personality, philosophy, and prejudices.

I never prophesy, but I would wager that this book will be read by countless readers with the gusto as great as I felt myself.

And to those who, in these days of fakes, might be doubtful whether it's not all too good to be true, let me say that in February, 1927, I had the pleasure of meeting the "Old Visitor" and his editress, in Johannesburg; and that he is in very truth the "character" herein disclosed.

INTRODUCTION

T HIS is a true story of a real man. So real that I have thought it necessary to alter names here and there, including his own surname. The Christian names I have kept, being loath to part with them: the first so redolent of the pre-Norman days from which his spirit seems not yet to have emerged, and the second mounting guard, so to speak, over old half-buried instincts of the Catholic, and ready to see him safely through the door of Heaven when the more barbarous Alfred fails to impress Saint Peter.

In his own words: "Aloysius? 'Tis a saint's name. It's our custom to give a lad two names. One to make his way through life with, the other to be bugled out when he knocks at Heaven's gate. That'll be the end of my travels. Unless there's room for roamers there too. One can always hope there's some forethought for human nature, be it Heaven or Hell. A feller that's been a prospector, always with his eye somewhere else than what he's standing on, won't be too agreeably placed on those golden floors they speak of."

When Aloysius Horn first swam into my ken I was about to settle down to a morning's work on the stoop. With notebook and pencil, it being then ten o'clock of a bright Tuesday, and peace in the air, I approached the doorstep full of the possibilities of Chapter Fourteen, which, before breakfast, had loomed very clearly.

On the mat stood an old man whose footsteps, coming up the eight steps from the garden, I had not heard. He was simply there.

He held a cluster of wire kitchen goods in his hand, neatly made and shining coppery in the sun: gridirons, toast-forks and the like.

Regarding me with a mild, but, as I now know, an all-seeing eye which dwelt on my possibilities, he began the business of selling to a person not wanting to buy.

The battle was short. I pleaded a kitchen replete with toast-fork and gridiron. I said I was very busy. I maintained that it was my principle never to buy on the stoop, which was my only study.

With an abstracted eye on my notebooks he said mildly that it was a good habit and that he could well understand it. To show that his words were no idle boast he shouldered his bundle of goods and turned to the steps with a cheerful "good morning."

But of course the battle went to him. Flinging victory away, as England nearly always does when it is hers, I raised my voice to stop him.

"I believe I *could* do with a new gridiron."

There was something I could not bear in seeing that ready acquiescence with failure. What a reward, I thought, for a man too courteous to argue. Too English to bargain, bully and browbeat; to wheedle, whine or weep.

I suppose he knew this was coming. As if it had been his cue in a play and he had retired to the wings for a moment, he turned back and off-loaded the wire goods at my feet.

"Why, certainly, Ma'am. It is natural to all to experience a change of mind. Over little things as over great. And both you and I are no more than children of nature."

That mild voice, rising, as I now know, from a past as infinitely full of repose, of restlessness, of action, of hidden hoards—spectres of bones and wreckage—from the past as the sea itself: as full, if so I may put it, of the quality of timelessness, that quality which keeps every roamer, from Ulysses to Columbus, and from Columbus to—to Aloysius Horn, awash between year and year as if the shores of time were forever theirs. Cradled like gulls, safe on the battering winds which are the breath of life to such as they.

Even after taking the gridiron I again nearly let him go. My head was full of Chapter Fourteen. My notebooks and pencil felt full of life, leaping, as they say, like the child unborn.

But it was not for Chapter Fourteen they leapt and smote. I see now that they were trying to attract my attention to greater opportunities.

We had said our mutual thanks and adieux. The old man's steps were again turned to the road when he paused and said: "I could tell you how to make oatcakes if you'd like me to, Ma'am. You'd find it useful for that ting you've bought."

It was at that moment I said to myself: "This man is an artist. Having successfully sold a thing, he is not basely content with the money. It is necessary to him to put a sort of bloom and finish on the transaction which will lift it from commerce into art. From barter to friendliness."

I listened to the only way of making oatcake, told with such zest and love that I said: "You must be Scotch."

"Born thirteen miles out of Glasgow, Ma'am. I should say you were perhaps Scotch yourself? You are fair."

"English," I said, briefly.

"Oh." The old visitor eyed me closely. "In that case—"

There was a pause.

"When I say I was born in Scotland, Ma'am, it's not to say I'm a Scotchman myself.[1] They're a poor lot, taken all in all.

---

1. In that delightful book *Cambridge Cameos* the Master of Christ's reminds us that Charles Kingsley was born in Scotland, Devonshire or the West Indies according to the audience he was addressing. The same diplomatic instinct will surely, then, be forgiven in an old, friendless man, intent on the serious business of "seizing food" as he puts it, in a town hard as gold. We are further told by Sir Arthur Shipley that in a biography of Mr. Gladstone the reader is assured that the great man "was born more or less in Scotland." So Aloysius Horn, also a Lancashire man from the day of his birth near Preston, lied in distinguished company.

Lancashire's always been good enough for one of the old Fist-and-Spear. My name's Horn. Aloysius Horn of the Fist-and-Spear."

I bowed and told him mine.

He sighed, as if this exchange of decent civilities had set something moving in his brain. His eyes, those farseeing, expectant eyes of age, gazed through me mildly. Washed free of definite colour, as is the way with the old, they were still large and clear. Contemplative eyes, set in large sockets. Calmly observant, they yet seemed fixed on the invisible.

"Aye. The old Fist-and-Spear. Ma'am, I could tell you—I've seen—"

He came nearer, his outstretched hand all but touching my shoulder, his face gone under some influence of which I had not yet the secret. I know now that it was the rising pressure of a soul making its last effort to express itself before the walls of age and senility closed in, to leave its shape and texture in a vanishing world.

He came closer as he spoke, looking as Columbus might have looked as he begged from door to door with his head full of spaces of land and sea. The waxen skin and high, wide skull stretched over with parchment and a few gray hairs; the white beard, longish narrow and pointed; visionary eyes that had seen a world and seen it whole—an imperishable picture.

I stood still as the Wedding Guest; or as when a bird comes nearer than usual—say a heron, as you stand on the banks of a stream.

"Africa, Ma'am. Africa—as Nature meant her to be, the home of the black man and the quiet elephant. Never a sound, Ma'am, in a great landscape at noon—only the swish of elephants in grass. Lying still there in the water, too—and me the first white man (nay, I was a lad) to pry upon their happiness.

"Bound by the rites of Egbo, Ma'am, to be blood brother of cannibals. Look at my thumb, cut when I was eighteen in a fight with a savage and never grew again. Me? I've seen the skulls in the Josh House. Blood brother to the priests, where no white man had ever been until I came...But I was only a lad.

"And I knew Nina T——, the cruelest woman in West Africa...So they say. So they say. But her hair was dark auburn....

"Goodness she was, in the Josh House there....

"Why, I was only a lad when I took that other poor lady's body down the river to try and get safe burial for it at Kangwe. Well of course they'd never seen a white woman before, up at Samba Falls. Very natural they should need such a unique body for *muti*. What won't any of us do for magic? We call it luck now and that's the only difference. A hundred miles I took her, and no mishap from the arrows.

"A lad of eighteen has a natural reserve of chivalry. Aye, it grows like a flower in him then—"

His voice slowed off, as if he stopped to look at something in his mind more intently. Something that was incredibly far away.

"Why, Ma'am, you may not believe it but I can talk French: *Oui, Monsieur, je baragouine ce jargon-la toujours assez bien pour me tirer d'affaires dans le commerce.*"

He spoke like a parrot, as if he had been using the same phrase on many doorsteps.

"French, Ma'am. A language for the meager-hearted. If God ever made a worse colonist than the French, he hasn't let me know about it. It takes more than a little straw hat and a cigarette and a thimbleful of absinthe all set out in a neat little office to open out Africa....

"Aye, when a young lad first hears the dawn-cry of the gorilla and covers his ears...And when he sees slaves—women—

"Seventeen I must have been. Or was it sixteen—I can't remember clear.

"But I must not keep you from your work, Ma'am. I'll be getting along. Good day to you."

I came to from my swound and hastily rang the front door bell, which was somewhere near my right ear.

When Ruth appeared, my coloured housekeeper and friend, I whispered, "Tea, please, Ruth. Very strong, and don't pour it out. This gentleman will prefer to pour it out himself. Bread-and-butter, too—the homemade."

The old visitor was faltering forlornly on the edge of the steps, the vision all washed out of his eyes. When I said to him, "Won't you stay and have some tea?" He said, "Why, it sure would be very pleasurable," and sank down on the steps with a vast sigh of pleasure.

No, of reprieve.

Or was it the sigh of the artist at the moment of achievement.

I sat down beside him and said "Mr. Horn—your address, please. And can you make it convenient to come here to talk next week?"

The compact was made that, once a week, instead of trailing round with wire goods to the doors of vulnerable housewives whose husbands were away in town, Aloysius Horn should come and talk for an hour or two, earning a little more than could be made from a day's sales.

All this six months ago. The result of our talks is in this book and in others to come.

Just as he rose to go my eye fell on the shining gridiron and a sudden thought struck me. More than a thought, a suspicion.

"Mr. Horn," I said, "you have told me how to make oatcakes, but no one could make them on an open grid like this."

"Why, no, Ma'am, I admit the truth of that. 'Twould be against the law of gravitation if you took it literally." He spoke soothingly.

"But thinking you might be from the Land o' Cakes, I thought it would please. I have picked up a considerable amount of knowledgeable stuff in my wanderings, and if you'll give me a loan of a pencil I'll draw Botha's portrait for you."

He bent over my notebook for a moment.

"There you are, Ma'am. That's a bit of wisdom saved me an empty stomach now and again when Botha was fashionable. Smuts was never the rage in South Africa as Botha was. A feller'd never touch the heart as Botha did. Excuse me if I keep the pencil a moment longer. I'll draw you a pipe made from the beak of an albatross. All the go at one time they were amongst us sailors. No fanciful lad'd go ashore without one."

"But I thought you didn't kill the albatross if you wanted luck!"

"Only on the homeward voyage, that is. When I was a lad, any sailor would kill one on the voyage out. But not me. I was always one for the preservation of Nature when humanly possible. And believe me, Ma'am, when a lad that's seen nothing bigger than the gulls and herons o' Lancashire first beholds that great white apparition of beauty men call Albatross sailing the southern elements, he'll not be the one to drain it of breath. Six feet o' wafting snow—"

He began the descent of the steps.

"Good day to you, Ma'am. I must not outstay my welcome. I often suspect I'm getting somewhat childish. What with one thing and another."

He paused halfway down.

"I often think it was a happy fad o' Nature to throw a bright light on boyhood's days as you're getting old. Aye, she jumbles up the perspective a bit when you're over seventy and seen what I've seen. But it's all for the good of man. When you're in a lodging house at a shilling a day in the Golden City and find your own food, it's good to have your surroundings dimmed a bit or you might feel disposed to give way to complaint, which I should be sorry to do. 'Tis no gentleman's way to give way to anything but philosophy."

We had now reached the gate. He closed it carefully after him, raised his hat which, old and crusted, yet had a certain air of dog about it, and crept uprightly away, eyes on the ground, with the smooth and careful gait of some old men.

I returned to my table and wrote the notes now used here.

For the first two or three weeks this old visitor fluttered round in a circle of subjects like one, as he himself said, somewhat childish. He repeated himself over and over, as the aged will, forgetting what he had told me.

"Egbo, Ma'am? I've been blood brother to the cannibals. No need to say been. I still am. Nothing destroys the bond but death. Cannibals...the most moral race on earth. The women chaste and the men faithful. Aye, I've lived amongst 'em like a brother, a lad clean and safe. Safer than what he'd 'a' been in London and other centers given over to civilization. Victoria Street, Westminster and so on. If you doubt what I say, look after the fight I had on the Ogowe river....

"Why, I can speak French, if you'll believe me Ma'am: *Oui, Monsieur, je baragouine ce jargon-la toujours assez bien pour me tirer d'affaires dans le commerce.*

"A poor lot, the French. Dogs in the manger. Snap up a bit o' good land half the size o' Europe and stand yapping over it for their taxes and duties. So taken up with yapping they forget to develop it.

"Did I tell you I'd heard the gorilla first when I was a lad of seventeen? Or was it eighteen...He's mad, they say. The natives'll always tell you he's mad. Something shaped in his brain that's similar to the mistakes in the brain of a madman. Nature's always got a hankering after experiments.

"Ma'am, did I mention to you that I've seen a white woman goddess of Isorga? Nina T—— her name. But best not mention that name. I've no wish to betray the tragedies of a noble English family. A handsome girl. Auburn...her hair was. Dark auburn. Seventeen I was. Or was it eighteen...."

It was not until the third or fourth visit that the idea came to me how much less wasteful of time it would be for the old man to write his adventures in his own way and for me to devote two hours or so of his weekly visit in making notes, not of his adventures so much as of his outlook on life, and all sorts of experiences which would never come into any written account of his doings on the West Coast: and to use such notes as a sort of chorus between his chapters, somewhat after the manner of Mrs. Markham's History.

The plan worked well. All unconsciously I hit upon the key to unlock an extraordinary memory which the struggle for life, as age advanced, had almost closed up forever. How nearly lost it was will be gauged by the fact that even at the fourth and fifth meeting he began our talk by reminding me—as if I had never heard of them on the previous occasions—of the four or five things branded on his brain as a youth: Egbo, Nina T——, the wicked French, gorillas, his shortened thumb, he still wove into a vivid monologue, varying the order in which they came into his mind and seeing more and more of the detail of the past as he dwelt upon it.

Sometimes a look came in his eyes as if he had met, in his memory, some old face or scene he had never thought to see again. For instance, it was not till his third visit that he remembered du Chaillu's musical box and compass. He had begun with

Nina T——: "Aye, she gave me the warning that I was to be attacked. She stood on the bank and I was in the old *Pioneer*. Livingstone's boat, that had been. At the engine I was standing and my men all in proper formation along the bank in their canoes. She stood there and called me to come ashore. 'It's not safe for you,' she said. Aye, she remembered a little English. A strange look she gave me. Eighteen I was. Perhaps seventeen…Did you know I can speak French, Ma'am? *Oui, Monsieur…'cré nom de Dieu, puis que je vous dis qu'il n'y a rien à declarer!*

"Aye, but the rite of Egbo's a safer accomplishment than French when you're hunting ivory. French is a language writ in water on the earth's surface. Water *and* scent. And if the English in pursuit of top-dog happen to have left a little bloody writing here and there, there's no man that is a man but'll agree 'tis a better medium to write in than this *chypre*, as they call it, and their little dregs of absinthe…. I found du Chaillu's musical box in one of the chief's huts up there. Musical box and his compass. There was still a bit of a tinkle in it when I saw it. 'Trovatore' or something. Picture of a lady in one of these chignons. There's a weakness, Ma'am, in all dago music, and never more so than when heard in a cannibal's hut.

"'Tis notably thin stuff. But, as magic, a notable addition to voodoo in that part of the world. That and the compass he left. Aye, they feared that little trembling finger more than the sounds in the musical box. Too quiet to be very reassuring…. The mariner's compass. One of Nature's discoveries that'll never be commonised by the sons of men. Aye, something about the edicts of the mechanical."

If regular once-a-week talking unlocked the past and admitted me to a strange jumble of memories of which nothing was ever begun or ended, it is very certain that the regular writing down of his adventures on the Ivory Coast brought back the mechanism of a vanishing intellect. Just as artificial respiration may bring back the breath and the life, so did the use of pencil and paper induce life to return to the dying intellect. The assurance that what he wrote would be read with interest brought back whole tracts of memory, and of knowledge lost for want of use.

He wrote on Mondays, a day when every man left the doss house after the strain of Sunday, and when there was no one about his path and about his bed and spying out all his ways: ways which, to those who only knew him as Zambesi Jack, the old wire seller, must often have seemed those of a madman. Now, after six months of it, the writing fills his whole mind. It is a tremendous obsession, this saving and cherishing of memories that have flowed so near the edge of oblivion. Not only has the new task filled his mind in the daytime but it wakes him in the night. Taps him on the brain with some recovered picture of youth, some old song or line of poetry which gives him no rest until he has recorded it.

"Ma'am, I've had a great loss. I woke in the night—I suppose it must have been a dream—and saw us all lively in our beds in the dormitory at St. Edwards. On a summer night it must have been—didn't seem quite dark yet. There was a boy I knew up in the corner there—I knew his face and I should 'a' got his name in a minute—sitting up and singing a song we all knew in those days—and I was just beginning to wake up and sing it, to get it right and look for the matches....

"That feller in the next bed thought I was having a dream and the hollering he made to wake me up put it all out of my head. Quite a nice feller, a bricklayer that's out o' work from drink, but lacking in imagination. It's a notable loss to the book. Bright as a picture it all was, until I woke and felt myself in the dark. Beds about me sure enough but not occupied by boys. Aye, they've gone again, into this so-called limbo of forgetfulness."

Another day the loss was a more serious one.

"I was just listening to Tommy Bamber describe the fight off Galveston. He was hidden in the withies along the shore—and a feller comes in drunk and wakes us all up, knocking things over in the dark.... Methylated always makes 'em so silly. Not like authorized spirits. It's only a fancy drink for the demimonde. Ladies with yellow hair and apt with hysterics.... But it might come again to me if I think about it closely when I fall asleep."

In such chancy ways has this book grown.

The arrival of my colleague once a week, with a roll of eight to a dozen foolscap sheets closely written in pencil (his week's work), and with all a writer's restlessness to see its effect on a reader, and the writer's irresistible desire to map out the next chapter, became almost as big a landmark in my week as in his. That next chapter: seeing it always in scenes and phrases that had taken possession of the mind; scenes that have been his for sixty years, lit up in the wane of life by words and phrases that often filled him with a blaze of excitement as he spoke them aloud to his audience. Yet never did his words and phrases retain that same living quality when the time came for him to pin them down to paper. Elusive as his dreams, they only fell out unconsciously during speech, that speech that was like the release of a long-dammed torrent.

I can see why words which came naturally to him in speech appear so rarely or so transformed in his writing. For one thing, the atmosphere of doss house was pressing heavily all about him. Even the literal atmosphere of doss house, in this country, is one of extremes, too hot or too cold. Without the encouraging environment, the proximity of a listener, he was like flint without steel. For another thing, he would, at his age, entertain an old-fashioned idea that the written word must be elegant rather than colloquial.

It is no accident, this Victorian style of his. As will be seen in the conversations, he thinks a very great deal about Style. And that is why I have altered nothing in his written narrative, but have left it untouched, as I, or any writer, would wish my work untouched. To have written, at his age, and in such surroundings, with an empty pocket (and, I fear, at first often an empty stomach) such a vigorous account of his life on the Ivory Coast fifty years ago, is achievement enough without any officious painting of the lily or gilding the gold on the part of his chronicler. But when I realized that his best literary quality is in speech rather than in the written word I certainly then began to take notes of his conversation much more carefully. If I have presented our conversations in the form of monologue rather than dialogue it is because, by repressing my own share, I have been better able to get the tone of Aloysius Horn when in full spate.

Spate is the word. No words of mine will make clear what a tremendous outpouring this weekly talk of an hour or two has been. It is an outpouring of a past into which not a soul remained in the world who wished to gaze with sympathy or interest. And if it is a past which not always—some may say not often—reflects the tranquil scenes of the virtuous life; and if at times the reflection is distorted or mistaken by reason of the great distance of years over which he is looking backwards—and over what leagues of land and sea, what worlds, of faces, black and white—much will surely be forgiven an old man who had already prepared to meet Death in the dumb way of the patient poor, life all unspoken in his breast like a saga unsung.

Whatever his shortcomings, whatever his record, Aloysius Horn is no sniggerer. I have never heard him laugh with cynicism, nor speak with any expression of slyness or a naming look. The double-entendre is invariably accidental in his speech, and is only remarked as such by myself and the reader. Had it not been so, this literary partnership could not have traversed so many strange byways and entered occasionally such doubtful company. One or two of the old man's experiences and expressions of opinion in this book were told to my husband on days when I was absented during part of the visit: prefaced, in his unfailingly punctilious manner, by some such speech as: "You will understand, Sir, being of scientific turn as you are, that there are some things no gentleman could speak of to a lady, which yet should be trumpeted to the world."

My poor old friend keeps his Victorian illusions by the simple expedient of never reading.

Our weekly conversation has always followed a meal prepared, as much as is possible in this country, in the English tradition. Grilled chops, nice raw steaks, cold beef and pickles, potatoes baked in their jackets, thick pea soup, buck—I should say, venison—with jelly, Cheddar cheese. All this is part of the scheme I followed of loosening an English tongue. Ruth, my cook, so caught the spirit of the adventure that one day she said: "What about stewed pears, Missis? Do you think they would be English enough for Mr. Horn?"

"Ruth," I said, "it is an inspiration. But they must taste of cloves and have a faint aroma of orange peel about them. We used to have them at Sunday night supper after church when I was young and it was autumn, and I feel sure Mr. Horn must have had the same. They might remind him, too, of family prayers and prayer-books lying about the hall when you go to bed feeling a bit excited and yet melancholy."

"Yes, Missis" said Ruth, and returned to the kitchen to try and capture that Victorian flavor.

Tobacco and a weekly tot of brandy have also played their part in unlocking the past; from the day, a very hot one, on which I said to the old man as he crept up the steps, "You look very gone-in today. I think you'd better have a little brandy to pick you up." To which he replied: "Ma'am, I should appreciate an incentive. We get nothing but this so-called tea and coffee. Poor stuff, when you're seeking an inspiration. I should sure appreciate a more useful drink. From Ben Jonson downwards, the use of an incentive has been recognized as nothing less nor more than natural in the interests of literature."

But long before he had this classic habit "'a babbled o'green fields" as the old do. The fields, for Aloysius Horn, are not only green but must be growing in good Lancashire earth. Yes, 'a babbles of Lancashire. With all the passion of the exile caught in the meshes of old age, his eyes forever turn to his county. The end of the rainbow, his span of life, stands, to his eyes, in Lancashire soil, touching the gold of Lancashire hearts. The other end is on the banks of an African river in the gorgeous peace of fifty years ago, a peace whose primeval depth was still unrippled.

PUBLISHERS' NOTE

Trader Horn's own story follows,
exactly as written by himself. At the
end of each chapter Mrs. Lewis has
added, in quotation marks, his conversations
with her as she took them
down at the time.

ᴄᴗ Chapter I. ᴖ

DUCATED at St. Edward's College, Liverpool, where I met as young companions Julian Venezuela of Venezuela, South America, Little Peru, son of the Peruvian President, Etienne Vangoche of Bogota, two nabobs from the cream of the Negro Republic Haiti in the West Indies, other sons of the most prominent people in Brazil, likewise the Count of Zeres in Spain (where the most of our best sherry wine comes from). We were, I think without a doubt, the most cosmopolitan group of youngsters ever gathered together for commercial education. I was only eleven years of age when I entered the school, some of my schoolmates of the same age, but I believe the old idea in mixing the young Britisher with his brothers of every clime was to make him cosmopolitan, and naturally we soon learned each others' language.

I was not long in the college when I could speak Spanish, Portuguese, and French and I also picked up their characteristics, which are diametrically opposite to those of the slow, young Anglo-Saxon. Their maturity is quicker and they do not think as we do, coming at hasty conclusions, and therefore hard to manage as a community. Most of these lads became famous in the history of their various countries, as they received impressions of better judgment than their own, and this I can assure you has been a world's factor for the best, as far as the American Republics are concerned. We were taught French, Latin, Greek, in fact had a regular Oxford tuition by first class professors. However, nothing my parents could say could stop my ardor for travel and I chose the West Coast of Africa, which was the best field for adventure I had read of, as the interland was practically unknown. Slavery was rife, as well as piracy, the animals, such as gorilla, elephants, and many others were known to exist, but their habits, characteristics, etc., had only been guessed at, and the mistakes made in the true description of the gorilla were many, and I may say to this day he still bears a character he in no way deserves.

We will now say goodbye forever to college life and associates and transfer ourselves to the deck of the good ship *Angola*, which was a steel vessel built regardless of cost specially for West Coast trade, using both steam and sail, classed A1 at Lloyd's, and was the commodore boat of many ships owned by Hatton and Cookson, an old and rich firm of traders, in fact by far the largest and richest on the West Coast. Their sphere of influence extended from Bonney Brass to old Calabar, also up the Niger River as far as trade had any influence. Also, all coast ports along Cameroon, etc., embracing Balanga, Eloby Island, Gaboon, exactly under the equator, Ogowe River, later explored by Count de Brazza, whom I often met when older.[1]

----

1. It is obvious that in his narrative Mr. Horn has run all his experiences together with only a vague reference to date. My impression is that he arrived on the West Coast about 1871 or '72, at the age of eighteen. That he spent more years than he can now remember in learning the rubber and ivory trade, both as a clerk and in actual travel on the rivers, and that at the time he met de Brazza he would be about twenty-

This river is the river I traded and hunted on for many years, is the home of the gorilla, in fact Pongo was shipped from there and was sold by the captain of the *Angola,* Capt. Thomson, whom I sailed from Liverpool with for the sum of £500 (five hundred pounds sterling). This was the first gorilla which ever reached Europe alive, and lived for quite a time in Germany, being resold to a German firm. The Ogowe River empties into the Atlantic Ocean one day's sail south of the equator, and from this river came most of the valuable cargoes of ivory, as much as 50,000 pounds weight being shipped in one season. The elephants are mostly hunted by the M'pangwes, Fans, and Ashiwa who speak the same language. These tribes inhabit the north bank of the Ogowe River nearly to its source and are all cannibals. I lived amongst them for many years, but for safety sandbanks and islands were the only safe camping grounds. Boys were supplied by the firm I represented, Hatton and Cookson, and we were well supplied with rifles, mostly the Old Snyder type, a few other rifles, and shop guns were always kept handy in case of surprise attacks, and we were frequently called on to defend ourselves in this uncivilized country. These cannibals are by far the finest type of all the Negroes I ever met, are good hunters, fine workers, and have no slaves. They are also very moral and I never knew a cannibal woman who was not more than faithful to her husband and children. I made many good friends among these men and have had many a tip to be on my guard, when the man who gave this warning invariably risked his life in doing so. In fact, they never forgot a friend and would come long distances to sell me their ivory and ball rubber. They

---

three or twenty-four and well away from boyhood. In a man who has never spent more than a few years in one spot, and who is now looking back over a crowded vista of half a century, this vagueness is hardly to be wondered at. Still less if we remember how elusive a date can be, even in a well-ordered house lived in for a lifetime.

would also take a good-for in writing for a bag of salt or keg of powder. And, of course, they always got what was owing to them.

―――――――――――――― ∽◯◇◯◯ ――――――――――――――

After bidding a fond *adieu* to my brother, I had time to look around the good ship SS *Angola*. The last of the cargo was being stowed away and all hands were busy getting things shipshape. The owners gave a last word to the captain, shook hands with all of us, and departed. A few minutes only were spent in clearing the dockside and, accompanied with a shower of seagulls, we steamed out into the Mersey. Liverpool was soon left behind with her forest of ships, and as the shades of evening closed over us we were well away. Sails were bent and with a full head of steam and a stiff breeze with us we soon outdistanced the many sailing craft and steamers which were bound for every clime and port. I retired early, and on waking in the morning fit as a fiddle, I found the decks washed and scrubbed, ropes coiled, everything in place. Our friends the seagulls were busily engaged picking up tidbits thrown over from the well-stocked cook's galley. Two of the largest of these birds, one with a damaged beak and one minus a few wing feathers, were always nearer the vessel's stern than the rest, and to me they seemed to fly with less effort than the young ones, which moved their wings more in their efforts to snatch from the sea a little food before the older birds had it. As the Welsh coast was kept in sight we saw many points of interest. The next day, the foreign-bound ships became fewer, but we had a good view of some Cornish fishing boats engaged in catching pilchards. A main boat bound for the Cape of Good Hope signaled us, we raced her but found her leaving Funchal Bay just as we entered.

There is a charm about this Land of Eternal Sunshine which makes an impression on the mind of the Britisher as no other place can. On first nearing Madeira you pass three islands, called the Three Deserters, a grand name whoever found them, mantling surfs and spray mount the islands at all times, sometimes reaching as high as fifty or sixty feet, the towering peaks are nearly always sunlit, and numerous seabirds make their homes amongst the crags and cliffs of the higher summits which are always sun-clad after sunrise. A glorious picture, the cliffs of Madeira, also sun-tipped, can be seen on passing, casting glimpses of green and blue velvet from the verdure growing on these cliffs, the beautiful lines of which are a gift of nature of this island alone.

The captain and I were the first to land. The telegrams for L'pool (All's well, etc.) were delivered. Two ponies, which were waiting, we mounted, and after visiting Reeds Hotel, the principal one in Madeira at that time, we rode up the mountain road to Mr. Latours [the Governor?] (pronounced Latas). The captain, who was an old and frequent visitor, introduced me to Mrs. Latour and her daughter, who was a little older than myself. The mansion was built in the Old Portuguese style by this old Aristocratic family and was charming in the extreme. Cool at all times, both in build and furnishings, nestling in the cool shade of the mountains from which Morocco-wards one had a fine view of the city of Funchal and plus that a fine sea view. With a kind invitation to come and stay with them at any time, we bade *adieu* to this kindhearted people, and after riding the steep zigzag roads of the mountain were soon onboard our trusty vessel, which by this time had taken a supply of vegetables, fresh water, etc. The bird sellers and traders were quickly moved off the boat's deck, the anchor raised, and we put out to sea immediately. Quite a number of singing birds, mostly canaries, had been purchased by the crew for barter and exchange at the West Coast ports we were about to visit. The Peak of Tenerife next came in sight to the east of us, and we passed several boats bound for Europe who invariably signaled us. Next we ran into shoals of flying fish, many of these falling on deck and were taken to the cook's galley. They taste exactly like mackerel, and can only fly till their wings are dry. Mother O'Cary's chickens next began to follow us. They are found in Equatorial Africa and are said to make their homes on wreckage. They are like swallows and are swift flyers. Several ocean eagles floating high in the air with their long wings stretched and motionless volplaned like airplanes and were steering towards the West Indies, wither the sailors told me they were bound. They fly swiftly and continuously. The sailors say no man knows where they nest.

Cape Palmas was the next place of interest. The palm trees show well out on the point of the Cape and are a landmark for sailors. The coast is low, while a fringe of surf ruffles it and makes landing dangerous. Sailing southward I could not make out much sign of life, only a few seabirds followed us, while several large sharks patroled the ocean and can be seen several miles away, as the back fin and tail every now and then shows out of the water like the sails of a small boat. The heat of the sun kept us under the awnings, which were stretched aft and forward, but in spite of this, the skin over my neck, arms, and face began to peel off and I was gradually receiving a tan, which grew stronger till I had lost all signs of the rosy complexion I had left England with.

I felt overjoyed when we cast anchor at early dawn about one mile from the shore, and fifteen minutes after firing the bow gun the Kroo boys began to come off and make things interesting during the three hours we stayed. Their canoes are well shaped for surf riding, and danced like so many corks on the surface of the water. A large canoe now came alongside with the chief on board. He brought presents of palm cabbages cut from the top of the palm trees and tasting exactly like cabbage when cooked. He also brought palm butter from freshly boiled palm nuts, and we had palm oil chop for breakfast, a beautiful dish which was greatly relished by the passengers. The Kroo boys, about three hundred, were engaged to take the place of boys returning from various posts, and we distributed them commencing with the River Niger, and the last lot were put ashore at Gabenda, at the mouth of the Congo. Each gang of ten boys had their own headman or foreman. The boys from Grand Cess were the finest body of men I ever saw in any country, muscular and well-built and splendid workers, they were never known to complain, always laughing and joking and caused no trouble whatever. The crew of the good ship *Angola* were now replaced by Kroo boys, who handled everything like born sailors and replaced the whites, who were put to work on easier jobs, like washing winches, splicing ropes for slings, sail-making, etc. The boys returning from other parts of Africa were paid off on the return of S.S. *Angola,* mostly in powder and flintlock guns, as they were at war with the Liberian Colony owned by the Government of the U.S.A. joining the Kroo coast on the south, and many a yarn of their battles with the Yankee boys were doled out to us. All Kroo boys were tattooed with a broad blue stripe, which extends from the top of the forehead to the nose. They all have two top center teeth filed at an angle, so that they could easily be known if they were captured by the slavers who would resort to all kinds of tricks to get them on board their schooners.

A lively trade was carried on during the time we were anchored with the natives, who brought curious carved canoe paddles and all kinds of native-made utensils. All the boys engaged were stood in line and were given English names such as Flying Fish, Bottle of Beer, Pugnose, Mainsail, etc. They likewise received a number. This being done, the gun was fired, the chief retired and the rest of his following lowered their purchases to the canoes below and then dived overboard. The anchor was run up and we streamed away leaving this laughing crowd of naked Africans behind us as we sailed southward. The land was still low, in the distance a few palm-clad hills were visible with stretches of rough grass. The small inlets where mangrove fringed the banks, which were faced with golden sands, were played on by brightest sunlight. The small waves and surf beating them shone like silver and had a charm which lent beauty to the landscape.

After rounding Cape three points down and leaving the Ashanti and Gold Coast behind us, we steamed to Bonney on the river of that name, one of the many mouths of the famous Niger River. Here we anchored and immediately began to discharge cargo for the company's agent, Mr. Knight. The most powerful chief in that part of the country, Oka Jumbo of Bonney, now came to pay us a visit, accompanied by a large retinue comprising several chiefs, the sons of this old king. They were well dressed in European clothes and some of them spoke good English, having been taught by several roving sailors. They were more than friendly with me as I was the youngest trader they had ever seen. Oka Jumbo wanted me to stay in his family circle, offering me all kinds of inducements. These African nabobs drank champagne copiously.

H.M.S. Consul now put in an appearance and several topics were discussed, such as the war between Oka Jumbo and the river chiefs, who were interfering with the free exit of palm oil, which was, by far, the most important trade on all the west coast of Africa at that time, more than half a century ago. Although this African potentate was said to own many thousands of slaves, he was generous and goodhearted, and stood well in the eyes of the British Government. Some years before this, an old Bonney Chief is said to have sacrificed 300 slaves in one day because a slave had the audacity to shoot a parrot in a large sacred tree which stands alone on the right bank of Bonney River, and is looked on with awe by the natives.

Several sailing craft, mostly schooners, sailed by us upriver-bound, whilst others returned as the tide changed. This is, I think, the most pestilential and fever-stricken coast in the whole world and has received the well-merited name of the White Man's Grave. It was not by any means an uncommon occurrence for ships to return from upriver with white hands down with fever, genuine

Blackwater. Here is the home of a native secret society called Egbo and woe betied anyone who offends an Egbo man. I will describe to you later some of the inner secrets of these societies which are truly terrifying.

———

"How do you like it, Ma'am? Writing's always been a bit of a furor with me. Writing and roaming. Some's born with one thing and some another, and I was born with the gift of roaming. Aye. But there's always something calls you home. And when home has had its way with you, that other voice is heard that's only heard in the ears of some races. Wanderlust is as compact a word as the ultimate end of things; be firmer friends for us than the Frenchmen. The Teutons and us English all speak an understandable language. I'd as life make an *entente* with the apes as with France. An ape is surely God's picture of the unstable man, no doubt put up by Providence as a warning to all and sundry. Aye.

"What did the French do in Africa? Make not much more impression on it than a treeful of monkeys. Wouldn't work themselves and shied stones at those who did. All those heavy duties…No trade possible…They were always glad enough to see an Englishman plant his vine or his fig tree—in an allegorical manner of speech. Meaning ivories and rubber, excuse me—and then down they'd come and take full advantage of what they'd never 'a' done for themselves.

"Such a thing, now, do you say, Ma'am, as a sacred tree on the West Coast? [I had recently read *The Emperor Jones.*] Why, sure. The Ju-Ju tree is what they'll have no liberties taken with. Three hundred slaves sacrificed for shooting a parrot in a Ju-Ju tree. Aye, they make no bones about the tree being sacred. A fine upset it must 'a' made. 'Tis an error to imagine that Ancient Britain had the monopoly of tree-worship. It's a notable fact that there's no worse savagery springing from religion in Africa today than what we ourselves enjoyed in the heyday of the Druids. Aye. The black man's a fearful savage we say, when we see him crucify a man head down. Head down, and with one leg lower than the other. Then off with his head, and bowls set for the blood. Eighteen I might 'a' been. A lad receives a terrible imprint at eighteen, and Lancashire far from sight...But when we cry 'Savage!' we're forgetting the stone of sacrifice still standing on the hills of England on which white men and yellow-haired women were killed by white men for the benefit of religion. Cruel method it was, too—breaking the spine across it like a stick against your shins. I don't remember seeing any place of sacrifice in Lancashire—the Vikings were not much troubled with gods, and other superstitions—but there's quite a few over in Yorkshire. Cross the Odda from one side and you'll not know the language. Something barbaric about it.

"You like my first chapter, Ma'am? I thought it would sure tickle the public to hear what a tropical lot we were at St. Edward's. Novelty's what they want in America, if not in England. A lot of the names seem to escape me, however. Sometimes when I wake up and find myself laughing and talking with some of 'em I'll just think of it but if I'm not smart it'll fly away. 'Tis like capping a butterfly. There was that feller whose father owned the pitch lakes at Trinidad—rich as Croesus he was. Whether 'twas he or Little Peru, used to have a guardian come up from London twice a year—I forget. Nice gentleman, 'd take a party of us to the confectioner's for pastry and ginger beer. Or hire a landau for the afternoon. Then there was another feller's guardian, nothing would suit but taking two of us out sailing. It was sure more of a treat then roaming the town with a full stomach that was more than likely to cause trouble. Ship owners' sons from the ports of the world, a good many of those fellers, with agents at Lloyd's to keep 'em, such little fellers, looking not too easy in their foreign-cut clothes, and speaking no

English. I sure felt pity for them sometimes, and me with all Lancashire for a home, and Frea not far away. But the matron was a lady of kind heart. She was there only to watch the little fellers. First thing she did when they drove up from the docks was to take 'em away to get English clothes. Dressed speckless they were, and soon learned not to cry, or spit at you when they were angry. 'Tis fortunate for the world English habits are more catching than the so-called Latin influence. Not but what my best friend at school didn't come from Peru. He was the only one I couldn't lick.

"Well, Ma'am, I mustn't detain you from your duties. The past is always entertaining and never more so than when you're left with too much time for turning it over. If you'll excuse me, it shall be *au revoir*."

I held out may hand and said, "Goodbye."

He looked at it dimly for a moment before grasping it.

"Goodbye, did you say, Ma'am? Aye then, *goodbye*! I've not heard the word for some years, nor shaken a friend's hand, excuse me. 'Tis a sustaining thing to hear it again when you live as I live, in the light of philanthropy."

༄ Chapter II. ༄

I WAS NOT sorry when we steamed away from Bonney, the smell of palm oil which we had taken onboard added to the discomfort produced by the heat and vapors which were always thicker before sunset, whilst midges, mosquitoes, and various winged insects caused one continual annoyance. Flocks of gray parrots flew over us bound for their roosting places, keeping up a continuous screeching. Once well away we had a view of the Old Calabar Coast and soon left behind us our winged tormentors. The next morning on waking for our shower bath, which was supplied us from the ship's hose, we had a distant view of the Cameroon mountains, which are very high. Sailing midway between Princes Island and the Ivory Coast we passed Gaboon and many lesser landings where Hatton and Cookson's flag could be seen saluting us from the shore as we sailed past bound for Gabenda at the mouth of the River Congo. Arriving at daybreak, we sailed to within easy distance of the shore, boats were immediately lowered and we were soon sitting down to an early breakfast with our good host Mr. Phillips, our firm's representative.

Gabenda was a pretty place, the few houses being built in the Old Portuguese style were cool and artistic. Everybody here could speak Portuguese, and although I could understand the conversation, I could not speak well enough to reply. At this stop we discharged cargo and took on a miscellaneous one. After bidding our new friends a hearty goodbye, we turned to the north again, calling on our way up the coast at Fernandez Vaz and other places. We reached the main depot of our firm at Elobey, four or five miles north of the equator. Here we took on a large consignment of ivory, ball rubber, as well as flake, some palm oil, also ebony, dye wood, etc. Our agent's name was Mr. Carlisle, a good-hearted man, a gentleman of the first water. He held sway from Batenga on the Cameroon coast, as far as Fernandez Vaz. He soon told me that as I was the youngest trader on the coast, he meant to take special care of me, and that my chances of success in life were far better than I imagined, and he would give me every opportunity for forging ahead. The *Angola* left after two days stay with a very large and valuable cargo. One of the company's steamboats, the S.S. *Batenga,* arrived as the S.S. *Angola* left, just in time to signal good luck. A cargo consisting of gunpowder, guns in cases, Manchester prints, etc. in bales; also hardware, boots, clothing, and salt, etc., was soon anchored off the beach of one of the chief centers of the West Coast trade. The post was in charge of Mr. Jobay. The stores and buildings were large, whilst the dwelling portion was a fine, well-verandaded building beautifully situated and only 200 yards from a fine sandy beach. The place was fronted by a large garden and was shaded by giant palms and coconut trees. As I was sent to Gaboon to make a special study of the ivory and rubber trade, I was put in charge of the ivory and India rubber store and had for my assistant Ritiga, chief of that portion of Gaboon city. He was an old experienced trader and soon taught me how to buy ivory. Most of the natives who came to sell ivory were M'pangwes, cannibals all, and traveled long distances. Most of them were tall, muscular fellows used to hardships and dangers. All had filed sharpened teeth, were marked on their faces or necks with some distinguishing marks. They were all well-armed with guns, spears, and large native-made daggers. Many of them wore scars on their bodies of old wounds, wore loin covers of skins, and were as wild and picturesque a lot of savages as you could possibly find any-where. A skin pouch was carried filled with all kinds of smoked meat, including dried smoked rats which they were very fond of. Ladlike, I was curious to know what they carried for food and they were not choosy, everything they said was *bechit*, their name for food. Monkeys of various kinds were delicacies. They also carried a wild bean, which they chewed in the same manner as a white man does tobacco. I tried some of it and found it to be first class. It reddens the lips and mouth and they claim that a few of these beans are sufficient to stave off hunger for several days. Each lot, as they came in, took up separate camping grounds, all old feuds and bad feelings were put on one side whilst selling their ivory. Each tusk was weighed generally. The large ones, running sixty to seventy pounds, were the most difficult to buy. Each tusk represented so many flint-locked guns and so much gunpowder and so many bags of salt. After the quantity of these had been agreed upon, guns so many were roomed (native term) or exchanged for brass and copper rods, lead bars, spiral wire plates, brass neptunes, trade boxes, knives, razors, files, various kinds of bowls, and other arti-cles always kept in stock. The art of trading was to get the natives to exchange cheap articles for dear ones so that it kept one busy talking and bartering, sometimes for an hour or more before the prices of the largest ivories were settled on. The lesser ones were easily bought whilst large strings of India rubber changed hands very quietly. Native-made daggers, spears, a large variety of leop-ard and monkey skins were a part of their trading stock.

These hunters often brought in live animals: monkeys, chim-panzees, and once in a while a young gorilla, likewise baby elephants. These African elephants are more trouble than they are worth, as it is impossible to tame them, whilst the young gorillas died of stomach troubles. They are reared on human milk and *nyondo*, a species of wild shallot or onion they cannot live without, so the natives said. In fact, whilst hunting I found that where you find gorilla colonies, you will always find *nyondo* patches. These so-called men monkeys always like to live in valleys, making their homes where you find the mammoth water vines. These vines are full of delicious cool water and it is really the greatest boon to travelers whilst marching through the forests. I have often seen them over twelve inches thick and full of water always cool. The *cedika*, and many kinds of fine large nuts, he is also fond of. You will never be troubled by dysentery whilst using the water found in these vines and the gorilla, being subject to stomach troubles, is taught by nature to use it. The chimpanzee is also found in these glades and is said to breed with the gorilla, producing a monkey called a *colocamba*. In all my travels I never saw a *colocamba*, although I offered a good reward for a live or dead one. So I put this down to the imagination of some dopey hunter.

———

"How do you like it, Ma'am? I shall sure get into my stride before long. It's not the first time I've turned a hand to a job of writing. I used to be able to toss off a good panegyric in my day. When old Matthew W—— died they came to me for it. Nothing but a brewer, but a man of heart in spite of it. It came easy, that's what it was. Sound of the soil on the coffin tapping on the ear—the straining of the cords like the pulling of heartstrings, etcetera, and so forth. Easy stuff to do with a little lapse of the imagination. Oh, aye.

"Lullabies are easy, too, with a bit of practice, although not so useful as topical. An eye for topical will earn many a drink you'd 'a' had to go dry for. We earned quite a nice little sum out of Tutankhamen when he was in the limelight. Feller I know who had a pretty sympathy with the guitar went partners with me. I wove out the poetry and we both managed a bit of a dance. A knowledge of hornpipe'll come in for most occasions. Yes, Ma'am. It's in the nature of this life that no portion of one's make-up is ever waste product. I'm not saying there was much college intelligence required in that little turn—words *or* dance. But if you're a student of humanity it'll be abundantly clear that intellect displayed in the Golden City is never likely to earn a bed. *Homo stultus* in hotel bars and me dancing before 'em for a living. Me—that's seen the unrolling of an African river for the first time before a white man's eyes…Kingfishers I could hardly count on both hands for variability. Gay as popinjays. And the great panorama of elephants at full leisure where the banks were trodden down at the watering places…Aye. Othello himself couldn't have seen more of the world.

"I could take you there, Ma'am. I could navigate you anywhere on the rivers that fall to the sea near Gaboon. Half a day from Muni River to Gaboon where John Scott lived. He shot a nigger in self-defense and was imprisoned by the Spanish. Died of ill-treatment in prison. 'Twas on account of this Carlisle refused to trade with the Spaniards and moved away. A thorough gentleman, Carlisle, and the first man to trade on the Muni. A wild lad, but college-bred, which is an advantage in all commerce with savages if not with dagos. All Latin races being somewhat lacking in perception. A great trader he was, one of the old breed that were like kings on the coast. Talk of Leopold with his ladies of the demimonde—any English trader of those days could 'a' sat on a throne, safe amongst cannibals, sooner than what Leopold could, if he'd had the pluck of a louse to come and see his territory. Aye. The traders were the imperial breed, and no gold froggings to label 'em.

"In those days there was an old man-of-war in the mouth of Muni River. Did odd jobs and so on. How long could you live in Gaboon if you didn't look out for yourself? That man-of-war—'twas like having a good mastiff on the doormat.

"Muni River…*Mime j'ra Gogo*…

"'I know that far off place.' That's what I'm singing. Tis a song of Muni River I used to sing. It means 'A young man like me, I'm tired of seeking places that are far, far away.' Aye, the natives there were melodious singers. A beautiful language, theirs. More words to it than you'll find in Anglo-Saxon. The vocabulary of the Greeks could hardly be longer. They called me River-Hawk when I was on the Muni River. Muni River. It means 'You shake as you dance.'…

"If only there was something at the end of life that isn't philanthropy. Something that, when a man's mapped out a wild river in cannibal country, it'll not be overlooked in the latter end, nor his record smothered under black philanthropy. Aye, if we'd think of death as the hand of nature it'd be no worse than lying down to sleep in a cornfield. It's when the parsons trick out a natural process with all sorts of common regalia like heaven and hell, that it becomes something to fear. The worst of it is, when Death has to walk through a doss house looking for the number of your room, he'll not be wearing too kindly a look. He'll not like his company. Such a child of nature as he is must surely prefer the country. Aye, I'd rather fall in with him on the sea itself than between four walls, even if it were the Pope's ante-chamber. 'Twould be a natural spot to every man that is not *Homo stultus*. Some getaway for the soul is necessary and that can only be found in the open, whether air *or* water.

"There's no denying that Death does his best for the sailors. There's less than half of them die in their beds. The undertakers'll never encourage a man to go to sea. The sea's the sailors home, and it's there he'll be found on the ultimate day."

ᴄᴊ Chapter III. ᴊᴄ

ONE OF the most interesting natives of Gaboon was Old Man Pipi, brother of Chief Ritiga. He was a great hunter and also chief medicine man, and had some of the most wonderful cures. There were many diseases that the natives were subject to. One was a species of heart disease and Pipi had a sure cure for it. If not attended to in a reasonable time it was fatal. A pain through the body in the region of the heart was a sure indication of this terrible malady. Pipi would press the painful spot with his finger and watch closely after the finger was released. Once he felt sure of the location, he drew from a small scabbard made of skin, an instrument like a flat bamboo needle. This he inserted two or three inches deep between the ribs he had selected, always piercing from the side, right or left as the case might be. The operation was so skillfully conducted that the patient showed little or no signs of pain, was cured instantaneously to stay cured. As I watched this operation many times, I am certain. Pipi and I were the best of friends and though it was forbidden by the tribe for a father to show anyone but his son his craft, he always explained and showed me how he did it. The next wonderful cure to this was a small worm in the eye which was very painful. Pipi would wait till it appeared wriggling over the ball of the eye below the skin. He then took a small sharp bamboo needle and quick as you could think had the small worm, about one-half inch long and as thick as a silk thread, out on the end of the needle. Always cured, the patient went away smiling.

Whilst hunting one day I walked into a swarm of midges. They attacked me in both eyes, and by the time I had walked about three miles homeward, with violent pains in both eyes, which were swollen and inflamed, I met Pipi coming towards me. He had been informed by a native of my misfortune, and hence his haste to help me. He bade me lie down, and in a few minutes had returned with a stalk of a plant that looked like hemlock and was a light green and hollow in the inside. This he sharpened like a quill pen and, pressing it with his finger, dropped a couple of drops in each eye. The effect of this was smarting pain rather sharp and violent, however in a few minutes this had all disappeared. I could open both eyes and was cured without further operation. I asked Pipi to show me this wonderful plant and this he did. To me it looked like poison hemlock, so common in Lancashire, England, and like it, was hollow in the inside. I next took *crow-crow* which is a blistering, hard to cure. It is very irritating and formed a solid scab covering my arms from the shoulder to the hands. This Pipi cured by hot emulsions of a sprinkling of a black powder called *eriko*, the native name for ebony. In a few days I was completely cured.

Pipi had other cures, but these being the most common, I am certain I am correct in my statements. The old man also told me of the wonderful medicine men I should meet later on when I went trading on the Ogowe River. The Ivilis, he said, were wonderful doctors; this I found to be true. Natives who had leprosy went there to be cured. I knew one Gaboon chief who was afflicted with this disease. I met him two or three years later in the Ivili, which is situated on the south bank of the Ogowe, about eighty miles up, and is said to be a famous place for the cure of leprosy. He looked all right to me and I complimented him on his good luck in going there. He showed me the only patch of the disease, which was still showing on his right hand. There was a slight blotch about three inches round and looked to me, then a young-ster, like thinly dried Epsom salts. I was cured later on, of my first dose of West Coast fever, by one of the *ojangas*, or medicine men of this place. The cure consisted of small red berries and produced heavy sweating. It took several days, but thanks to this man I have not had a dose of fever since. Cured to stay cured is what he told me, and although I have been for many years in some of the most pestilential spots on Earth since, I have proved immune, where sound healthy men have died. Of their witchcraft, etc., I will give you a good description later. White doctors, I found out, have a lot to learn about these diseases, and it has often occurred to me that some efficient man would confer a great benefice on humanity if he would only risk a little time in research on the wild river Ogowe. I was cured of bad gunshot wounds and spear wounds by these natives, no white medical man being available at the time. I can show you my first wound on the left hand. As I had hold of the top of the native's gun at the time, and it went off, I received a wound which pretty nearly tore off my thumb. This was cured by hot bark emulsions, and the wound was filled with the white of a cricket. Like a cockroach trod underfoot, the white of the stomach come out on pressure.

Worm in the leg is another disease which I have seen cured. This worm inhabits the leg between foot and knee. The *ojanga* finds the head by carefully examining for a small swelling; this is lanced or cut carefully. The head of the worm is then secured between two pieces of soft pithy wood and is turned once and the wood nipping the head of the worm is then securely tied by mak-ing a turn of the wood each day. With the head part of the worm secured, the patient gradually loses the worm.

As each tribe has a cure for the diseases most prevalent, amongst them the cures are quite numerous. Dysentery is cured by enema of a pepper (called *togolo*). The water vine, which contains at all times pure cold water with a very agreeable taste, will be found healthy at all times and will be found in the glades along the lakes and rivers. This is always used by gorillas and chimpanzees and where it is found you will find their homes. The wild *nyondo*, or onion like a shallot, is also readily eaten by gorillas young or old. Natives declare this biggest of all apes will not live without it. Wild coffee, also a species of sugar cane and a species of red banana are found. The coffee is first class and is used in Gaboon.

———

"I've been doing a bit for the doctors this time that'll provide an interesting novelty. Aye, I'm a humanitarian and that's why I like to remember the medicines. A certain modicum of medical knowledge should be in every man's makeup. George Bussey knew his *Materia Medica* or he couldn't have reported the passing of the Anti-Vivisection Bill in a readable manner. George Bussey, the friend of Dickens. They went through Poverty Square together, if anybody did. Aye, they sure took rooms there for a time, and it wasn't on the first floor either. Dickens, and a lot of other fellers like that. Why, they'd go to Day and Martin's blacking factory and gum labels on the bottles for two and six a night, working right through till the small hours. Bussey lived at Albany Road, Camberwell, in his better days. But when he was fighting for a footing in London, before he became Master of Hansard, he and Dickens'd come across many a day when they'd have to keep away from the Old Portugal in the Strand. Too many fellers they knew there and they hadn't got the money for the drinks. They'd walk all the way to the old Fox under the Hill at Dulwich to get a cheaper drink and a bit of bread and cheese by themselves. He was a good feller to me, was George. Aye, he'd a big heart for the young. And what I know of literary procedure comes from him…

"Aye. That Old Portugal was always a great house for newspapermen, poets, betting men, and so on. 'Tis an axiom of nature for all men who live on their wits to gather together. Fellers that like every day to have a different flavor.

"I thought you'd like these notes on medicine, your husband being a scientist will sure appreciate it. I've always had a bit of a soft spot for men of science. Got the taste when I was on the Coast. Dredging party came along in a nice little vessel all fitted up for wrestling with the secrets of the deep. What is it that feller Byron said? 'Ten thousand fleets sweep over thee in vain.' Grandiose stuff, but it never stood in the way of fellers like those I met on the Ivory Coast when I was a lad. Scientific gentlemen with nets and spirits o' wine and what not. The head of them was one of the Professors of Science. Nice party of fellers, though. Very interested in nature they seemed. 'Twas like talking to children to answer all their questions. I could tell 'em a bit about some of the lakes I'd been on, where you can see to the bottom same as peering into a dew drop. 'Twas a pleasure to hobnob with such a party. Drawing so much life from nature myself, it sure made me understand their ways.

"There's a simplicity comes from the worship of nature, same as from goodness. That poor missionary lady…innocent as a child she was…'Why, Mr. Horn,' she says, 'what's the matter? Isn't God here just the same as in America?' 'Twas when we were walking through a cannibal village. They'd never seen a white woman before. The only one within a thousand miles was Nina T—— that was goddess in a Josh House. Did you know I'm blood brother to Nina T——? Yes, by the rite of Egbo, Ma'am. Not that she was lady fair, although her father was an Englishman. Her mother was an Octoroon from Princess Island. But English blood'll battle through. Nina's hair was auburn. Dark auburn. And her skin was pale, no darker than many a beauty in London.

"I must be going, Ma'am. I must buy a bit of wire on the way out and be selling again in the morning. Tuesday's a better day than Monday for selling stuff that's not wanted. The women're a bit edgy on Mondays, but on Tuesdays they've got over the worst. There was a woman last week asked me why I didn't go to the tradesman's entrance. One of these weighty daughters of Israel that's only just getting used to having a house to play with. I soon calmed down her furor. I don't always take the trouble but I felt like amusing myself. She bought two lampshades she didn't want. Aye, the old Fist-and-Spear could always meet a situation even if it has to be in the slums and so-called suburbs of the Golden City."

ও Chapter IV. ও

AVING GIVEN you a slight idea of the character of natives who inhabited Gaboon and their powers to cure the most prevalent diseases with herbs and plants, I will describe to you, if possible, how the white traders as well as the natives were situated under the French Government. It must be remembered that at the time of my first few years on the Coast, the French were not as friendly and could naturally not be so to the Germans as they were to the Britishers. The sting of their great defeat at Sedan, the Occupation of Paris a thing they had deemed impossible, was still green in their memories and this fact was a great help to us English traders, as the big German house of Carl Woerman of Hamburg who were the only real opposition, were straining every nerve to gain possesion of a fair share of the trade of this part of Africa.

Whilst the British and German trades were contending for supremacy in the ivory and rubber trade, the French trade was insignificant compared to these two giants of commerce. The feeling between the British and German races to each other and trade rivalry made no difference in their friendship to each other. Both took their success or defeats in gaining trade in a goodhearted sportsmanlike manner, and when the day's work was over visited each other and even cracked jokes as to their various mistakes and vied with each other in hospitality. Mostly from Hamburg, they were a fine lot of men, these Hamburgers. I liked them immensely and during my trading days I found them a jovial lot as we sat in the evenings and discussed matters. I found they thought as we did and were people who, sooner or later, would hold together. The French were entirely different and I found all the Latin races to be so. They were too fond of military government, the governor having all powers invested in him and handled all civil rights as he thought fit. Outside the City of Gaboon you would never see a soldier, only customs-house officers, with a guard of Senegal soldiers here and there in a few trading spots on the coast. The upcountry traders all fought their own battles, which were frequent with the natives who were lords and masters of their various domains, as much as they ever were.

By far the greatest number of natives who occupied Equatorial Africa were M'pangwes and their territory was immense, stretching from the coast and following the north bank of the Ogowe River into Central Equatorial Africa, yet unknown. They paid tribute to no man and were entirely free in every sense, and did not know or care about the Frenchmen as the great majority of them had never seen a white man, whom they looked upon as a great curiosity. I have entered many a M'pangwe village followed by a crowd of laughing women and children anxious to get a look at the white man, whilst those who happened to be taken by surprise would clear quickly out of their houses and hide behind trees, etc. I had visited most of the rivers running into Gaboon harbor. These were the Como, Remwe, Belagona, and a few smaller ones which are inhabited by Fans, a tribe of the M'pangwes. These people all cut rubber and there were quite a number of ivory traders also dealing with the natives, for various firms in

Gaboon. These natives were a dangerous lot and would often fire on the trading boats, which plied to and fro from the coast, and wars with one another were frequent.

Having learnt the ivory and rubber trade, I was sent to Adoninango, the furthest upcountry post of the firm. I boarded the *Pioneer*, a large paddle steamer belonging to Hatton and Cookson. As the rainy season was now over, this was the last trip this boat could make up the river for six months or more. We had a grand view of the coast sailing close to the shore, as the sea here is deep and there are no reefs or dangers to be encountered. Coming to Cape Lopes, which we doubled in the finest of the weather, we entered the river Ogowe and in a couple of days anchored off the town of Angola. Cape Lopes and this river mouth is inhabited by the Ceringus, mostly pirates and slave traders, and was then considered the most dangerous spot on the coast, especially to small sailing craft. Leaving Angola, we were soon in a well-inhabited country, and passed quite a number of villages each day. The Camma boys occupied the south bank of the river, and on the north bank were Ivilis and Shekhanis. Further upstream we passed Galwa and Okelley villages and then came to M'pangwe towns, both on the right and left bank. The natives all cheered us, crowding the banks as we passed. On the point of an island we now had a view of Carl Woerman's splendid depot where there were large numbers of natives trading at the time. In a few minutes we drew up at the pier of Hatton and Cookson's trading depot and were received by the agent-in-charge Mr. Sinclair. All were busy in no time, landing and checking cargo, and in a few days the steamer *Pioneer* departed with a full cargo made up of ivory, ebony, ball rubber; also tongue and flake rubber. Mr. Sinclair was a tall, well-made Scotchman from the Orkney Islands and was a hard worker. He had an assistant named Mr. Surrey who took fever shortly after I landed and died. I had full charge of the ivory and India rubber which came in, and I must say we did double the trade than the depot at Gaboon. On the arrival of a new bookkeeper named Gibson, and most of the trade being over on account of the fall of the river, I was put to work on surveying the Ogowe, carefully noting the position of the main channel from the mouth to 100 miles above the trading station.

———

"If it's facts you're wanting I can give facts and novelties, too. They are the basis of solid interest. The English set a great deal of store by facts, but if a book's to be sold in America, you must keep an eye on the novelties. I know America. Best not throw too high a light on some of my experiences on the Coast. It never does to give good folk a shock. Aye. Talk of dreadful scenes.... A young lad brought up never to think of evil nor read it in a book—and he gets to the Coast at eighteen…seventeen it might 'a' been…he feels revolt, Ma'am. The shock of it's like to make him sick. He'll shy at everything, like a colt first driven through the streets that's known nothing but the fields. Aye. Even the cruelty's more than he can bear, although in those days I used to say my St. Edward's prayers every night, same as I did in our dormitory. Renchoro, my M'pangwe boy, used to say 'em too. He'd watch me very close, and listen, and in course of time he'd be down on his knees when I was, and making the same sounds as well as he could. Many a paternoster he's sent up. A fine feller, Renchoro. His father was a chief over a bit of Africa the size of all Britain. The great Onlooker must have had many a quiet laugh at the sight of us two boys.

"But it takes a pretty strong prayer to shut out matricide. Not but what they'd have to get permission from the priests at the Josh House to do away with 'em. Then they'd gather a few friends together and chuck somebody's old mother or granny into the river, at the age when in Lancashire she'd be just right for a shawl and a good cup o' tea.

"You couldn't do anything, any more than you could stop a funeral in Lancashire. Seemed like you could neither run away nor shut your eyes…. You just had to shiver and try not to blubber in front of 'em. Some of the old women would battle out and try swimming but 'twas never for long. The crocs in those rivers, who take up a stand near a village, are too lazy to attack a bather or the woman coming for water. They're too well provided. Sometimes you'd even see a floating body. If 'twere a woman she'd be face downward. 'The woman's modest,' they say amongst the natives, meaning that in death she takes up a modest attitude. A man'll always float face up, as if he'd not turn his face on death.

"I hope I've not been too discursive on the great subject of this so-called expansion. It doesn't do to say too much. But if its truth you're wanting, I can tell you the French have never learned to spell the word. Expansion! The biggest stumbling block to trade known to civilized man. The most rapacious nation, consistent with inactivity, the world has ever known. Nothing more than funguses sucking life from a healthy tree. Why, they'd change their duties easy as putting a fresh song on the piano desk. Rush the tax off matches and clap it on something else. That's them. 'Unstable as water, thy name shall not excel.' That's them. I like a little allegorical speech now and then. Used to excess, 'twill lose its effect. I was taught that by George Bussey *and* at St. Edward's. But chosen with an eye, it'll form a spotlight in any narrative.

"That *Pioneer* I'm writing about was Livingstone's old paddle steamer. Fine boat, with a stand of arms and plenty of brass fittings. Fancy sort of cabin. Aye, when you're apt at dispensing hot air in the drawing-room meetings of Piccadilly, you'll get supplied with luxuries for travel. Why, Livingstone killed more men than ever I did, with all me rubber and ivories. Human life was nothing where the Bible had to go. Ladies in Hyde Park praying for 'im and handing on the wherewithal, while we traders had to struggle to open up a country in decency. When I go out to trade I go out with a gun and some Manchester cottons, not with a Bible. He sure was fortune's favorite.

"I must soon be making a move on.... Did I tell you 'twas Renchoro that showed me where George T—— was buried? Aye, he knew where George T——'s slaves had settled and he got T——'s own old boy to come and point it out. Nina's father.

"I've told you about Nina T——, goddess to the Isorga? Aye. It sure gave me a strange feeling to see those eyes looking out from a great mask at me. I was a lad then. Eighteen I might 'a' been. Well—good day Ma'am."

"Mr. Horn, tell me—how did they look?"

He came a step nearer, an expression on his face which, in a young person, would be called shy.

"Ma'am, there's some things it's difficult to capture with a word. I should say her eyes were kind but piercing. Aye. Kind but piercing."

ꙫ Chapter V. ꙫ

*I*WAS PLEASED to have Adoninango, as I was completely my own master. Following the main channel of the Ogowe River was a huge picnic. I had charge of the river trade and visited most of the up and across traders, taking stock of the amount of rubber, ivory, etc. I likewise bought many large canoes big enough for river trade. I selected a large, well-built canoe and took twenty of the best boys, six of whom were old experienced hunters, as my crew. I was well filled with rifles and ammunition, food, and trading goods to pay current expenses with, as money was practically unknown on the river trade. I was well supplied on my first trip, which turned out most successfully both for myself and the firm I represented.

I chose early morning for a start and the sun was not yet visible when I met Herr Schiff, the representative of Carl Woerman and Co., and discussed matters with him for a short space of time. The old man gave me the best of advice, as he had been a long time with his firm he knew what he was talking about, and I found his fatherly advice did me a great deal of good. So bidding a most fond adieu, I was soon far away, traveling very swiftly along the river channel. The Ogowe was full of strange life and sounds at early dawn, in fact, was a veritable zoo let loose. Hippos would scurry from the papyrus swamps into deep water, crocodiles would slide from the banks, and clouds of white-winged seabirds would rise from the banks on which they laid their eggs and raised their young, having come from the ocean for this purpose.

By noon we had entered a small creek which led to Lake Azingo, and before sunset I was having a good hearty supper on the shore of the most beautiful lake in the world. No wonder the canoe boys sang *Imburie N'gange* (Spirits of the lake listen to my song). The creek leading to the lake is arched over by vines, from which hang all kinds of vegetation which was simply crowded with flowers of all shapes and hue. As the trees on both banks were high, there was lots of space between this natural archway and the water and terra firma, which was one mat of varied colored vegetation. Birds of all descriptions flitted to and fro. Now the beautiful crested crane would rise and fly away and kingfishers of all kinds disturbed would follow them. The most beautiful bird in the world, the *pippio*, which is one mass of green and gold, finds a home here. This bird is highly valued in London and Paris. Butterflies all colors and shapes are also to be found in great numbers. Sitting perched on the outstretched branch of a large tree were several large owls, they were very tall and looked just in place as they sat motionless with their large yellow round eyes fully opened looking vacantly at nowhere. These owls are perfectly blind in daylight. Last, but not least, I must mention the monkeys, which quite enjoyed our visit and cut up all sorts of antics for our entertainment. Before entering Lake Azingo, we came on two native canoes, the occupants of which were engaged in spearing *manga*, a species of seal which is found only in the lakes of the Ogowe district. The forest surrounding Lake Azingo furnishes ebony second to none. Here also is the cross-country path to Gaboon city. As I carried the mail, I dispatched a runner as soon as I arrived.

The native villages are inhabited by the Bimvool tribe of M'pangwes, who make quite a good revenue from ebony cutting. The trade of this district was entirely in the hands of Hatton and Cookson and many tons of ebony are shipped yearly. This is also a great rendevous for gorillas and elephants, besides many other species of wild animals and birds. A very large species of water lily, not unlike the Victoria Regia, is to be found amongst the aquatic vegetation. This lily is sensitive.

Leaving Azingo just before sunrise, we were soon well away towards the main river. I have seen many lakes in many countries, but should anyone ask which is the most beautiful I should answer Azingo. As we neared the mouth of this enchanted waterway, my boy pointed out towards a clearing on the right bank. On looking where he pointed I saw three gorillas, one big fellow and two smaller ones. I grabbed my rifle, and could easily have got the big fellow, possibly all three. The canoe, which was traveling at a big rate of speed, spoilt my shot by passing some large trees, and when I next saw these man-apes they were too far away. They were just entering the thick bush on the other side of the clearing. They traveled at a speed that surprised me, they are very quick-sighted, and have a knack of turning corners which is surprising, and will put every rock or tree possible between the hunter and themselves. As they bounce along, the feet hit the ground at the same time or shortly before the hands. The knuckles, which are covered with thick callous black skin, are used instead of hoofs. The large males make a kind of side motion. They can bound at any angle, and I have often seen them make a complete turn in the air in order to get a look at the hunter.

By sundown we arrived at a large Galwa village, situated on the north bank of the river. Here was a skull house or large native Josh House, supposed to contain an Izoga, a sacred human being who never died. This Josh House was situated some distance from the village, and as the sacred rites were being held at the time no one was allowed near it, especially the stranger or the uninitiated. Some of the boys were quite eager to join this Josh so I gave them full permission to do as they wished, in fact I was curious to know all about this Josh or God-man and mentioned this fact to their chief. He said I will see what can be done, and on his return told me that if I waited till the following evening I could *gingina*, or be received as one of them. A special ceremony would be necessary for a white man, and I would be told what to do, on entering the Josh House. To this I agreed and had the pleasure of being initiated. I needed a rest and occupied myself drawing the river chart till the evening, the time for my initiation.

What I saw in that Josh House was such a surprise to me that I shall never forget what took place. These ceremonies always take place in the evenings. I was told that the power of Izoga for good or evil was supreme, and would always help me to get what I wished. Further I could *Ranga Yasi* (swear by saying Yasi) which meant calling Yasi to witness what I said, and I would be believed by all members of the fraternity. I was the first white man to become a member.

"Aye, we're getting to the pith of it now. I'd 'a' been able and willing to write more if they hadn't stuck still another feller into my room. Came in drunk at two o'clock in the morning and said he was Colonel M——. I didn't mind that, if only he'd a gone out when the other fellers did next day. But he stuck close. One of those staring fellers. 'Twas cold and he hadn't a coat. I have to wear the coat you gave me night and day to save it from being collared by some poor chap hasn't got one. 'Tis a poor sort of place. Aye. One good word I can give it—there's no lice. Whatever one's walk of life there's still something to be counted as a blessing. The rich are happy when there are no mosquitoes. For the poor there are greater mercies.

"I thought you'd sure like the portion on Lake Azingo. I can see you're fond of nature, excuse me. Kingfishers, Ma'am. Kingfishers.... Aye, when I go to one of these so-called cinemas, I stand a bit of it and then I come out. Rivers I've seen where no white man had been. It'll take a world of cinema to wash that out. Like a snake with green sides. The middle stream its silvery belly. The crystals of the dew wetting the fine air at dusk when you're watching the transfiguration of the mountains. And kingfishers, with their toppings of bright gold...

"I was a very curious lad, always wanting to know things, you understand. Nothing to read, and having only a Scotchman to talk to, it seemed, you may say, natural to turn to nature. In addition to that, he was always too absentminded about his wife to be bright company for a young boy. One of these strict Presbyterians, he couldn't get his wife out of his mind. Always clapping a hand to his forehead to see if he'd been running a temperature. Not been married long. In the Orkneys he'd left her...

"Peter Nolan, our engineer on the *Hiawatha*, he died from being a Catholic. Something in the throat. I should 'a' died too if it hadn't been for Egbo. Nice feller, Peter Nolan. His folks kept Nolan's Toffee Shop next to Stephenson's Monument. Aye, if it hadn't been for Egbo and the wild witch doctors of the neighborhood.... If the white juice of the cricket is apt to cure a wound. I'm not breaking my heart for Harley Street. And come to a fever, there's none knows better. Make a fomentation of the cotton that's under the bark of the cotton tree and wrap you up in skins and it'll sweat any megrims [migraines] out of you. Aye, Peter Nolan put Catholicism before the wisdom of the savage and he died of it. The witch doctors are quite handy with the throat. They use the wild pepper for that. They'll fold it up like snuff in a sort of little pipe the shape of a cigarette and blow it down the throat.

"Aye, if that poor feller had given himself like a child to the science provided by nature, suitable to the occasion, he'd 'a' been living now, as I am. I'm one of the lucky ones. Here I am still and even philanthropy can't rob me of my memories and my pride in navigating a river or two. Charting 'em, too. Ha! I could tell the Admiralty a thing or two about their little mistakes at the mouths of some of my rivers…."

↶ Chapter VI. ↷

THIS PORTION of the river belonged to the Black Cammas or Nkomis. The king of these people, who were numerous, was Remb Injogu, the elephant of the Cammas. His younger brother was Isogi, which means the Buck. Isogi was a slender and sickly man, always complaining of his sufferings, whilst Remb Injogu was stout, always in good humor and always half intoxicated. A regular King Lear. His wives and children were many. He was always laughing and passing jokes, had no cares or worries, and was greatly loved by his people. He was a perfect opposite of his ever-wailing brother Isogi, who was always attended by witch doctors whose incantations could be heard by night and day, calling on the various deities to ward off the evil spirits that bewitched the chief. I left him very early and after visiting Remb Injogu, I continued my way down the river, and by now had reached the first village of the Ceringus; here I saw the women making cord from the giant cotton tree called the *joungu*. These trees were very high and were a beautiful sight. They were 60 or perhaps 100 feet high, and their tops were loaded with beautiful, white, long staple cotton. In the branches of these trees was a colony of pelicans. The legs of these birds projected out from their nests as they sat hatching. The males fed the females, who never seemed to leave their nests while hatching. Father pelican is very good to his wife, and there was a continual procession to and fro of these huge birds. They are great fishers, and carry their catch in a yellow skin pouch which, when loaded, hangs like a bag under their bill. I shot four of these birds. Their breast tastes like chicken. The fish they carried in their pouches looked like salmon trout. Thus for dinner we had fish, flesh, and foul. I bought a number of cotton handbags and one large hunting bag. These were beautifully made and designed and would sell well in England.

It was about sunset when we arrived at the old slave town named Angola, where we were received by the old chief and his people. The same evening we saw a native *conjo* or theatre. This *conjo* was held in the open air and we all enjoyed the performance. The actors were the Akowa bushmen, a strange race of natives. They are dwarfs averaging about four feet in height. They are splendidly built and are better looking than the average native and are lighter colored. They first gave an exhibition of conjuring.

Some of their tricks were wonderful. After making a bow to the assembled natives, one of these dwarfs took a bow and arrow, shooting the arrow straight up; this he followed by a second arrow which stuck in the end of the first missile. Of course the second was fired with greater force but was a splendid shot. After this, another arrow was fired at his comrade's head. The missile went in, piercing the left cheek and protruded out of the other side. The one with the arrow through the cheeks then paraded round the circle of visitors who loudly cheered the performance. After several other tricks had been performed before a highly delighted audience, these bushmen left the arena, returning later dressed in raffia kilts. They then gave us the best exhibition of dancing to music I ever saw. They danced the native sword dance, then the native dagger dance, both of which are really wonderful. The dagger dance was the best. These long knives were placed, handle down, in the ground from which they protruded about a foot, each one being close, about a foot from the other. After nimbly dancing around these daggers on toetip, keeping time with the music, the dancer quickens his pace, toe dancing in and about these dangerous weapons. The dancing bushmen's feet move so quickly and gracefully in and about these knives that it seemed a miracle how he missed cutting his feet. This feat was loudly cheered.

The next dance was a spinning ball dance. Spinning round on one foot, the performer then danced on his hands, then hand and foot, running round a circle like a raffia ball or a ball of string. Looking on one could not tell or see either head or feet. The performer was loudly cheered amid great laughter. Now came the crowning feat. A hole about two feet in depth was hastily dug and in this was placed a stout banana leaf chosen from a plant by my friend, the chief's son. I helped to plant it. The dancer now executed a *pas seul*. Firstly he gave us a muscle dance, moving the muscles of his breast, first the right one then the left one, always keeping time with the music of the native harp. Then the breasts, first right then left, began to pop in and out, the stomach began to keep time after this, the muscles of the arm, then the left eye, right eye, then left toe, right toe, all keeping time with the music seemingly without an effort, then the right eye, then the left eye. We all cheered. Now he turned adroitly half round, all the muscles of his body answered his wish without effort. Next he commenced to bob up and down from the ground, firstly at four inches, then a foot, then he bobs up and down like an India rubber ball, always in time with the music. He then spun like a top on his left toe, keeping the right leg extended at a perfect right angle. No lighter than a feather—one mass of motion—he leaped in the air and danced on the swaying banana branch until turning a complete somersault, every muscle in his body still moving, he lighted on the ground. We all more than cheered him. Was he human or what was he? Some said wild cat, some said monkey. Myself, though I could never understand why, I came to the conclusion that like a man, he was a little bit of everything. As the bard says, the flower of all creation.

The performance ended, the Akowa left the town. We all made up a collection for them and they were pleased. Where did they go to? Nobody knew, nobody ever lived who knew. Once away they were never seen again. All I could bring myself to believe was that they were the survivals of the fittest, the Paleolithic man from whom we are all descended. I have furthermore come to the conclusion that these few men who live where nobody knows are the only remnants of a race who are our true ancestors and probably these few dancers and conjurors are the only ones left on Earth. If not, where are the others? They are light-skinned and have good European faces. Although they are pygmies, they are pretty nearly as intelligent as ourselves. Their tricks are the result of thought, their weapons are more deadly than ours, viz the poisoned arrows which they can shoot pretty nearly as quickly as we can an automatic, and always with fatal effects if meant to be so. If I am wrong in my assertions concerning the Akowas, I would be pleased to be corrected.

The next day I was busy making firewood contracts, giving orders for large canoes, and buying farina, dried fish, etc. I was greatly assisted by my boy, who was very intelligent, honest and really loved me as I did him. I had taught him to speak and read English. As he was the son of a Camma chief who lived near the sea, he was the owner by birth of a salt claim which we found was being worked by his brother, a slave trader. It had always been my custom to say a prayer before going to bed in the evening, he would kneel down also, he always slept near me. If we were in a dangerous locality he would sleep near me, he would rise on the slightest call, wake my cook, and attend to me hand and foot. We naturally discussed Izoga. Was she a white woman? She was, he answered, because he knew her father who always went to Princes Island to meet the mail steamer, which called about three times a year. He had come to Cape Lopez when my attendant, who was named Renchoro, was a boy. His wife, who came with him on a small steamer, was white, he said, but not so white as the daughter whose name was Nina.

The trader was an Englishman and had died suddenly leaving his store and everything to his wife. He had left three boys and one girl, Nina, who was the youngest. The oldest boy had sailed away on a schooner and was nearly grown to manhood, and along with him went Yousouf Carriala, a Mohammedan slaver and dangerous pirate. This was after his stronghold had been shelled and burned by a British gunboat, a slave catcher which used to patrol the coast. The dead English trader's name was T——. The two other boys died, leaving only Nina and her mother Mrs. T——. Shortly after the death of her husband, she had married a famous witch doctor. This witch doctor took little Nina and her mother away. Was it Nina that was the big Izoga that never died? He said he was not certain but he had heard his father say it was little Nina. T——'s slaves, ten in number, came from Old Calabar and were liberated on the death of Mr. T——. They had, since the death of their owner, lived on his *pindi* or plantation, and as they all had wives and children, formed quite a little colony and made quite a good living gathering mangrove bark for tanning leather in the small rivers. They were not allowed to make salt, as the real owners of the country reserved the right for those who were freeborn only. Where was Hon. T—— buried? As all the white men who died on this part of the coast were buried on an island situated at the main entrance of the Ogowe River, I told him we would visit this spot as soon as we had finished our business at Angola, as I wanted to learn the truth about Nina and her mother. He said the best people to give me all the information were the liberated slaves on the plantation. I found all he said to be correct.

As the old channel of the Ogowe changed every year, I had orders to take great care in following the deepest one, as there were several entrances or mouths of this river. I was to find out the deepest waterway so that a large vessel could make an entry at low tide. If this was possible it would be a great savings, as there was deep water at all times as far as Angola, where the vessel could be met by a small tugboat which arrived later on. As this tug was very powerful and could be used anywhere where five feet of water could be had, she proved a great saving in time and expense. As this boat was sent out after I had recommended the scheme to our agent Mr. Carlisle, and proved a great success and was a step towards Top Dog, I felt quite proud after I proved it to be a great success. As there is a silvery lining in every cloud, there was always lots of amusement if you were not of a serious temperament constituted for the world's battle. As for myself, I found pleasure and amusement always around me. The Akowa dance had put us all in good humor. As the Akowa dance proceeded palm wine, nature's own intoxicant was supplied ad lib, and as a natural consequence made everything look best, but like other fermented drinks if taken too freely caused the drinker to have double vision, in fact he enjoyed the performance twice as well under the influence of Membo palm wine as if he was a temperate man. A more black cosmopolitan crowd I never saw in any part of the world, and I have been a professional globetrotter. This bunch of humanity included pirates, slave traders, slave owners, and many others. They had all come to see the *conjo* or theatre. All conventionality was cut out. As regards the performance itself, executed and arranged by pygmies, it was a huge success and has the world of conventionality beaten to a standstill. The incidents which occurred at this famous *conjo* are always green in my memory, and as I received the impressions made on my mind by this performance in my youth, I have reason to believe they will always remain.

"It'll be a ponderous work, it sure will. But it's weaving out very nicely. Aye. Facts is what they want…facts; with a little bit of old times for sentiment. Looked at from a distance, the past is often as good as fiction. The past is what the Americans amuse themselves with. 'Twould tickle them to death to hear that our elocution teacher at St. Edward's was Edwin Booth, the brother of the feller shot Lincoln. His name'll spring to me in a minute or two—southern family, always a bit sensational whether in acting or reality. *Wilkes* Booth. I thought I'd catch hold of it.

"Nothing but the best at St. Edward's. Individual attention is what was carried out there. Aye, they did their best with me, there's no denying. But I heard Dr. Roberts say, "I'm sorry for the Horns, that lad's so wild." Tuke R.A. taught me oil painting. I took prizes for it. Nothing's ever wasted in our intellectual makeup. I made a couple of pounds with a copy of "The Stag at Bay" only about three years ago…The proprietor of the ——— Bar had a bit of a fancy for Landseer. Thought it'd look well on the walls when he'd had the place done up with paint and paper. I was glad to take on the job, I was beginning to find the *kopjes* a bit more than life-size, looking for gold and so on.

"And that French feller La Marre. You remember *La Marre's French Grammar* perhaps. He was a fine teacher, too. I can remember a whiff of French still. I can speak the language when necessary.

"But you'll always pick up stuff in real life that'll outdo the grammar books in common sense. That's why it was so good for us to meet lads from the outlying portions of the globe. Peru was my friend. Little Peru we called him. The only feller could lick me. I sure had a natural liking for the lad that was better than myself. He had Inca blood in him on the mother's side. His father, a man of the name of L——, was governor or something similar. Afterwards he became what we should now label a Silver King.

Some o' the biggest silver mines in Peru. Could fetch up a revolution as easy as coughing. Aye. Money to spend in Liverpool on men-of-war, either new *or* renovated. A lot of money to be made, always has been, in supplying these little places with fighting ships. 'Tis easy enough to nurse things up to a head—excitable places like that. A good agent that knows his business.

"I know the shipping business from the inside as they say. Aye! 'Tis in the veins. My great-uncle Bill, him that had land in Jamaica and was the last of the privateers, and my grandfather, John Horn, started the firm. Hamlin, Horn and Hamlin. Know it? Aye, the world knows it. All me uncles and cousins I've ever had are in it, same as they were in the Alabama Syndicate. My Uncle Richard was killed in the fight off Galveston. Water fighting's natural as mother's milk to the English. As for Lancashire—the Vikings owned nothing but water till Vortigern incited Hengist and Horsa over to do a bit of fighting against the Scotchmen—so-called Picts and Scots. Aye, nature gave the waters of the world to the Viking. 'Tis his religion. And that part of a man's religion which is convenient, that he'll never drop.

"Well, Ma'am, if there's nothing in this new chapter you'd like explained—I'm always open to questions. I think I told you that that girl Nina T—— will be the pivot of the book. It sure was a bit of a shock to find the daughter of a good English family doing her duty as goddess to Isorga. They called her cruel, but 'twas surely not her fault that she had to see so many fearful doings. Even the smell of blood can get commonplace. Every enemy's head had to be brought in to put on the great pile of skulls there. There was a swarm of bees up under the roof. If they attacked a stranger 'twas all up with him. It was thought they sensed a bad nature. Been there for years they had. Bees have odd notions about some people, but always quiet and gentle with me. Aye, if that poor feller, George T—— could 'a' seen what his little daughter'd be put to…Honorable George T—— he was. I've seen a likeness of him, taken at Cape Coast Castle. Biggish feller, in a helmet and a good mustache. There were some letters too, from his mother. Begging him most pitiful to come back…

"Well, good day to you Ma'am, I'll not overdo you with recollections. Let's call it *au revoir*."

ᴄ **Chapter VII.** ᴐ

EVERYTHING was quiet in the sacred village. My boys, who had been initiated the previous day, all wore a Sunday smile. I had finished two sections of my map and was highly pleased when the old chief called on me. He told me that after many calls the spirits were pleased at my request to join them, he also instructed me to follow all his edicts. This of course I promised to do. As we entered the temple which was then clouded with smoke from the *yos* or bush lights. (*Igo* from which the lights are produced is the bark of a vine loaded with gum, commonly called incense and has been used from time immemorial in religious services. The smell produced was delightful.) There were three nests of sacred bees hung up one hundred yards or so from the temple and also under the roof, and should you be stung by one of these on entry it was an omen which would prohibit you from further egress. After passing these, wild invocations both weird and fantastic were very audible to me, and I must say had a weird and fantastic effect on my mind. On entering the temple, which had an ornamentation of human skulls, and likewise two small pyramids of the same placed on each side of the doorway, I was confronted by a row of masked objects hideous to behold. I was then seated bareheaded on a small seat composed of leopard skins. There were two objects the chief called my attention to, one was a square piece of crystal, the other was peg-top shaped and pointed at one end. He told me to place my hand on these objects, and that one represented fire (the red one) and the other water. This I did but could not help grasping the smaller one which was very heavy. I came to the conclusion it was a ruby of great value. After this there was great vociferation from the building, supposed to come from the spirits behind. The sounds were somewhat irregular and then again there was a conglomeration of spirits of delight. Now everything in the temple began to sparkle and placing his hand on my head, which I bowed low, he announced in a loud voice the entrance of Izaga. He then said *Dana te eo* (Rest in peace or Don't be disturbed). I noticed on raising my head a little commotion from those in goggle-eyed masks who were at the right and left of where I saw the Izaga (or native god). The chief then ordered me to stand up and approach the center mask. Whilst I was doing so the mask disappeared from Izaga, likewise the raffia hangings. There stood the God that Never Dies, the most beautiful white woman I had ever seen. Her eyes were large and had a kind of affectionate look. Although I thought there was pity in them they had a magnetic effect on me. Of course I was young, she looked like sweet sixteen, half-naked there she stood statuesque, dressed where there was any dress in somewhat Egyptian style. On her head she had a dressing of white hairpins made of hippo ivory inlaid with ebony. Her hair was auburn, and was plaited in circles and pressed on to the temples. Two ringlets ornamented with gold and green tassels fell down on each side of her shoulders, whilst high up on her forehead the hair formed a diamond-shaped coronet. A short leopard-skin kilt ornamented with snakeskin and dainty fur sandals with black straps formed the rest of the dress of this Izaga. I was kept waiting for some time, her large intelligent eyes fixed on me. Now a conglomeration of pleasing sounds filled the building and this was mingled with low music from the *ngombis* or native harps which are small, are made like the Egyptian harp but have only seven strings. A sudden cessation of music and muttering was followed by a voice which seemed to come from afar. The spirits were pleased and had made their decision. Distinct command now came from Izaga who said Rangasi. The old chief led and I repeated after him the words *Yasi Izaga*, at the same time striking my left forearm with my right hand. Although the sound came from Izaga, the mouth never moved, the eyes were fixed on me as before, and never moved during the whole performance.

The ceremony over, I withdrew, making a bow to this statuesque beauty. Sounds of sweet music filled the air whilst the clear sweet voice of a girl struck my ear. They were singing a beautiful song, *"Umbilla Nyone me Koka N'gala,"* White Birds from Over the Sea. That of course was meant for me. I was the first and, as far as I knew, the last white man ever permitted to join. Whether becoming a member was a benefit to me, I leave you to judge by what took place afterwards. The power of Izaga extends from Ashanti to the Congo, perhaps further. Every country has a different name for it yet the formation and religious rites are the same. On reaching the large hut where I was staying I had a good talk with the old chief, who told me I must always be kind to my comrades of the same creed. If at any time I was in need, I was always to lay my troubles before Izaga who would always make things right, give me peace of mind at all times, and help me in all my troubles. I thanked him and after giving him a few nice presents of merchandise, I withdrew, saying *Dwana ta so Ogio* (Rest in peace, my relative).

I rose early next morning as was my usual custom and was soon in the main river. Here we passed a small fleet of Nkomis who were taking salt they had made near the sea. This they traded with slaves at Samba Falls, far up the big river called Angani. They stopped for a few minutes' conversation, and then went on their way. I often met these men afterwards at Samba Falls. This town was inhabited by Ivilis and Eveijas.

On my way downstream I amused myself shooting mallard and other ducks. Droves of these frequently fly by and over us on the annual trip to the lakes and the headwaters of the Ogowe and Angani rivers. Next we passed a large canoe belonging to Chief Isogi, the melancholy chief. They had on board a young woman who had been found guilty of bewitching Chief Isogi. They were taking her for execution to the temple of the Ivilis, which I had just left. She was sitting upright, and looked quite resigned to her fate, which was certain. There was one more skull to be added to the temple. The executions take place immediately on the arrival. There is no further ceremony, only the executioner walks round the edifice carrying the dripping head held high whilst his attendants cry Izaga. This was the second victim executed on account of the chief's melancholy illness and, as he was a powerful nabob, being brother to the King of all the river Nkomis, these executions would continue until he had completely recovered.

———

"Aye, the book's about to be a *fait accompli*, as those French fellers say. Risen, one may say, from a gridiron bartered in commerce between two strangers. If you're framing a book to sell— excuse me if I seem to be too apt with advice—you must have ambition, which shows brain and the play of all the instincts liable to make the world beautiful. Facts are *stultus* without the brain, and the brain'll be *stultus* if not based on a choicy instinct.

"'Tis selection that's the crux, George Bussey says. And (if you follow me, Ma'am) if I have to gather together all that I know of Nina T—— and her father into a ponderous mass all in one chapter, and all the information re: nature and commerce in another, it would sure be an indigestible result. Chase the threads and then weave them into pleasing results in what proves best in the ultimate.

"I'm sure getting to the pithy parts now. What I've always wished to investigate is how a ruby came to be in Africa. Africa's got most of the gifts of nature but rubies is what she's never been given. As one of the oldest prospectors I ought to know. But if you'd lived on the Coast as long as I did, and that as near sixty as fifty years ago, there'd be reasonable solutions suggesting themselves. I've bought doubloons from the natives for a few yards of bright cloth. Aye. Got 'em out of the sand, they said. And once I bought three pierced pearls they said'd come from a broken ship that'd been half-buried near a river mouth more years than anybody knew about. Believe me, Ma'am, there's more than Spanish and Portuguese came down that way. What about Malagassies and others feeling the call Westward Ho! as Columbus did.

"The Malagash is a Malay, and in their catamarans the Malays have dared both east and west. Aye, the feller that has the catamaran is the Viking of the South and the water's his element. Why're the totem poles in Mexico same as those in Madagascar? Why is their hair and their features the same? Because *they are the same.* Get a globe, Ma'am, and see if the Malays weren't aptly situated for adventure east *or* west. And with such a gift of nature as the catamaran, safe as a gull and swift as an arrow, who'd to stop him from overtaking Africa in his wanderings? He settles in Madagascar like birds on an islet—what next but to set his catamaran to flight round the Cape and up the old Ivory. How else came that old ruin that has the looks of Zimbabwe about it? Bonded stones same as Zimbabwe. Aye.

"They may give out newspaper talk about King Solomon and the Phoenicians. 'Tis too fanciful. The Malagassies were handy for slipping over in their catamarans. We know they were experienced gold miners and when they grew to anything of a colony they'd sure build themselves an impressive fort. There's some feller in the newspaper tells us Zimbabwe was the work of Bantus. How then did the Bantu trek over to Georgetown and build a similar sort of monument? Bonded stones is what no African native ever thought of. He's hardly yet learnt to put two and two together in the building art. History is made up by tying links together, and one great link for Africa is Madagascar plus Zimbabwe plus Georgetown. This should sure be told to the world. It makes me sick to see how some feller's never traveled will stand and stare at Zimbabwe for a couple of days and then go home and write to the papers. Where's his proofs by comparison? Has he ever taken a scholar's outlook over the ruins in Madagascar? Bonded stones again. That Bantu vision of his is even more of a wildcat scheme than King Solomon. Isn't there traces of King Solomon all down Africa until you touch the equator? 'Solomon's Road' they call it. Pops in and out all down the Lake Chad Road. There's a tribe somewhere out there we used to call Sheba's people—smooth, Arab-type. Aye, I'm not saying that a mythologist like this Rider Haggard couldn't have dragged Solomon through equatorial country for his own uses. But what's the use of going against truth when you've got the Malagash in his catamaran to show it to you? Catamaran? I've seen him a bit closer than that. A poor feller we found in those old workings in Rhodesia. Three yards more to the left and he'd 'a' found a regular Bank of England. More gold than quartz. Most accomplished prospector, the Malagassy. He was sure on the right vein when the great Onlooker said 'Thus far and no further,' and niched him up there like a saint in the wall. Long black hair touching the shoulders—fine skull with a forehead clever as a white man's, just like the dead I've seen in Madagascar. The wealthy families there take their dead for an outing once a year. Mummied and dressed in embalmments. Aye, I've often met 'em supporting the corpse between them and telling it all the news. All a question of habit. That Malagash? He fell all to pieces when we touched him. There was his *batté** there, too. It had been cracked and patched up with raffia hemp—sort of linen—the same as they'd mend a *batté* in Madagascar today.

"Aye, the Malays beat Alexander. Look at the Sioux Indians over in California. The Incas in Peru. The Malays, I'm telling you. Look at their totems—that symbol o' three birds same in Madagascar as in Mexico and the same writing. When Dr. Karl Peters pored over it, and in the end couldn't make it out, he went melancholy. 'Twas on his mind. But they'd 'a' done nothing without that craft of genius styled catamaran.

"Georgetown? Why, sure, 'tis opposite Parrot Island. I could take you there Ma'am. 'Tis a lonesome outlook when you get there. Nothing in nature's so full of solitude as the spot where Man has been, and gone again. The natives'll not go near a place like that.

"Aye, 'twas hot just there. I'd like to feel warmth again like that. Sometimes I feel I'll walk away with my back to the streets and the mines and ask the veld to receive me. 'Twould be my last bit of an adventure, to see what Africa'd do with me. At any rate she'd be able to offer me a clean bed."

---

*Miner's wooden dish for washing gold (Ed.).

ॐ Chapter VIII. ॐ

EFORE LEAVING Angola for the Coast, I received my mail from Liverpool and reading this was a delightful pastime. As the waterway is wide and deep to the mouth of the river, there was no need for sounding, so that I had a delightful day. After my mother's letter, the most important was from a young college friend. We were always together at school and he felt lonely after my departure for Africa. He was born in Peru, South America. He was the son of an Englishman who had wandered to Peru and had married an Inca chief's daughter and become the owner of a famous silver mine. He had died and had left a tremendous fortune to Little Peru, who was my best friend and always remained so. Besides his affectionate letter, he had sent me two long six-shooters, specially made for big game shooting. One of these was especially good, was sighted to 500 yards and was the best small weapon I have had. A supply of ammunition for these small arms was always sent and arrived by each mail about every three months. The river at the commencement of the dry season was crowded with waterfowl, ducks of many varieties, flamingoes, cranes, etc., in great variety. I amused myself shooting these, especially mallard ducks, so that we always had plenty of table birds for food. My boys were always very fond of these and always had good appetites.

By about noon we were at the seaside. And thanks to my good attendant Renchoro, we found a nice little village nestled in a large *pindi* or plantation owned at one time by the father of Nina, the goddess. On his death he had freed all his slaves who had married and formed quite a colony of peaceable natives. The chief of these liberated slaves spoke English fairly well and showed me a little casket or box inlaid with mother-of-pearl, which his master had put in his care. On opening this I found two old faded tintypes. One was T—— and the other was a lady that might be his mother. T—— was well-clad and wore a hunting jacket and hunting leggings. The other photo was a bust and on her head was something that looked like a small ornament of jewels. The face and the rest of the bust was so faded and indistinct I could make nothing of it. In the box I also found a letter from T——'s mother, a very affectionate letter and she had begged him to come home, etc. The contents of this letter I shall never divulge for conscience sake. A small copybook, etc., told me that T—— had taught little Nina how to write. This I was pleased with, as Nina would have perhaps not have forgotten yet. This I found later was correct, as far as reading went, so that I could always smuggle in a short note to the goddess when I used to visit the temple to make a wish. It was customary to make a visit by Isogi's congregation. The supplicant generally had his wish granted if his present was sufficiently large to please the sprits, whom I found easy to satisfy. I bought the casket and contents from the old slave for four bottles of trade rum. This old slave also pointed out to me the island where his master was buried at the entrance to the Ogowe River. I visited this and easily found it. The stone had been broken to pieces, the grave had been opened, and being only a few feet from the edge of the island was gradually being washed away. I removed this with what remained of T—— to the center of the island, but was surprised to find T——'s head had been removed entirely, together with portions of the gravestone, which I put together, but I could not have understood the inscription on it if I had not had T——'s mother's letter, which however proved a clue to his family and likewise his standing with his people, who held a very prominent place amongst the British aristocracy.

Vessels entering the river were forced to use the main channel, which was deep at low tide and went close to the island on the north side. This island was a good landmark for entering vessels and could easily be told, as there were two tall decayed *upas* trees on it, in which a colony of huge vampires made their home. These trees were easily seen from a long distance seaward and made splendid beacons but gave the island an uncanny appearance. I felt more than sad that T——, a piece of flotsam and jetsam like myself, should have such a last resting place. But it was Mother Earth, and I laughed inwardly when I asked myself the question: Will your finality be as good as his. I also found T——'s marriage certificate with his wife's name. They were married at Prince's Island and T—— had first met his wife in Madeira. They were legally married. The goddess had, I should say, every right to whatever property or title would have been her father's, as her elder brother was killed in Northern Nigeria by a British patrol who came up with Yousoff Carriala and his band of Morocco desert thieves. This I proved to be true by the Nigerian Protectorate Border Patrol. T——'s son had fought it out with the rest, as the law of nomads is no surrender. He was killed on the Lake Chad Road.

The Ivory Coast, where I now found myself, was skirted with long islands and there was a navigable passage from Cape Lopez nearly as far south as Fernandez Vaz, and these islands were called *itovas*, pastures for animals. Almost any time of day whilst sailing through these channels one could see herds of *nyari*, wild cattle, grazing peacefully in the *itovis*, whilst the Congo buffalo and many deer and antelope made a home here. These islands were infested with *injogus*, or large leopards, many of these were man-eaters and were more dangerous than lions. Two specimens of beautiful tree-leopards were also to be found here, and likewise many kinds of rare birds. Gorillas were plentiful. The leopards, so the natives say, will not attack gorillas, which were quite able to defend themselves.

Whilst I remained here I always made my home with my boy Renchoro's brother, whom we found busy making salt and preparing salt fish for the slave traders. Most of this salt and fish was sold at Samba Falls on the Angani River. Samba Falls was then the largest slave market of the faraway hinterland of the Ivory Coast. These slave traders were the light Cammas; the river Cammas were called the black Cammas, and although the same tribe of natives, the ones born near the ocean were much lighter than the ones born inland. These two tribes of Camma boys were about the best fighters on the Coast and were always ready and willing to go anywhere with a trader. I was there with strict orders to find an entrance to this waterway or canal, as the loss incurred every year by landing cargo to the trading posts which were to be found as far as Gabenda on the mouth of the Congo, was very great on account of the surf which fringed the Coast. I had been supplied with an old admiralty chart and although I found a few entrances that could be entered by small sailing craft, these were dangerous and useless as far as steamers drawing seven or eight feet of water were concerned. I nearly got drowned following the instructions laid down in this chart. I had left my large canoe some distance away from the entrance of this new river mouth as the small surf canoes built by the Camma people were safer and more easily handled in the surf.

At the entrance of this supposed channel, which I called No. 2 south of Cape Lopez, were several *roches de baleine* or whale rocks. These are formed by caves extending from the river floor to a few feet below oceanwards. The entrances to these caves are large and point to the sea, whilst the outlets are much smaller. These caves, on being struck by a large wave from the sea, force the water out from the surface inland to a great height and look like the spouting of a whale. There was one very large one right in the middle of the supposed entrance. Here I lost my small canoe, which was hit by a gigantic breaker. Two of my boys went through the cave mouth whilst the remaining four of us were thrown out to the left of the whale's head, clean over the barrier reef. As the tide was running inward we all easily swarm to shore, landing on the sandy beach of the *itovi* about a quarter of a mile above the *roche de baleine*. We were all sound, except one boy who had a small piece of the skin of his head hanging down, and as this was covered with coarse black hair would have made a good ink pad. As I had a small medical outfit, I soon patched him up. The small canoe went upstream in two halves but my tin box, in which was my compass, was recovered by some fishermen, so my loss was small: only leadline used for sounding was gone with the admiralty chart. I was glad I lost that admiralty chart, and felt I would do unkind things to the man who made it if I had had him on the island just then. The boys, who I had left in my big canoe, could hardly stop from laughing, dancing, and pointing at the wounded one who they said came through the water and flew up the river like a bird. We all enjoyed the experience and I had surely found the admiralty passage through mouth No. 2. If any of the august gentlemen composing the admiralty department doubt my story, let him take the risk in finding the entrance charted, but I would strongly advise him to steer clear of the whale rock.

After drying ourselves and eating a hearty morning's meal we all felt as fit as ever. Only we all decided that it would be foolish to bother ourselves with any more river entrances. We now commenced cleaning up guns and getting things in shape for a few days hunting, as I wanted a quantity of dried meat for my boys' rations. As I had quite a lot of writing to do I dispatched Renchoro and ten of my best hunting boys with weapons and ammunition to secure this meat, and it was not long before the sound of gunfire could be heard. They returned about four o'clock that afternoon, having killed twenty head. The fishermen who had now joined our party agreed to cut up those dead *inyari,* etc., for one-third of the meat and hides, and commenced operations at once.

We made camp in a beautiful grove of tall redwood trees and feted and feasted ourselves on tidbits of the animals shot. The fishermen were joined by some of their friends and by sundown we were surrounded by a veritable butcher's shop. Large fires were made, as the island was infested by large leopards which made the night hideous by their screams and howls which have an unearthly sound. Early next morning I was out with four of my best hunters, two of us made a large circle so as to have the wind against us whilst the others were to work up slowly carrying the animals and wind towards us. After walking a few miles, myself and boy mounted a little knoll of rocks and had a beautiful view of the *itovi,* which resembled a natural park. There were several large buck and two large *nyari* shading themselves in small groves, but I could see no leopards. I had a splendid view of the animals as they passed and, as I was out for leopards, I let them graze in peace. Some of these animals skipped and frolicked about as they passed and, as I was always fond of seeing the handiwork of Nature, I was well repaid. I returned home without getting a leopard, although we found plenty of spoor. I found out by practice that the leopard is very cute and, like myself, only believed in still hunting. On returning to camp I found that Renchoro had killed a beautiful dark tree leopard, almost black and very rare. This I afterwards sent by next mail to my bosom friend Little Peru.

"How do you like my version of the whale rock episode? A comical interlude is all to the good in literature as in real life. Doesn't do to weigh the thing down with tragedy. The Americans won't stand it. That's why I wove it in after finding T——'s grave. Aye, that old boy of his didn't want to go near. He told Renchoro that they often saw the Englishman walk up and down on the beach on moonlit nights with a little girl in his arms. Seeing that the dead was so restless, it's not strange they wouldn't go near the body. Very fond of the little girl he'd been, the boy said. Always teaching her letters out of a little picture book. Nursing her on his knee when he sat writing letters at the back of the store. 'Twas likely, at the latter end, he didn't feel too safe about her running about near her mother. Who's to know whether she....

"Did I tell you she was an *octoroon*? Princes Island woman. Aye, there sure was a missing link in the family escutcheon. Lots have it, but it doesn't always become known. There'll be great curiosity amongst the English aristocracy to know who George T—— was. I know how inquisitive they are. When I was a young feller in England I was in a position to enter into the feelings of the *haut ton*. They have a naturally inquiring disposition. More than you'd think from exteriors. And there's some it'll touch on the raw. When this book comes out, go and turn up the cushions in Lady ———'s boudoir and you'll find it hidden there. She'll not be talking too loud about her relations on the West Coast. Not that she'd mind the color of 'em. 'Tis only Anglo-Indians and other colonists get faddy about that. But what about Nina's children turning up one day for a share in the property that should 'a been George T——'s? Aye, there's something in the general makeup of the English that'll set property before kinship. If God Almighty was to ask for a corner of the Park to Himself, He'd not get it unless He began turning a few unpleasant miracles.

"The vampires'd look well in a cinema. None of the fellers trading would ever go near that island if they could help it. But you know what lads are, full of curiosity not to miss anything. I had to go and see the bats I'd heard so much about. Very unpleasing to the eye—hanging like an old garment that's been drawn through a sooty chimney, full of crumples. About eighteen inches long. A foot to eighteen inches. Better be strictly accurate and say eighteen inches. The Americans resent inaccuracy—especially in weights and measurements. If I were to take this story in to an American editor he'd say 'This vampire of yours, was it, or was it not, eighteen inches?' Aye, they like you to know your own mind. Not that I can pretend to have handled a vampire. There's something about them forbids the kindly feeling you have for a little bat flitting about on a summer evening like they did in Lancashire when I was a lad.

"Those trees…. 'Twas said they were some kind of *upas* tree, supposed to give out unhealthy fumes. If so, they'd poisoned themselves, too. Dead as mutton they were, except for the bats hanging under the boughs. Good sentinels for the dead. But they couldn't guard them from the sea. The sea thinks nothing of *upas* trees. Nor the dead either. They'll all be gone by now—trees and all. Washed out into the Atlantic, same as poor Tom Keating. One o' the best skippers on the coast was Tom. But the pirates got him and he was buried on the island where George T—— was buried. 'Twas quite a proper burying ground for the fellers that fell to the fever or killed themselves with square-face. Aye, my second visit to the island was when Tom's daughter sent me out some seeds from the garden and a little tin box of English soil. She thought he'd be happier under English soil. No use taking the seeds but I took the soil over. 'Twas too late. The sea'd got Tom Keating. So I just sprinkled the soil out over the edge o' the waves and said 'Here's love for you, Tom, from England.' I had to write and tell the girl 'twas all right. No need to say he'd gone. Women set a great deal by grass and wreaths and etcetera and so forth. But I reckon Tom was glad when the sea let him loose. He'd been a first-class sailor, first and last."

ঌ Chapter IX. ঌ

I WAS READY to return to Adoninango, our chief depot up the Ogowe River, and had given orders for an early start at dawn, but that evening I received a message that the Camma chief, Renchoro's father, would visit me next day at sundown. Another leopard hunt was my next day's fun. News had reached us that an old leopard had killed a slave girl close to a cane brake where she had gone for a nice calabash of cool water at a clear spring which was situated in the middle of the cane brake. This leopard had paid yearly visits to the seashore and had caused the death of many women and dogs, always attacking them near the springs when they went for water. It is a strange fact that most of the human beings killed by leopards are women.

Early dawn on rising I found a motley crowd of slaves and salt-makers. They were armed mostly with guns and spears and were making merry on palm wine. Renchoro and I were accompanied by a slave who was armed with a formidable long *assegai*, and had seen the leopard just after he had killed the slave girl and knew exactly, as it proved shortly afterwards, the tricks and moves of the man-eater. The rest of the party, accompanied by five dogs, formed a circle round the cane brake and soon the drive began. The slave boy took a stand about 150 yards from an old withered hardwood tree, with Renchoro about 20 yards on our right. Here we remained prone and kept in the edge of the long coarse grass, which the beast always made for when hunted from the cane brake.

We had not waited long before a keen-eyed slave pointing to a knoll or mound about 800 yards distant where the leopard was situated between us and the animal drivers. Then he disappeared as the yelling spearmen and dogs approached. I might have killed the brute at 800 yards but was afraid I might possibly miss my distance and kill one of the beaters. The next time I sighted him was jumping into the old tree near us. He executed this move so rapidly that I did not get a chance to shoot. The next moment I had him as he raised his head to get a glimpse of the barking dogs, which were now close to us. The bullet struck him just at the juncture of the spine and head. My boy now shot him low in the spine and the slave rushing forward threw his spear into the animal's body. I asked him why he had done this and he laughingly assured me that a leopard will play dead on you, especially the man-eaters.

As he hung limp from the tree fork, he looked dead enough but I was cautious to go near the monster, which the natives declared was one of the biggest they had ever seen. Now one of the most amusing sights ever I saw took place as they removed him from the tree. A circle dance around him took place, some brandishing their spears as they danced, calling on the spirits of those to witness that they were revenged. Then a procession to our camp on the seashore took place, insulting jokes were addressed to the monster, such as these: We hope, leopard, you enjoy your visit to our camp, we will make you welcome. You seem to have fallen in love with our women, you have a good taste, but now, old man, we will see how nice your meat is.

After breakfast, we decided to divide our force of hunters. One half, under Renchoro, were to shoot meat for his father's reception, as he was always accompanied by two large war canoes and had a large retinue of relatives. The other half and myself were to hunt for tree leopards. We took the five dogs with us. The meat-hunters hunted the north side of the island, whilst I and my party took in the south portion, and the beaters and dogs kept well behind us so as to avoid accidents. Small buck and other animals fled before the beaters, the leopards took cover in the old trees. They are exceedingly clever, these tree leopards, and are hard to find or drive. It was nearing sundown before our efforts were rewarded. The beaters decided to try the bush along the seashore and they had not proceeded far, when from the thick out bounded a fine dark leopard, nearly twice as big as the dark animal shot by my boy previously. I could have killed him as he ran within 200 yards of where I had taken a stand. He sprang into an old tree and lashed his tail from side to side as he calmly waited for the dogs. One of our five dogs was a half-bred Spanish bloodhound, and soon found the leopard in the tree. With their noses pointed up towards him, they yelled savagely. This was just what I wanted to see—a fight—five dogs to one leopard. With gleaming eyes and lashing tail he now crouched, and, making a spring to the ground, he bounded from dog to dog and then sprang into his tree, when I shot him.

He had inflicted terrible wounds on the dogs, one of them died shortly afterwards from loss of blood from wounds like knife cuts that were deep and near the neck. The other three dogs were also gashed about the back and body, and the wounds looked as if they had been made with a knife. So rapid were the motions of the brute, that one could not tell how he had done so much damage in so short a space of time. For his size, he is the most dangerous animal the world possesses and can kill a man as quickly as he can a dog. His claws are the weapons he uses. And my hunters told me once he jumps on you, your chance of life is very small. Fixing his fangs in your flesh he sucks blood at the same time, rapidly working his hind claws, you are soon torn to death.

As the sun was now about to set, I had a look at the barrier reef which seemed to be lit up with silver and gold, whilst the spray thrown up by the whale rock glinted like a shower of river diamonds of first water. Taking along my dead tree leopard, we returned to camp and found all engaged in roasting meat and making ready for a feast. Shortly after our arrival, the chief's canoe, accompanied by two war canoes, arrived. The meeting of my boy and his parents was very affectionate, especially the mother, who was glad to see him now a grown man. The chief was pleased to see me and told me the Camma people would always do their best to help me in any way. His three daughters, and also Renchoro's sweetheart to whom he was betrothed, came along with the chief.

The harps now began to play and the drums to beat, and in no time the *conjo*, or merrymaking and feasting, commenced. Palm wine was consumed in large quantities, dances of various kinds were indulged in, and it was early morning before the chief took his departure in the moonlight. The Camma people like to make their journeys in the moonlight, which is almost as bright as day in Equatorial Africa, so that one can easily see to read a book provided his eyesight is normal. I left the merrymakers after the chief had departed, and got a few hours rest as I wished to start up the Ogowe River with the change of the tide, which is felt as far as Angola and is a great help to traders.

By far, the most amusing native I ever saw was a black dwarf. His face was exactly like a good-looking gorilla. He was about four feet in height had a tremendous chest, whilst his arms were unusually long reaching beyond his knees. He had a long body well-supplied with coarse hair, also a large mouth decked out with beautiful teeth, the eye teeth were very large. He could imitate every move of the man ape and caused more amusement than anyone else at the *conjo* or dance. He would take a banana I gave him, peel it clumsily like a gorilla, whilst he grunted and rolled his eyes around at great speed under this thick protruding eyebrows. This done, he would run backwards and forwards always using the knuckles of his hands and always using his feet in galloping, so that they met the ground before the knuckles of his hands. He would then turn over quickly an imitation stone and would commence grunting with pleasure if the imaginary insects under the imaginary piece of rock were to his liking. He was clever indeed and was born on the high Congo. As when he was young, he was a mischievous youth. He was sold into slavery by his father, who he said was a good old man but could do nothing with him. He was sold several times and eventually reached Samba Falls, where he was purchased by his boss, the saltmaker, with whom he never intended to part, as his master was always kind to him. He had purchased his freedom twice. His master had taken him far down the coast and sold him to a Portuguese, but he had run away and returned to his master. The second time, his master happened to be hard up. He had been sold by agreement to a man on the Cameroon coast but ran away, meeting his old boss on his return. He had always returned to his master, thus buying his freedom twice.

As I had made all my preparations for my return up the Ogowe, I left early next morning by the light of the moon. My canoe, which was a large one, was built for both sea and river sailing. The wind was blowing half a gale, so I decided to sail up the river and give my boys a rest. I had a good set of sails, one of which was especially large, and as we had the wind and tide with us, we went up the river in record time, landing at Angola shortly after noon, so we must have been moving at tremendous speed.

We took in sail at Angola about three P.M. From this place I dispatched four men with my overland mail, which went via Lake Azingo. Needless to say, I had written a long letter to Little Peru, my bosom friend, telling him all about the goddess and who she really was. I also told him that for her sake, I had determined to take away the large ruby and replace it by an imitation. It would be risky but I would chance it. He could sell it in Liverpool or New York after he had it valued, and with the money realized we could educate Nina, whom I intended to steal off later on. I drew a sketch of the precious stone and told him to have the imitation slightly pitted so as to show weathering. I must have the two imitations by next mail, if possible, as I would make the attempt soon to change the true ruby for an imitation. Once I had it in my possession I would send it to him so he would have plenty of time to change it into cash. I told Peru I thought the best market for the big ruby was Tiffany's, New York, USA. I also gave him a good description of the English girl Nina.

In due course I received the two imitations and a most affectionate letter from my South American friend. After transacting what further business I had, I made an early departure and, as the wind held well, I was soon far away up the river, as I used both paddles and sails. I passed the villages in quick succession and was at the mouth of the creek leading to Eliwa Mpoloor big lake, where we had many rubber and ebony traders. There is grand shooting round the big lake. I saw an animal feeding near the banks that looked like a leopard with black spots on a light yellow ground. I shot the animal and we all had a laugh, as the supposed leopard had hoofs like a horse and two small tufts about two or three inches high in place of horns. The natives gave it a name but I have forgotten it. I sent the skin to England to one of my sisters, who was very pleased with it.

There are a great variety of birds at Eliwa Mpoloor, and I shot some fine specimens of crested cranes. The head-topping or crest was long. I sent these feathers to England and they were classed second to none. I was asked to supply them to a London firm at a good many pounds sterling an ounce, but I declined the offer and afterwards only killed the birds I required for my friends in Lancashire as presents who valued them highly. I stayed two days at Eliwa Mpoloor and went gorilla hunting on the second day. I managed to shoot one large female, one out of three we met in a grove. The animal was sitting peacefully playing with something near her, close to an old tree stump. She was only 250 yards off when I fired. She fell forward, dead. The bullet had gone through her head from temple to temple. On approaching we found a young baby gorilla which had gone to her breast immediately as she fell. I felt great sorrow at this sight and made a resolution I would never shoot another of these animals with their babies, it looked too much like murder. I sent the little one to Herr Schiff and it lived for about six months or so and seemed quite contented and happy with its new home, but like nearly all the young gorillas in captivity, died with stomach troubles.

"Aye, the dwarf will provide the novelty. I sure thought he'd come in well in this chapter. His strange antics provide a little relief. I've often wondered at his origins and I sometimes wonder if it's been my destiny to set eyes on that so-called *rara avis,* the missing link. Renchoro, my boy, could never take his eyes off him. All the boys were the same, crowding round. He was above par as a draw, that dwarf. Nice feller, though. Affectionate to the core.

"Aye, the Americans must have novelties, whether in search of one of these breakfast foods or in literary matters. I'm not saying it's good for them. Bacon for breakfast and Shakespeare for reading've been good enough for Lancashire and England, generally speaking, for a number of generations.

"What's that, Ma'am? Do I believe Shakespeare was written by Bacon? I've heard the idea spoken of in London, but if you'll excuse me sounding somewhat harsh, that's one of the most foolhardy notions that the mind of man could conceive. Newspaper talk, I call it. One of these dodges. It's well-known that the monks

wrote Shakespeare. Our astronomy professor at St. Edward's—
nice gentleman, I forget his name but he went out to Australia to
study the transit of Venus—howbeit he always said to me 'Aloysius,
my boy, your Shakespeare will carry you wherever you want to go.
Read between the lines. And remember 'twas not one head but
many that represent Shakespeare.' 'Twas the priests, who else?
What human man could have learnt so much without the confes-
sional? 'Tis a universal grasp of the genus Man never likely to have
been wasted on one brain.' Aye! Of *course* they kept him supplied!
I dare say they were glad enough to earn a regular bit of money
from the feller for the powerful stories they could give him. What
they did with the money is not for me to say. We're all human. And
there's a truism you can't get over.

"No, I can't be said to be strictly Catholic anymore, Ma'am. You
forget the animosities of religion when you're living a life close to
nature. These orthodox quarrels're a difficult thing to understand
when you go home and you've been living happy with a
Presbyterian trader shooting gorillas. Strict, *he* was. He'd never go
near the Josh House, Sundays *or* weekdays. A man without a natural curiosity. Aye, too much quinine drinking. Always warding-
off. Any new fancy medicine'd please him, long as they were
labeled preventive.

"Aye, that feller Sinclair belonged to a genus nature never
intended for trading up the river. That poor lady I took down from
Samba Falls would 'a' done better at it. A natural provision of
courage is the right outfit for those parts, trader *or* missionary. She
was a gallant woman. A bigger impression on the savage than any
Countess'd provide. Or that woman I saw in Rhodesia, Lady
Florence Dixie. Wearing bloomers'll make little impression on a
lion, unless a little natural curiosity.

"That forbidden hill, where they used to throw the slaves down
from the rocks. 'Oh, what a place for a mission, Mr. Horn!' she
says. She was looking up like one of these saints in a picture.

"The only white woman I met on the Coast except Nina T———. She was goddess in a Josh House. But I've told you that before. But I'm forgetting Madame Fischer, that little French-woman who kept a little store and sold mostly drinks out of it to officers. A proper poison shop in a climate like that. About thirty-five she was. If she'd had anything of the mother about her she'd not have provided young fellers with a death warrant. Aye, the Latin races are hard, even to the females. If she'd been a Liverpool woman she'd 'a' said: 'Nay, lad. Better make yourself scarce out of here. Better let me make you a nice cup o' tea now.'

"That stove you gave me is sure a godsend, Ma'am. A man's not to be called homeless while he can kindle a flame of his own and call another feller in to it. Well—I'd better along to *au revoir* before I wear out me welcome."

๑ Chapter X. ๑

HE WATER of the lakes is wonderfully clear, so much so that in many places you can see the bottom plainly. These lakes are joined together by swamps and one could possibly travel by them from Lake Eninga to the country inhabited by the black Cammas. Looking round these lakes at the perfect shadows of villages, canoes, trees, plantations, etc., it gives one the impression that you are floating in mid-air. The effect is wonderful. There are no passages to enter these lakes large enough to permit large steamers or boats, on account of the narrowness of the inlets. Submerged rocks in places make them dangerous, although I could use my sail and had very little paddling to do. The lagoons extending east and west for many miles are skirted by large groves, the tall trees of great variety support a dome of foliage of various hues. Butterflies of many shades and colors flit around, whilst parrots of various kinds make a home here. The prettiest of these is the Kiombo which is green with a beautiful headcrest and in captivity makes a beautiful talker, but is not so hardy as the east coast Pretty Poll, which will live nearly anywhere.

The varieties of beautiful fauna and flora to be found here beggars description, whilst a zoo let loose inhabits these places. The people inhabiting these lakes are Galwas or Eningas, who cut rubber in the interland lying south, whilst ebony is to be found nearby in abundance. The country is ruled by small chiefs, many of whom I visited. They would invariably trot out their wives and you were told to pick out one or more and not to feel lonesome in his town. This is looked on as a matter of course by all the tribes, except the cannibal tribes who are absolutely moral. I found trade was excellent; nearly all the trading posts needed new stocks, whilst most of them were even able to pay their debts with the stocks of ivory, ebony, rubber, etc., besides a not inconsiderable quantity of tortoise shell they had on hand.

I left the big lake before daybreak and soon after sunrise was in the Ogowe River, which was very low. As we passed the big sandbanks, huge crocodiles slipped into the water from the banks on which they had laid mouth open, whilst the Tick birds picked their teeth free from insects, etc. Hippos were numerous, while waterfowl, herons, egrets, and many other birds were busy feeding on the fish that come yearly in great numbers from the sea to spawn. The crocodiles grow to a tremendous size and I measured some of them, especially one who often could be seen on the long sandbank near Adoninango. From the top of his tailmark on the sand to his nose he easily measured over thirty-three feet, was olive green in color to dark mud green, whilst his jaws were crooked so as to give him a fine hold of any animal he once closed them on. No one had ever bothered him and I have often passed him at less than a ten-foot distance, he would then walk leisurely to the water's edge and would slip into the river quite unconcerned. His skin was spotted with dark brown spots. We passed several large Galwa towns on our way and the youngsters, as well as many of the grown-ups, would bid us good morning. *Mbolo Tangi*, good morning, white man. I did not care to call at any of these towns as they always took whatever they had for sale to the trading stations where many of their men were employed as canoe boys to traders.

I had a good sound sleep on the sandbank that evening. The sandbanks in the open river are always the most desirable camping grounds, as generally a cool breeze blows over the sand after sundown and makes the night air deliciously cool and refreshing. A swim in the river or lake every morning makes us feel fit and ready for breakfast, which we always had early. I then gave the canoe boys a tot of rum each, took a nip myself and always felt ready for everything.

Leaving the camping ground before sunrise, we were soon in sight of the long island where the German trading post is situated on the eastern point. The left waterway of the island takes you to Adoninango. The island is, I think, twenty miles long. We felt we were nearing home once more. As we were turning from the big river we suddenly came to a standstill, talking ceased, I grabbed my rifle, so did Renchoro. The left-hand river was about a quarter of a mile wide and leisurely walking along the edge of a sandbank was a huge bull elephant making directly for our side of the river. He was about the tallest one I ever have shot. His skin hung loose about his sides and legs which reminded one of mud-colored overalls. His ponderous and nodding head carried splendid large black ivories, whilst his large ears moved slowly, keeping time with his leisurely stride. He entered the water about forty yards from us. He then took up a trunk full of water with which he sprayed himself with ears erect. He continued this process several times, turning the end of his trunk so as to make a circular complete shower bath over his body. We had a fine view of him.

The old rascal elephant was well known to the natives who dwelt on the island. He had paid them yearly visits from time out of mind. He was a night prowler and had killed many of the natives on his rounds and he always destroyed more than he could eat. This dangerous pachyderm was called by the nickname of

Ojuga (which means hunger and starvation), producer of want and hunger. I could have shot him and probably killed him whilst he was crossing the river, but he always held his head in a position to make the eye shot dangerous, as the swag of his head was difficult to keep time with, and I had been taught that the behind-the-ear shot is instantaneously fatal.

An elephant cannot see still objects. On he came slowly towards us and turned to the right twenty-five yards from us, but he held his ears too close to his head for me to take a bead on the fatal shooting spot. As he left the water he headed for the rocky hillside quite close to us and commenced to climb upwards, but gave me no chance for a sure kill. Up he went, and as the hill was very steep he seemed to be climbing a ladder. He took his time but never stopped. He was a splendid climber. About one hundred feet above the water he trumpeted, his ears were up but he was tail on. As the path was small and dangerous, he had signaled ahead that he was coming and wanted a clear road. Suddenly he turned with ears still up and I fired. No result. I fired again with a rifle quickly handed me by my boy, who was good at the job and always behind me loading up. Another shot behind the ear, no result. He quickened his pace and disappeared. I jumped to the sandbank with my boy and as I pointed my rifle the rascal fell backwards—the shots had taken effect.

He was quite 200 feet high when he fell backwards, bringing what seemed like the hill with him. Down, down he came with a few tons of loosened rock and a cloud of dust with him and fell into the river about ten yards from the canoe, with his head on the sandbank and his huge body in the water. We had all cleared away, the canoe boys diving like frogs from a log. When we all had ceased laughing and the dust had cleared away, we found he was quite dead, the hind portion of his body being covered in a pile of rock and dust. My deserted canoe was now adrift going downstream. So I gave strict orders to Renchoro for everybody to get busy. I gave them a good tot of rum each and guessed the weight of my prime black ivories after measuring them at 150 pounds, which was a good guess as they scaled 156 pounds when taken from the head.

The chief of the island inhabitants was sent for, and made his appearance in a large war canoe. This was the celebrated chief Efanginango (Fear none but my own people). He was a fine old man and he and his people were M'pangwes, the same race as the M'pangwes of Gaboon. He was chief of a very superior race to those surrounding him on the mainland, who respected him, but he kept aloof from them and when he and his people were not disturbed, he and his people were not fighters from away back. His bodyguards were well armed with both guns and spears. He shook hands with me in European-style and said he was forced to congratulate me on my luck. Why do you call it luck? Why my son, he said in pure M'pangwe, I have known him when I was a boy and I have speared him in the left side in a fatal spot, but he went away and cured up. We hunted him high and low, as I was then growing wild *illotos* (bananas) and he visited me the next year. Two of my slaves who were near shot him at close range and he turned and trampled them both to pulp but escaped, although we followed him for two days. He has led a charmed life. He had been hunted by my father and grandfather, to whom he was well known, and here he lies, this rascal of all elephants, Ojuga.

As I had promised my boys the meat of the brute, they made a trade with Efanginango for mats, native hats, and a large leopard skin cape or blanket like the one he now wore—quite a good war gain, I thought. In turn, I bought this from them giving them a good price for it, as it was perfect and made up of twenty large-tree leopard skins. The chief's people now began to arrive in large numbers from the island, bringing with them *ijos* (bushlights) and a good supply of palm wine, and in no time fires were lit and there was a full-blown muscle dance in progress—men in line, girls on the other side; one couple would trot out and shake up the sandbank, whilst the rest sang the hunters song *"Oh' Oh' Ricine Njogu macula go wala!"* (Translated: Oh Ricine—a famous hunter of bygone days—the elephant has fallen into a trap.) In other words, has been caught napping.

The chief had skins spread on the sand, on which he and I sat and watched the *conjo*. The musicians were about the best I had heard, their wild music sounding well on the open river and the *ngomas* or native drums. They kept this *conjo* up till next day. The tusks of Ojuga were laid at my feet, as well as the *oqinde* or tail. This I offered to the old chief who gladly accepted it. Whilst he spoke holding up the trophy, the *conjo* ceased: My people, I have accepted this *oqinde*, which must always be kept in honor amongst you, in honor of the visit of this white man whom I am proud to welcome. I order you always to help this white man at any time, and he is always welcome to my home at any time. Loud *vabus* or cheers were the answer to this nice, timely little speech and at a nod from the smiling old man, the *conjo* proceeded.

Elephant meat was now handed round and whilst the chief and I regaled ourselves on French brandy, the rest of the dancers drank rum and palm wine, whilst the bank was covered with small fires, above which hung chunks of elephant meat being roasted and smoked at the same time. Old Efanginango and I now became very friendly, he was about the whitest native I ever met, his jokes were great and I had to laugh outright at some of them, and we eventually drifted into the history of old elephants.

This old man told me that the old elephants always had a favorite *ogey* or spring of clear, cool water, generally in a grove (the one I had killed would surely have made for one of these which he thought was situated a little west of Lake Azingo), whilst a young elephant, when badly wounded, invariably died near the creek crossings or watering places he was used to as bathing and cooling resorts. Not only that, but the younger elephants would be killed or badly beaten off if they approached the *ogeys* or springs resorted to by the rogue elephants, who were invariably chased off from their own herds when they were useless as breeders, the younger bulls uniting to chase him out. This, he said, he was doubly sure of. The old ivory, green and colored ivory, was always dug up from around these places near a spring and was always full-grown ivory, whilst he could not remember finding any small *scrivellos* or female ivory in these *ogeys*. Thus I had what I think is the truth about the old story of elephants burial grounds.

The chief and I turned in about midnight, although the *conjo* was still in full swing. The chief and I, after eating a hearty midnight meal cooked sandbank-style, took a duck and *dorus*, and rolling ourselves up with our heads resting on a skin-covered sand pillow, were soon in the land of dreams, and, as we were two sound sleepers, we did not wake until dawn.

———

"No thank you, Ma'am, I'll not be needing the screen today. I like to see out while I can—at my age.

"Aye, there's something about old Sol's rays that nobody ever thought of. I am instructed by Nature to put my head in the sun. 'Stay in the sun' is her message to the world at large. No need for these fellers to agitate the world with their so-called violet rays. 'Twas nature's teaching in the twilight of the world's history. Even on the Coast I never wore these fancy sun-hats you see on the cinema. Just me ordinary.

"Every cow-puncher of my day wore a soft-hat. Of course on the coast, helmets were the thing for the religious, missionaries and so on. Fancy tourists'd not be without them, and magistrates'd find them a bit more imposing. But for busy men there's nothing beats an English hat. Thirty-five years ago they were sending out hats at $100 apiece for Mexicans. Aye, English-made hats for

Mexico and Peru. Not a hidalgo nor a well turned-out cow-puncher but fancied he ought to wear an English hat. In the Persian Gulf, too, I always wore one. They're handy, whether there or on the Coast as at Frea. Me grandfather's house in Lancashire, the sun was up early there in the summer. We used to lean out in our nightgowns, four in the morning. There'd always be a thrush on the lawn tapping his snail shell on a stone. 'Twas a fine sunny room and you could climb out on to a porch. There was one of these prancing dobby-horses pushed up in a corner. We'd all had him. There was a bit of the plaster broken off one of his fiery nostrils, but he moved all right.

"Aye, when you look at nature's surroundings—those lakes I'm speaking of are clear as dew. Strange apparitions you'll see if you keep your boat still and look down through the water. Nature at her task and a young lad like me surprising her at it, that'd never been seen by blue eyes before mine. I could never get me full of staring. I was always one for finding out. The strange picture of nature'll entrance any boy more than simple bloodshed.

"I'd have me gun with me but often'd go back without a shot fired. 'Twould 'a' been like taking a man unawares to shoot those birds bright as popinjays. They didn't know me for a man. Homo sapiens with a gun'd not shattered their trust in nature.

"Aye, when you're a lad confronted with the eye of Nature, your thoughts're pure as the day when you sat turning a picture book before you could read. I'd sit there staring in the water—and one day I saw a strange birth of the dragonflies. All those creatures—sort of caddis it was—in dozens. A regular school, climbing up on the gunwale out of the water. I was near the bank and there must 'a' been some water plants touching the boat's bottom. And after they'd got dry in the sun there came one bright drop of water on the tail-end of each. Then it shot a tail out and unfolded itself and shook out its new wings's if they'd felt crumpled in the packing and turned all fancy colors before my very eyes. 'Twas like the sun pouring color into them that'd been kept empty. All colors you could name. And eyes—beautiful. They seemed to look at you, and size up the scenery before they'd make up their minds to launch out. They stayed for near an hour on my boat and you could see them getting strong and quivering their wings for life's pleasure. Then they flew off on their swift errands, catching mosquitoes.

"Increase your dragonflies and you'll lessen your mosquito output. Over the water, always hunting mosquitoes. And in the dark shades of the forest you'll see them at midday, always hunting mosquitoes. Aye, the balance of nature—leave it alone and it'll function to perfection. But to see 'em climb up was a strange apparition. I've seen a kind of carp, one that could move out o' the water with some rudiments of legs he'd got. In process of evolution towards a lizard is how I diagnose him. Got the land hunger, as they say. On the move, same as Abraham with his flocks and herds. Aye, 'tis the great instinct of man and beast for movement that keeps the world spinning over and over in space. And the sun that burst the dragonflies on my lake'll not forsake me in less favored circumstances.

"Excuse me not noting the time, Ma'am. How did you like the narrative of the rogue elephant? In the world of literature you're dust and ashes if you haven't got a background of facts. What people may not have realized is that the elephant is a mountaineer. Nimble as a goat once you get him on rocks. 'Tis nothing for him to put his four feet together on a tub in the circus. He can perch on the smallest patch of a rock and never be clumsy about it. Aye, he has the brains of a climber, with the mind always on what's before him. That rogue elephant had likely been a young feller in those parts when Prince Charlie came strutting to Preston. And none to gaze on him then except savages. 'Tis handed down as a duty, to kill him, and part of the family lore to know his whereabouts.

"Aye, nothing so savage as the creature forsaken by his kind. An elephant's too human to enjoy solitude, same as a bull. All he can make of it is to get into mischief, same as humans. Tramping and trumpeting about until the swamp holds him too fast, one day when he's gone to drink as usual, and he can't pull his great weight out. Aye, I can feel for the feller now. 'Twas a grander death my gun provided for him. More majesty in that ponderous fall."

◌ Chapter XI. ◌

ROSE EARLY, the *conjo* was still in progress and Efanginango rose at the same time. I told the old chief that I wished to reach Eninga Lake before sundown that day as I had business to attend to there. He said he would like me to stay a little while at his village, as he wished to pay my boys for the elephant and also give me some food for my journey, which was the custom of himself and his people. We arrived at his village, which lay back from the riverbank about a mile, in a short space of time. His town was quite picturesque, being built near a small lagoon or lake, round which were his plantations. The houses built by the tribe were far superior to any I had seen since leaving Gaboon. They were built generally above the ground and the floors were made of split African bamboo or palm, nicely inter-woven so that they gave slightly when walked upon. In many of these houses the women were weaving mats of many designs that were well designed and pretty. Here Efanginango gave me some specially prepared palm wine, which was really a beautiful and refreshing drink, and with this I was served sweet pudding made of stamped monkey nuts or peanuts mixed with ripe bananas and boiled like a sailor's duff, but instead of being tied in linen it was wrapped in green banana leaves, and to me tasted delicious. Before parting the chief begged me to call on him when passing and I could always count on his friendship and his peoples'. After a hearty handshake, I bade the old man adieu and was soon well away to Lake Eninga.

I thoroughly enjoyed my visit to this village. I arrived at Carl Woerman and Cos. about midday and had a hearty welcome from Herr Schiff and his new assistant, Herr Boome. We all had hearty laughs at the many comical incidents that occurred during my trip. Especially my boy's trip through the whale rock. As I wanted to finish my journey to Eninga, I promised Herr Schiff an early visit when this was over. Eninga was reached about one hour after leaving my best friends. And I had quite a good reception from the Eninga boys and their blind king. Here I also met Nina's father-in-law, who claimed to be doing wonders for the people. He had raised a dead man to life and had also found a charm which, if worn round the neck like a necklace, would prevent anyone being killed by gunshot or by a bullet fired from a gun. He was very friendly with the Eninga king, and years before that he and some of his ilk had persuaded the chief to have his eyes put out.

The old king was stone blind and believed he could transport his spirit to any part of the earth. He was always surrounded by numerous clients, some of whom were suffering from numerous kinds of ailments. Some of these people were medically attended to by the witch doctor previously mentioned, whilst others were supposed to be bewitched. For small or large payments, the king of Eninga agreed to transfer the malady of the patient to the body of the man or woman who had bewitched them. This he believed he could do, as being blind, he could talk to the spirits by day as well as by night. The natives believed him implicitly, as he was known to have effected some marvelous cures, which could not be treated by the famous witch doctor.

I had not much business to do at Eninga so I did not stay there long.

It is a beautiful lake and, as I have previously mentioned, joined Eliwa Mpolo, etc. The water of these inland lakes is quite clear and all surrounded by groves and *impondis* or plantations, and, as they are only a few miles distant from the trading stations, the Eningas supply more than half the food required for these large trading stations. Whilst the Eninga chief was busy chasing up witches, the crafty witch doctor, who was passionately fond of rum, with which I supplied him liberally, kept incessantly telling me of his marvelous cures and charms. Under the influence of Bacchus he went fast asleep. That gave me a good chance to tell my boy Renchoro to go through his bag, as I wanted to look at his stock in trade. This resulted in the discovery of two black lead balls and a few pieces of magnetic iron strong enough to pick up a needle. These I kept. I had discovered his secret of being shot at without receiving any injury, as the black lead or graphite ball split up into dust on being rammed home with a steel ramrod, and the bigger the charge of powder you put behind the dust, the more it pulverized, so that fired at a distance of sixty or seventy yards you stood no chance of being hurt.

I told Renchoro to get out a bottle of Old Dom, which I used as a pick-me-up occasionally. He then roused the witch doctor and, as he asked for a bracer, I served him with a stiff tot of Dominican. I did not see the arch scoundrel again till about sunrise, and as the boys made ready for departure he drank rum and Old Dom until we bade him adieu. He told me he was about to sell his charms to the M'pangwes and begged me to advertise him, as he knew I had great power with the Bimvool, who stood in great need of enlightenment. This of course I promised to do, for such a great benefactor of the human race as he. He felt elated with my answer. I could not say goodbye to the blind king as he was asleep and supposed to be chasing witches.

We were soon clear of Eninga and well on our way to Adoninango. I told Renchoro all about the black lead trick and that he had better go over to the Pangwe town and see Matam, the son of the chief, and tell him all about it. And not to forget to tell him that this rascal was visiting them to sell his charms and make a display. At this we laughed, but I never thought this little joke would end so fatally for the raiser of the dead at Eninga.

———

Needless to say, I had a great welcome from Sinclair and Gibson, his young assistant. Immediately on arrival I handed over my tin box with charts, state of trade in various places, etc., and the new passages I had found opposite Isogi's and Remb Injogu's towns. I also told him that on invitation of the Pangwes at Lake Azingo, large bodies of their friends, all rubber and ebony cutters, were fast settling round the lake so that the trade in the near future could be easily doubled. In fact there was one good-sized village had already reached the coast, and as this trade would all come to Lake Azingo, we would be badly in need of a small tug or steam launch of small draught, powerful, and built to burn wood. Such a boat had been ordered but had now become a real necessity. This and other business information I had brought with me was joyously received by Sinclair, who urged me to take a couple of weeks holiday. He congratulated me on my trip and confessed the knowledge I had imparted to him was new and certainly must be attended to at once.

We had a revival supper and a singsong, and the next day found the chief and his clerk busily engaged on the homeward mail. About six o'clock that evening I received a visit from Matam who wanted me to come out at once, as the Azingo witch doctor had appeared amongst them and was about to give them an exhibition before selling his charms. This I mentioned to Sinclair, who advised me to go by all means, as the M'pangwes of the Bimvool were by far our best customers and as I knew their language so well, they were reluctant to sell their rubber and ivory to anyone else. Sinclair had a great eye to business but little knew what I had up my sleeve. I asked for a few presents for the chief and was told to take anything I wished and charge same to Trade Diplomacy. You know, he said, all is fair in trade, love, and war.

On arrival at the Bimvool town we went immediately to the grove where ceremonies, dances, etc., took place. Here I was greeted by the witch doctor of Azingo. He was awaiting our arrival, as Matam was to fire the gun and my presence would add some charm to the scene. He was ready for the performance and I gave the old chief, who was Matam's father, a drink of Old Dom. Then I drank, Matam drank, and the witch doctor took a big gulp, which made him close one eye for a second.

The old chief now lifted up his short spear and ordered *Bimvool taba se*, which means "All sit down." This order was obeyed immediately. The witch doctor then stepped off the ground about sixty-five yards. He then handed the ball to Matam and told him to load, which he did using the steel ramrod. The witch doctor then began waving his arms and making sounds as if talking to the spirits. He then said, "When I stretch both arms and look at you mouth open, fire." He now stretched out both arms, looked towards the sky and Matam fired. The rascal witch doctor made half a turn and fell dead. Matam had slipped a ball into the gun unseen.

Such a roar of laughter followed this incident. The old chief called for order and everything was quiet immediately. These cannibals have great respect for their old chiefs and obey them implicitly. "My children," he said, "you have seen today what a great *cuckverrot* (talkative idiot) this man has been. He came here to show that he could not be shot by a M'pangwe and ordered his own execution. I tell you, no man's medicine or charm can stop a bullet fired by *ajuna-ie-limba*, a man with the twisted hair. (*Anjuna* is the battle cry of the M'pangwes.) Now tell his people who came with him to take this fool away and tell them not to come here with their charms, but go elsewhere to people who are as great fools as themselves."

The meeting dispersed, still laughing and joking at the dead witch doctor's expense. The M'pangwe village was crowded with ivory hunters, as there was an elephant drive about to take place. The animals were about twenty-five miles away and were being lured into an enclosure several miles in circumference. Once in the enclosure, the trapped animals have no chance of escape, as the hunters—in force—close round and form a ring, which is seldom broken. About 150 animals composed this herd, which were looking for fresh pastures, and those migrations took place yearly, and always in the dry season. Had they not been interfered with, this bunch were heading for the southern shores of Eliwa Mpolo. But the M'pangwes, always on the *qui vive,* generally get them before they arrive at the promised land.

In these migrations the hunters say the young elephants are led by the old bulls who have made the trip before, and, like migrating birds, when they are lonesome they go to the interior and fetch back fresh inhabitants for the districts they live in. No one but the drivers ever go near the enclosure. The animals are coaxed into the enclosure by food being placed at intervals on the way to the trap. Their food consists of wild *illotos* (small red bananas), *cedika* nuts, palm nuts, banana leaves, and a variety of choice foods loved by the elephants. These foods are also distributed in the enclosure and help to keep the animals quiet. Without this they would easily break down the enclosure which is very weak in places and makes one wonder why they do not break through. The food must have a very quieting effect on them. I left the village the next morning with orders that as soon as the elephants were trapped I should be warned, as I wanted to see the animals before the killing.

Herr Schiff was more than glad to see me and we spent most of our time that day and part of the night in making plans for future trade, for our mutual benefit. As the trade in ivory, rubber, etc., was increasing by leaps and bounds it was more than ever apparent to anyone who had an eye to the future that keen competition up-country was absolutely ruinous for both firms. United we could have done better, but being two opposites the best we could do was to have a plain understanding as to our modus operandi in the outdoor trade. It was I that first broached the subject, and Herr Schiff concurred or gave his reasons why not. Mutual help in distress was one of the main subjects and also no encroachment on each other's territories. To this we both agreed, and whilst I and Herr Schiff were in the interior the agreement was never broken, and furthermore, we found for each other up the river and were twice as powerful as we would have been working at loggerheads. As time went on it became a glaring fact that our private agreement had saved many lives and made trade possible in places where otherwise we should never have been able to hold our own singly.

I turned in and slept soundly that night and was awakened early next morning by Matam the hunter that the elephants were in the enclosure. I made all haste, and after breakfast took an early departure to see the fun. Herr Schiff gave Matam an order for a young elephant to be delivered at his trading post and this was afterwards delivered. Young African elephants are difficult to sell as they never become properly tamed but Herr Schiff wanted one for a friend in Germany. On arriving at the trap or enclosure, we found the hunters around the enclosure. Small fires were burning at intervals in a huge circle from which rose a dense smoke, whilst some of the native spearmen walked to and fro near the circle. The elephants were leisurely walking round the trap, whilst many of them were eating the food that was placed there for them. We had quite a good view of them whilst the M'pangwes were watching their actions, especially the larger ones, which would give trouble and had better be killed as soon as possible.

I followed Matam into the enclosure with five of my best hunters and we cautiously made our way to a spot covered with large trees and concealed ourselves. Here we were quite safe, as the animals could not follow us, as the space between the trees was too small. Any large opening had previously been closed with thick stakes firmly driven into the ground. After a short while, two large tuskers came well in short range. Matam's gun rang out and down fell one elephant whilst I got the other, whilst a large grown cow charged a small piece of our fort which had been enclosed, and with such force that she nearly succeeded in forcing an entrance, but she was soon dispatched. It was some time before the big ones came our way, whilst firing had now opened in several places. We killed quite a great number in this manner but all the larger game seemed to be giving the most trouble about the entrance to the enclosure. We decided on moving and giving a signal to the hunters on the outside they lifted back some brush so as to give us an opening. On receiving a signal I was the first to slip out and the rest followed one by one, and we all got clear without mishap.

Great caution is necessary as the animals were now on the alert and would charge anything moving inside the trap. We had the good fortune to see one large elephant break through the enclosure near the entrance as he had charged a retiring hunter. The M'pangwes followed him up, running and dodging like hounds. They are splendid hunters and are absolutely fearless. The big animal was soon made to look like a porcupine, as the barbed spear thrown with unerring aim found an easy billet in his huge body. He made for the river but was there met by the natives who were camped on the edge of the forest he had entered. These men seldom lose a wounded elephant.

As the shades of evening were casting long shadows from the trees, I decided to return home and I left this motley crowd of savages. On our return we met many native women, walking Indian-file through the glades and jungle carrying away elephant meat. These animals are much larger than the Indian, or in fact the elephants of Rhodesia, and are more ferocious. The elephants are mostly hunted in the dry season, as at this season they find plenty of food round the lakes and creeks and rivers. And as they are fond of bathing and good water, they roam in herds along these watercourses.

Of the world's yearly supply of ivory, I have heard it said by men who were in the ivory markets for many years, by far the most, and certainly the best, ivory comes from that portion of the west coast called the Ivory Coast. I have visited many of these elephant traps and could never understand why the animals did not break through the enclosure, as in many places it would have given them no trouble to do so.* All the information on this point was the animals are so fond of the red *illotos* (wild bananas), that after eating them they become probably tame, in the same way they say that gorillas will only make their home near *nyondo* patches. The *nyondo* is the wild shallot or onion.

The cannibal tribes are meat-eaters and always have a supply of smoked meat on hand. This they often sold to the canoe boys at so much a basket. These baskets contain about half a bushel and the contents consist of elephant meat, dried *enongos* (rats) about the size of small rabbits with round ears. Also a variety of monkeys dried and smoked. I have often seen gorilla hands, the hands, feet

---

*Mr. Horn once told me that for two days after being trapped, the elephants never stopped marching mechanically round and round the enclosure, which they could have trampled down with ease. This is reminiscent of Fabre's processionary caterpillars, except that the wild banana seemed eventually to break the spell. (Ed.)

and other portions of chimpanzees, etc. The M'pangwes seldom or never eat fish, and I never saw a case of leprosy amongst them or elephantiasis (swelled leg or foot), so common and fatal amongst the fish-eaters.

I arrived at Adoninango next morning, as I had attended the blood brother ceremony of the Fans. This is a simple ceremony, which consists of a man handing you a piece of sugar cane smeared with blood taken from the arm of your blood brother. My blood brother was Matam, who stood next to me in line. This simple ceremony over, I watched a cannibal dance. This beggars description—loud shouting and cries of *Anjuna i timba* rent the air, guns were fired in volleys in great time and roll-like, well-drilled musketry fire, whilst spear dancers painted all colors and shades kept time to a band of savages whose only music was a reed placed in the nostril. This sounded weird in the extreme. After this, I parted with a guard of spearmen drawn in two lines as far as my canoe, whilst my departure was heralded by cries of "Rest contented Brother of the Fans!"

On arriving at Adoninango, I received news that Count de Brazza would be with us when the waters of the Ogowe had risen, as he intended to visit the interior, which he did later and formed what is now known as the French Congo with its interior capital of Brazzaville situated opposite Stanleypool. So that between Stanley and de Brazza, they had taken in a country bigger than Germany and Austria with little or no trouble from the outside European powers.

"How do you like it, Ma'am? I'm too old for boasting and it's no fancy of mine that people like to read about facts that have lain undisturbed by the pen of man. Unsullied is my word. 'Tis a good word. Aye. Unsullied.

"That witch doctor's death provides a comical episode. 'Twas that feller poisoned George T——. Excuse me, but I'd rather not have the name mentioned. Brentwood, de Trafford—any name you like but we'll keep off T——, the father of the goddess. You remember I told you Nina T—— was in the Josh House, goddess to the Isorga. She had auburn hair somewhat above the average, although done close in the way of Egyptian classics it hardly showed to advantage. When the eye is used to the ladies' fashions of England, anything else seems over-romantic. My sister—Emily, not Edith—Edith was a Sister of Mercy—always seemed to fancy the chignon. An old maid. Lives next to Miss —— in Lancashire. It was surely a bit of a novelty for a lad to see hair done like a picture—ornaments of ivory and so on. Very pretty it looked, although she was on the pale side. A bit startling for a lad's been thinking of a bonny lass in ringlets in a Lancashire lane.

"Aye, that poor feller George T—— was only ill for a day, his boy told me. 'Master very well in the morning, in the evening very sick and cried out too often.' That's what he told me. And dead before midnight. Then the witch doctor took his master's wife away with him, he said. I told you George T—— had married an Octoroon from Prince's Island. A lovely woman, old John D—— told me. He'd been on the Ivory a donkey's years. Seen her once on one of his journeys. The little girl was eight or nine then, the boy said. Might have been younger—you know how a native can't be accurate about age, especially if it's a white person. She was given up to the priests of the Josh House to be trained as the goddess. He could never get near her after that. Not Victoria herself had a stricter bringing-up than a goddess'd have to go through. No choosing a Prince Albert for Nina. Strictly virgin is the law, 'n if you break it, you die. Aye, he couldn't get near her after that. He'd been fond of his master, that feller. He showed me the little picture book that her father'd been teaching her from.

"From Calabar, that witch doctor. A wicked feller. 'Twas he put out the chief's eyes. At the chief's own request, mind you. The feller'd told him that if he was blind he'd be able to see where his enemies were in the night and kill them. But any fool could see it would give the witch doctor a free hand if the chief was blind. With boiling water he did it.

"I admit it wasn't a gentlemanly thing to do, to look in the feller's bag any more than you'd put your hand in old Dr. ————'s bag that used to come to Frea. But no Englishman's ever a gentleman when it comes to taking what he wants from a foreign country.

"Pretend to raise the dead, that feller. All I can say is the specimen I saw that he'd raised'd had his nose plugged up with something to keep him alive before he'd been buried. Some sort of trance. Just cheap conjuring tricks is what he excelled in. You can picture that with a blind chief and all, that place was a proper hotbed of necromancy.

"That elephant hunt makes a pretty splash of activity. What's so peculiar about that way of catching 'em is that they'll walk round and round in a circle for a day or a couple of days, following the leader and never thinking of breaking through the brushwood. 'Tis only when they get exhausted that they'll turn and eat the bananas that lured 'em in. Then the beaters can manage them easily. 'Tis only if you want a bit of fun you go in before they start this procession idea. They make pitfalls, too, to catch single elephants. Dig a pit and cover it nicely with brushwood and bait it with the wild bananas. Aye, 'tis easy enough to catch an elephant, once you make up your mind to be no gentleman about it. When you've done as much watching as I you'll know how to treat the different children of the wilds. 'Tis a grand life—watching. It'll stay your hand, that's too ready to kill, when you're a lad. You've got to give an elephant his congé in no shameful manner. The lion, too—he's such a sensible soul. Dainty, too, like a lady over his food. It's only certain portions, he'll tolerate. The hyena now'll not leave two bootsful of his kill, or anybody else's kill. He's a coarse feller, no death's bad enough for.

"Why, yes, Ma'am, write to my brother, if you've a mind to. He's priest at ———. For myself I don't hold with letters. It's always been my habit to go home every six or seven years, when my bank balance was good. If ever I've been short on the Coast, I could always fall back on a few ivories. Same when I balanced me account for Sinclair. If it fell short, I'd always twenty or thirty ivories to depend on. Here there's nothing but philanthropy. I've no wish to go home with nothing but that in me pocket, instead of what I'd been able to seize for myself from the circumstances of fortune."

ᑐ Chapter XII. ᑐ

THE NEXT few days of holiday were spent in picking out posts for a new station, which was built about one mile below Carl Woerman's down the river, as our present location was upstream and we had the cannibals thickly settled close to us on the east and a troublesome tribe of Galwas on the north and west. It was a dangerous position to be in. In fact, the Galwas declared war on us, but these people were easily conquered. Mustering a force of cannibals, which I led, and all the spare force of native employees we had, we rushed their town, which was quite a large one. The M'pangwes advanced in two lines in extended order like Europeans, whilst a strong force of spearmen crept leisurely in the rear. The firing, which took place as we neared the town, was systematically poured in volleys like drilled troops and continued for some time as to give the spearmen a good rest at charging distance. The battle cry of *Anjuna* now rolled out and the town was in our hands in short order. There was very little loss on either side. The chief was captured and sent to Gaboon, where he received a sentence of three years to Senegal. This had quite a good effect on these troublesome natives. The loss on the Galwa side would have been heavy, but the cannibals had orders to wound and kill as few as possible.

Both Herr Schiff and Sinclair were very pleased with this little battle, which put an end to the small rows which were continually occurring and were often accompanied by fatalities. The precincts of the trading stations were afterwards sacred and no fighting was allowed there. Whilst engaged in picking out trees for the new station, my hunting boys came in with the news that they had sighted gorillas about three miles inland in a valley near a small creek. It was about noon when we came up with them and, as their hearing and sight is keen, it is necessary to use great caution if you want to get near them. Being still a youngster, it was my custom to watch the natural antics of animals and, as gorillas were easy to be had, I often went to watch them. We had a splendid view of this bunch. There were five: one mammy with a big youngster, two medium-sized, and one big one with an odd looking face, his eyes were more sunken and he had large bushy eyebrows. They were drinking from the water vines. One would climb up the vine, which was a large one, whilst the mammy stayed below and the youngster watched progress from fifty feet away. The vine they swung on was about twenty-five feet from the ground but held tight. They wanted either to pull a long length of it down or had some other object in view. Presently it gave a little and down came the lot. All lighted without mishap, and after a few moments the young ones executed a few turns and mounted the vine again. The two smaller ones first, then the mammy. Now the old man gave a grunt and, jumping clear of the ground, grabbed mammy round the waist. Mammy was fast held with the hands and feet and the old man swung around and now and then would give a high jink up and down. The old girl must have been strongly built round the waist to stand this stunt.

Eventually down came the vine. Instead of drinking at once, they all, baby as well, began to pick something like large wood lice from the fallen water carrier. Mammy was the first to break a hole in the vine, which baby began to drink or suck from. She then burst another hole, which must have been rather large as the water drenched her like a hose. She jumped back and shook her head, when one of my boys laughed and spoiled the game. As quick as lightning the youngster jumped on mammy's chest and off went the gang—all but daddy whom I had covered. He was quite a big fellow and I buried him in an ant heap. He was a fine speciman, not so tall as some I have shot, but he made up for it in chest measurement. The ants soon consume the flesh and leave a clean skeleton in short order.

On our way back we surprised a group of black monkeys, but they scampered off into the dark forest so quickly that all got safely away. These monkeys grow to a good size and their skins fetch a good price on the London market. The natives get them by still hunting and killing them with poisoned arrows. After being shot at they will scamper away quickly, always choosing the darkest shades and, as they are jet black, they are hard to shoot. They are curious, and after one is killed by a poisoned arrow they will break away but will soon return to see what has taken place. In this manner I have known a lucky native to get more than a dozen in three or four hours.

I returned to the station, and the next morning before sun-up I was off for the headwaters of this big river, the Angani, which lies about southeast from the Anjuni. My orders were to make a navigation chart of this important river and, if even possible, to continue above Samba Falls to Ashiwa, as down this river come yearly large supplies of rubber, ebony, and a little ivory. I slept on a sandbank near Njuki's town, a very powerful chief who claimed to own the river as far as Samba Falls. All traders call at Njuki's place and, as he was powerful and kept peace in the river as far as he held sway, he was considered a man it was necessary to keep on good terms with. I made very many trips up the Angani and very seldom had any trouble, and could always settle bother that occurred between our traders (who were many) without bloodshed.

At Njuki's town, in front of the chief's house, was a large spreading tree and this tree had been the home of beautiful parrots who made the air pleasing with their wild notes as they came to and fro. These parrots were never molested and were looked upon as sacred. The nights, which were mostly spent on the sandbanks, were deliciously cool and the river breeze chased away the flying pests such as midges, mosquitoes, etc. The harmless hippos could often be seen feeding on the banks and showed up plainly by a phosphorescent glow round the jaws as they chewed their food, whilst often the elephants made you aware of their presence by their low trumpetings and breaking off of branches. Many crossed in the night and it was not difficult to shoot elephants at their crossings, which where numerous between Njuki's town and Samba Falls. The river had been used by slave traders time out of mind by the white Nkomi of the Coast, who exchanged their homemade salt and saltfish for slaves.

The sandbanks were the home in the dry season of all kinds of aquatic birds. These were well-fed on the various kinds of fish which came from the far ocean to spawn yearly. The Okelleys inhabited both sides of the river and were paid tribute by both traders and slavers, but the amount paid was what the traders wished to give.

The next river of note is the Remba Koi (called *rembald* or long river). This river rises or runs far away through Ngilla, the capital of the Okelleys. The chief trade occupation of the people inhabiting the Angani is rubber that finds its way to the trading stations of the Ogowe and comes from the Angani and its tributaries.

The dawn is called by the natives *injuna,* or the gorillas awakening, as the noise they make commencing with a scream ends with a tremendous roar which can be heard afar, and is followed by a beating of the broad chest of the male and sounds not unlike a drum. Some of the natives I have heard imitate the gorilla to perfection and likewise his finishing grunts, which they say are his language.

After leaving the old chief's town we passed many villages which were all situated on the west bank of the river, whilst animals of various kinds held sway and roamed at will in the forests of the east bank which was a hunters' paradise, as the forest trees were tall and allowed an easy passage below their wide-spreading tops and afforded a welcome shade to the traveler or hunter. We passed several large canoes with their cargoes of slaves bound for the coast. Contrary to what you might expect they were a happy lot. Boys and girls mixed with elderly Negroes and their families all seemed happy as they knew that they were bound for the coast where they would be able to eat salt, saltfish, etc. In fact, I have talked with many old slaves who had dwelt on the coast for years and I never heard any who were not contented with their new homes and masters.

Count de Brazza sent word up the rivers and down the rivers for native slaves to go upcountry and live happily and in perfect freedom in his new town of Brazzaville. But after waiting awhile and advertising this amongst the natives, the amount of slaves who joined him were very few. In fact, not a canoeload, which I thought was very discouraging. In fact, as I already have said they preferred to stay with their masters rather than endure the hardships they had gone through in their inland countries which are practically saltless.

I had a splendid trip to the mouth of the Remba Koi, which is situated about one easy day's travel by canoe from Samba Falls. Here Herr Schiff had an educated Senegalese trader who entertained me royally. He had quite a large and well-stocked trading store and did a large trade with the natives of the Remba Koi. I called on him frequently and he always made me perfectly at home. After leaving this river the Ivilis are met with, and make their homes herein, the mountains of the Angani. Next came Samba Falls, which are not very high but are picturesque as they are wide. The king of the Ivilis has his big town here nestled in rows of small streets, along the hill on both sides of the river, whilst the rapids below are singularly beautiful with their eddies and swirling currents keeping time with the incessant roar of the falls.

The large *okilli,* or road for trade and slaves, leaves the mountain town of Samba and runs in a southeasterly direction and is the only road to the interior laying south of Brazzaville, and extends with its many branches nobody knows exactly where. Here I met many slave traders and, as we had many traders at Samba Falls and likewise on the main road, I felt more than at home at Samba Falls. The chief of the Ivilis was a very old man and had a great many ancestors according to his story, which he was ever ready to dole out. The cannibal tribes are good at this but their old king easily took the cake. He had a long lineage which would have shamed the book of Genesis.

I put in the night close to him and my temporary residence was well constructed, clean, and much better than his own. Early in the morning I rapped at his door and shouted in a loud voice for his *ncumbo* or list of lineage. He was alert and came out like a jack-in-the-box, spear in hand, and went through all kinds of antics, whilst we would encourage the old man by shouting *"Kangari"* if he slacked off for wind, and off he would go again. We had to stop him, as his story and how many forebears he had up to the time we called on him to desist already had shown that he was truly a royal chief and the beginning of his ancestry must have dated back, according to what he related in his *ncumbo,* to long before the twilight of history. His effort was rewarded by a good stiff wet of whisky which the old king really enjoyed, and it was laughable to watch the after-effect: the tight closing of his mouth and eyes, and the smiling after-effects that lit up his countenance. The Ivilis, and likewise all the inhabitants of the Angani, were passionately fond of liquor and the old king especially, and as he always drank his raw, I wondered what kind of an interior the old man had.

After an early breakfast I walked down the mountain to get a good look at the falls and the river beyond. At the falls I noticed a small gathering of people at the riverbank and, on inquiring, found that this gathering was for the purpose of witnessing the drowning of an old white-headed grandma who had outlived her generation. And as this was one of the laws of the Ivilis, I was powerless to stop it. I hurried down to the scene and was told that the man who had the legal right to drown the old white-headed woman had not arrived, but he soon put in an appearance. And after a little parley with the people round, during which the poor victim stood bolt upright and did not show any signs of emotion, the relative then seized her and tossed her into the swirl of the rapids below. This being done, they walked away without even turning their heads. I put my glasses on the water and saw her white head appear above water. She seemed to be a good swimmer but after a few more seconds she disappeared. This was perfectly legal according to the laws of the natives and happens very frequently.

—

"I hope you were interested in the technique of a battle with savages. Aye, whenever you lose a fight in Africa you're lost. There's no softness about nature. When you're driven from the herd it's for good. Pity's a fancy article Nature, in her wisdom, can only leave to humanity. She can't afford to handle it herself. Pity versus preservation of the race. That's all it is and it turned out to be a good system until Man thought he knew better than the powers that made him. In nature, as in international comfort, it's the balance of power that must be kept delicate as a hair spring. Big issues from small adjustments, like the big weight of steam I could get out of me engine if I respected its mechanism and remembered that its inventors knew more about it than I did myself. Handling any engine keeps a man off the wild goose track whether in politics or up a new river in so-called darkest Africa. Aye, the *Hiawatha* was as nice a little boat as ever was turned out. Nice brass swivel gun she carried. Hatton and Cookson were always lavish in their notions. That's why they got rich.

"They'd 'a' got somewhat richer if they hadn't had Sinclair in control. 'Twas like being tied to an apron string to try and develop trade under a man like that. Not that he minded *me* risking me skin now and then, but I could have opened out grandly if he had not been there at all. No conviviality in the man beyond an over-dose of quinine. Wanted to return to the Orkneys without a scratch. *I* could be scratched. Aye. Always looking at her photo. But a man shouldn't embrace cowardice for any woman and her ringlets. She'll not think the more of him for betraying his brother man *in extremis*. What Sinclair would never venture to believe was that with the river in white hands it would mean safety for us all. Commercial equality, whether for English, German, or French.

"Aye, rivers—you've got to learn from the noble savage the law of rivers. Make friends on one bank of the river and do it well and good. Then there's safe navigation. Neither in politics nor in real life can a man make friends on both banks of the river.

"But when you put one of these timorous fellows—feel your pulse and run for the doctor....

"Presbyterian he was, Sinclair.

"For a nature-note I've put in the rare passion for salt you'll find in primitive man. Bring 'em down from Leopold's country to the salt-pans on the coast and 'twas quite pretty to see their joy over such a wealth of it. If you gave 'em a bit, they'd cover it quick in both hands and run away and hide, for fear it should be stolen from them. Aye, they make some pretty songs about the salt when they first come down. Happy as crickets about it. All the salt-pan owners are rich in slaves—the slaves are so content with their surroundings. 'Buy me!' they used to beg, when they'd run away from Leopold's country, 'Buy me!' Believe me, Ma'am, a man's wealth is in his slaves. They fight for him and feed him. And their wealth lies in the comfort of having a master. A man that's got a lot of slaves is able to be a good master and not overwork 'em.

"Oh aye, they've got a native substitute for salt up where they come from. A plant called *izanga*. They burn it first and use the ashes for salt. But it can't taste stronger than soda. But it was not only the salt brought 'em from Leopold's country to work for Englishmen. Those fellers were chained to us by freedom more cleverly than they'd been attached to King Leopold by neck irons and other infamous ironmongery. Paid for out of Hell itself, that's what.

"'Twas at this Samba Falls I saw Miss Hasken sketching. Hasken was it, or Haskeyne—I've forgotten how she spelt her name but I mean the mission lady who went as far as du Chaillu. *She* wrote nothing about it. She simply died. No bombast about her. And on that coast she'll be remembered long after du Chaillu's works have rotted to pieces in the British Museum.

"'Why, what's the matter, Mr. Horn?' she says. And we were walking through a village with great big idols sticking up at every corner. Twelve and fourteen feet high some of 'em. Painted skulls everywhere. I put a bright smile on me, Ma'am, and walked beside her with me hand in me pocket grasping me revolver. Not that it'd 'a' been any use. They'd never seen a white woman. And what a sweet face that soul had!

"'God is everywhere' she says. 'Here just the same as in my home in America.'

"And me not daring to look sideways. 'Twas the first time I felt a coward. Aye, women have more than enough to answer for when all secrets are out.

"They'd think nothing so suitable for voodoo as a white woman's body. Something unique is what they pride themselves on. Did I tell you, Ma'am, that on the Coast the remains of the gorilla have just as much value as *muti* (magic) as the human body? 'Tis an interesting point for the so-called scientists. These fellers who believe we spring from the ape'll like that for a bit of evidence. Give 'em something to play with. What's any book, after all, but a compilation of facts plus ideas? And there's one of them."

Chapter XIII.

I WAS KEPT very busy for a few days visiting traders in various places in the mountains on each side of the river below the falls. I found one of our M'pangwe traders away out on the big slave road and as he was a smart, shrewd businessman, he very willingly showed me his reason for being there. All the natives who came by these roads with rubber or other produce paid *ibango* or toll to the Ivili king, and this toll amounted to quite one-sixth of the value of the produce. No native coming from the interior was allowed to sell without coming into the town and must be accompanied by one of the citizens whilst selling, and the toll was handed over immediately when the purchase was made. Many of the natives would creep into this man's store, and although they ran the risk of losing their purchases they would take a chance and sell their rubber either at the store or in the thick bush around it. The exchange was made very rapidly, and the trader got rich by this illicit business, which went on night and day. This was rubber smuggling. Slave traders also made a good business smuggling the slaves by circuitous routes to their boats. These slaves were examined very much after the fashion of a trader examining an animal. The most particular attention was paid to a slave's eyes. Those who had the evil eye were discarded. This disease or fault was called Devil's Eye.

Slaves were cheap, as the overseas trade in them was practically at an end. After the American war of the North and South, there was a strict watch kept on the Old West Coast slavery posts, especially by the British whose gunboats continually patrolled the coast and showed no mercy to slavers. This was a boon to the large trading houses, as the slaves were generally put to rubber cutting and that was the reason for the boom in rubber trade. Many useless slaves were drowned or done away with after their usefulness as rubber cutters was over. A slaver would often buy a father, son, and wife and leave the girl's mother behind, and as the old woman was aged she was generally drowned. This practice of drowning the aged kept the crocodiles and fish well supplied with food in the Angani River.

I made daily visits to the old king and we became great friends. I told him one day that I wanted to proceed up the river above the falls, as I wanted to see the white hippos I heard were to be found between the falls and Ashiwa, which I would also like to visit and to see them make the famous Ashiwa daggers and razors. He did not seem to relish this idea, as the privilege had never been accorded to a white man and this was a strict rule, but he would call his chiefs and would do his best for me. As I was only a lad yet, and was quite a professional coaxer and promised not to do anything without his knowledge, this request was granted, especially as I promised to do no trading or to interfere in any way with the sole right of trade he possessed. Paul du Chaillu, the man who had written a book on gorilla hunting, was stopped at Samba Falls and that was as far as he was allowed to travel. Here was found one of his compasses and an old musical box which had belonged to him, whilst the Ivili boys who hunted for him lived near the falls.

All my routine work being finished, I bade adieu to the old king and had my large canoe pulled up to the other side of the falls, and leaving a crowd of traders, slavers, etc., behind, I pulled up and across the river to an Ineya town. I was made welcome here by the head witch doctor and chief. This was a celebrated religious town and here I saw an old doctor carving a rather hideous wooden god. These gods were in great demand amongst the Ivilis and other natives, as they were supposed to ward off evil spirits. Here I had the pleasure of buying the largest gorilla skull I have ever seen and this was supposed to have great power in spirit land and, as I was an Isorga (Egbo) man, I had no difficulty in becoming the owner of it. The purchase price was three bottles of trade gin and a few other articles of trade. I eventually sent this to Gerrard, College Lane, Camden Town, London, and I realized it was the best figure I ever had for a gorilla's skull.

After leaving the Ineyas, the river meanders through the mountains and by noon we had passed several small villages, but the natives were very shy and cleared at our approach. The river was alive with bird life and I was greatly surprised at the quantity and variety of the kingfishers. Here dwell the smallest ones I had ever seen up to date and looked more like blue hummingbirds. Next at the entrance of a small creek or river we came on the white hippos, but as they were shy I did not get a chance of seeing them at their best, although one big fellow rose close to us and had a very light snout. I had no chance of seeing the rest of his body, but the portion of his head that showed up was certainly much lighter than the common hippo, and as they were sacred I left them religiously alone as far as shooting was concerned.

I spent a couple of days amongst the Ashiwa tribe and they were highly amused to see a white man. I watched the manufacture of daggers, etc., which were splendidly made and I bought a few fine samples, which I shipped to friends in England. The rubber cut in this part of Africa found its way to Samba Falls, but all cut in the southern portion of this country found its way to Cetta Camma or Fernandez Vaz on the coast, and as our firm had large trading stations along the coast I came to the conclusion that it would be robbing Peter to pay Paul to establish a large trading station in that part of Africa.

The rubber cut here is called flake, and is of an inferior quality to the Ogowe rubber. I heard that the Portuguese convicts who had large quantities of slaves cut a large quantity of rubber south of Ashiwa, and as these convicts were hard taskmasters and cruel to the poor natives, they had robbed and slaughtered their masters, and the country was in a state of ferment, as these slaves were well armed and had declared their freedom, which they were well able to hold. This was a good country to keep out of, I thought.

The Ashiwas are also coppersmiths and told me they got their copper from the Angani mountains, where they declared there was a plentiful supply. The dagger and razor handles I bought were ornamented with this copper. On my return journey, I again came on the white hippos but I never got a full close view of them as they were shy. The gorillas are plentiful here and herds of elephants roam unmolested in the mountains and valleys. Some of the mountains are very high and no doubt abound in all kinds of mineral wealth. I was fully satisfied with my visit up the Angani, as I had proved beyond doubt that to use the river above the falls as an outlet for rubber and ivory would be wasted money, as there was not sufficient trade to be done, and also that the big slave road will be the main outlet for trade in this part of Africa.

I was well received by the old king and the inhabitants of Samba Falls and, as my business was all transacted, I returned at once to Adoninango where, after making a full report of what I had seen and heard, I made immediate preparations for a voyage up the big river the Ogowe. My trip above Samba Falls and amongst the mountains was a surprise to Mr. Sinclair, who had always surmised that the river was the one and only route required to double the output of the Angani. But when he saw the map I drew of the big slave roads with their various branches, he completely altered his views and congratulated me for my foresight and perseverance in gaining the knowledge I put before him, and furthermore, he previously had told me I would not be able to proceed above the falls without a fight and had given me extra rifles, as he wanted an open river. When I explained that the only shot or weapon I had found necessary was the bottle, he smiled. The bottle had won and made friends where the use of weapons would never have won a complete victory and would have created everlasting ill feeling and, as Sinclair was a devout Presbyterian, I never mentioned to him the great use to me of the power of Isorga.

Next I visited Carl Woerman's and received such a lot of packages from Little Peru, as well as home letters, I was forced to laugh. After reading my home correspondence I turned to Little Peru's, who had sent two registered letters, one of which contained four fifty-pound Bank of England notes. The first package I opened contained three imitation rubies, well imitating the rough stone in the temple of Isorga, one especially came quite near being an exact duplicate. He had also sent a small camera and lens, some plates and also tin-type outfit, nitrate of silver, collodion bath, etc. Also a book of directions how to use same, likewise a small, dark folding tent, etc. I also received a small electric battery which caused endless amusement amongst the natives. Next case contained two pairs of ladies shoes, a couple of ladies dresses, and a pair of boxing gloves. I thought Herr Schiff would never recover from laughter when I unearthed the pair of silk dresses. In fact Herr Boome, his assistant, could not resist coming in on our solitude and on sight of the slippers and dresses he too laughed outrageously. I left Herr Schiff's after dinner and he was still laughing, as also was his assistant. After locking up all in my canoe locker, I bade them a fond *au revoir*.

———

"That was an outstanding gorilla's head I bought above Samba Falls. One o' the best. Aye, I did well with Gerrards, Camden Town, one time and another. Cross's, Liverpool, too, and some of the zoos'd take all sorts from me. The easiest way in the end is to catch 'em as infants and keep a slave girl for foster-mother. But she'd have not to feed her own child at the same time—the monkey'd kill it. Fearful rages they exhibit, even in childhood. Very choosy about the woman being clean, too. A gorilla's like humans in that way—can't stand the natural perfume of the Negro. Aye, if she didn't wash herself between every feed he'd not take the breast at all. Get sulky about it. They're rare ones for the sulks. Human as a man in that respect. If any philosopher were to give it thought he'd see there's nothing brings us closer akin to the apes than the tantrums we get into.

"Taking the infants from the mother? Hard enough, I admit, but the mother can get another child. No child can replace a fond mother. Only once I shot a mother—I think I've mentioned it. When she was dying she lifted her hand and put it on the baby. She—lifted her hand…No man that's not *Homo stultus* could stand it. I tried to make amends to outraged Nature. I gave the little one to one of the traders to bring up for me. Left him thirty shillings to get proper feeding for it from one of the slave women. Or it might have been two pounds. Meaning to let it loose when it was old enough—paying my debt to that poor mother that asked for pity. But it died in captivity.

"Aye, I sold some thousands of pounds worth in Europe—one thing and another. Chimpanzees are nice creatures to train. I had one for about a year and then I sold her to Crosses and they disposed of her to Manchester. I never knew it, but she recognized me one day when I was walking through the zoo there at Bellevue to see what they'd got. When I was in England it seemed a bit of home to go and look at the animals. Aye, she knew me, after three years—made a strange sound and leapt about and tried to touch me through the bars. I had a great talk with her and we soon had a big crowd listening to us. I knew her again by a mark on one of her arms. Aye, Ma'am, I met no one in Manchester I liked so well. I'd 'a' liked to take her back with me. I'd never seen one of my own catches togged up in a zoo. A very peculiar sensation it gave me. I never felt quite so keen afterwards on packing them to Europe alive. Dead and in spirits—that's harmful to no man.

"But there's always a risk in shipping anything in spirits. A man's a man for all that and you'll not find sailors differing from the rules of common humanity. They put Nelson in spirits after the battle. But when the keg was unpacked in London by the admiralty authorities, there wasn't a drop left. Bone dry. An unpleasant episode, when a man's saved his country, but they gave him St. Paul's as soon as they could. Aye. When you belong to an old shipping family as I do, you get to know history from the inside. Things that don't get put in the obituaries or the panegyrics. 'Twould never do to let the newspapers know everything. As George Bussey used to say, the truth is not always ornamental. People'll stand a bit of demimonde or anything else—come to heroes. But a little bit of reality such as what I've just related is best left to oblivion.

"There's a lot of nonsense talked about slavery. Whether it's degradation or not depends on the master. I never lifted my hand to a native in my life. The boy that needs flogging needs shooting. If I saw a boy was no good, I'd send him away within a few days on some pretext. You need an eye, same as you do for old china and so on. George Bussey's house was full of it, but his wife tried to hide it away as much as she could. Crewelwork and so on. Woolwork. That's what she had a fancy for. Old Derby was what George liked. And I knew a good slave as well as George knew a bit of Derby.

"'Tis a terrible thing for a lad new from school to see the slaves being examined before sold. Such an indignity as could never be matched in any hospital. The doctor being a scientific will understand better. There are things I could scarcely mention to a lady. I shall have to mention it to him [He did so. The things that were in Mr. Horn's mind were the terrible tests for virginity—a virgin being doubly valuable—amongst the girls and young women, which were brutally carried out in front of their forlorn groups of men, who in their turn had to undergo not only indignity but mutilation. As many tribes (among cannibals especially) are not only naturally modest, but have strict codes of morality, this must have been as bitter a tragedy as it would be to many civilized white people.]

"But that 'lurking devil's' a strange thing. Strictly speaking it's not a disease at all, but a sign of character. I wasn't too good at spotting it myself and I can only picture it to you as a slight cast in one of the eyes. Aye, in a country where magic reigns supreme, any little natural defect means a lot. They'd never try to keep families together, those traders. 'Twas a terrible thing to see them being separated. When a savage loses his kin, his heart breaks. He's got no newspapers and these so-called cinemas to cheer him up. All he knows of pleasure comes not from food, but from eating it with his kind. Not from hunting, but from hunting with his tribe. He pines like a dog. The first thing education teaches you is to walk alone. Aye, you can sure stand on your own spear when you've learnt the word goodbye, and say it clear.

"Aye, I must 'a' been the first man to try the river above Samba Falls. Where du Chaillu failed, I succeeded. When you're young and life's a bit of laughable fun, you can get your way easy enough. Too much Latin about du Chaillu. They've never had the knack of youth. As soon as nature makes 'em into men, they stop laughing. One of the greatest obstacles, whether on the Coast or in Lancashire, is to stop laughter.

"Kingfishers! Above par on that river. When a lad's eye's been trained to watch for 'em up a little brook in Lancashire, it's the first thing he sees on an African river. Those bonny birds, finer than dream-size. Threading to and fro in front of your canoe like bobbins o' bright silk. And those faraway mountains that seem pure of man...

"Aye, if I'd known minerals and their habits as I know them now, I'd never have borne to turn my back on them. Minerals. I was in a place once behind the Cameroons, where a piece of the hill had fallen down after a storm and disclosed cinnabar. Quicksilver. The natives paint their faces with it. But copper they smelt out cleverly in their little blast furnaces. Two-handed bellows—piston bellows—same as you find in ancient workings. Same as I found in the copper mine, Tati Concession. They make the bellows of monkey skins. Same old style as you find in Madagascar and Rhodesia."

～ Chapter XIV. ～

ON MY return I was met by a messenger in a canoe and he handed me a letter from Sinclair. The contents were: Mission boy belonging to Kangwe mission station (Presbyterian) has been killed by the Bimvool at Lake Azingo, the other boy was allowed to proceed. The news arrived by Old Dick, our M'pangwe trader at the lake. This boy belonged to the M'pangwe town about 25 miles from here, which is situated on the south side of the river. As you know these people well, I would like you to go and see what can be done, as they say they will declare war at once on the Bimvool if this boy is not paid for at once. The chief of these people is the grandfather of the boy; come immediately when you receive this.

Before I had finished this short letter I was at our pier where I met Old Dick, who told me the whole story. The boy called to rest at the village and was recognized by the Bimvool by fine raised tattoo marks on his neck. Old Dick tried his best to restrain the hostile natives, but to no purpose. After firing the alarm guns to call in the heads of the villages round the lake, the poor missionary lad was carried off to a grove and was there beheaded and eaten, whilst the other boy was allowed to go free to Gaboon with the mails.

As they continued their orgies and seemed to get more reckless as the night proceeded, Dick had made an excuse and had voyaged as quickly as possible to our trading post. On entering Sinclair's sanctorum I met the head of the American Presbyterian mission station at Kangwe hill, about four miles away. He seemed very much disturbed and told me he would like to have this matter settled peaceably. The boy who had been ruthlessly murdered was a clever lad about seventeen years of age and could write and speak English well and was the pride of the Mission and was exceedingly clever. I explained how I thought peace could be brought about at once, as Matam, my cannibal friend, had told me that although they would never bother these people down the river or interfere with their coming and going to Adoninango for trade purposes, yet they were deadly enemies and if they ever came up with them on Bimvool territory they would fight immediately and give no quarter. Furthermore, he said, that these river M'pangwes still owed them two ivories or two of their men, and if they failed to pay up the Bimvool would either kill two of their men or take two ivories.

To get the heads or headmen of these two tribes to come together would be the only way of securing lasting peace. This, I explained to the doctor at the mission, and he thought my plan was good. There was no time to be lost and it would be wise to first visit the M'pangwe town and see the old chief, and afterwards the Bimvool down the river, and bring them together at Adoninango. Mr. Sinclair walked down to the pier with me and I explained to him exactly what I would do to the letter. He bade me a fond adieu and told me not to be mindful of cost, as the two tribes were our best customers. As I had already thought this over, I told him that we must, on no account, let these two tribes fight out their differences as there would certainly be no trade as long as they waged war, whilst we would not be able to trade with Azingo once they commenced fighting. The Bimvool would be sure to win but would wipe out the large town on the other side of the river, whilst other tribes, the Okelleys and the River Nkomis, might be easily brought into it.

As I swung clear he waved his handkerchief and shouted, "you have it all in your hands." I smiled for response, the job just suited me. I waved my handkerchief passing Herr Schiff's and he sent Herr Boome to tell me to wait a minute. Herr Schiff knew all the news, he said, and was willing to help in any way. He handed me a case of home comforts and said, I know you will settle it as you have tackled the job at once. I lit one of his best cigars, waved him goodbye. I made express time going down the river, as the boys were the pride of the river and had had a good rest and we arrived about midnight at the big native town and, as I hopped ashore, I was met by the brother of the boy who had lost his life.

I was immediately conducted to the big hut of the chief, who said to me *Taba Se?* Shall we have a friendly sit down? I commenced business straight away by praises of the dead boy with whom I was well acquainted and told him I had left the white men at the trading post in sorrow and had come to see him at once on receiving the news. I then ceased speaking and opened a bottle of good rum. The chief accepted a drink, as likewise his counselors and relatives. After a pause, he said to one of his kinsmen at the end of the circle, Speak brother. A native bowl containing small wooden sticks was brought in, the same one I have often used in trading ivory.

The first headman spoke only a few words. If he thought rightly, I had come to settle a grievance in which they had lost one of their people and to show my respect for a dead friend. In that I was right. He sat down and the chief, without speaking, handed me a stick. He then motioned to the next counselor who rose and recommended war at once, but with the Bimvool only. He sat down. I spoke with some length. I knew these people and their language, also, I was exactly in the same mind as him, if he could show me how this could be done without hurting outsiders. War, I said, was a manly way of settling your grievances if you could do this without interfering or destroying the trade of innocent people, and how he would manage to do this I would like him to explain. The old chief smiled and ordered the good counselor to reply. He stood and recounted the wrongs done them by the Bimvool but failed to show me how he could make war without doing great injury, and after all would be no nearer peace.

He sat down and in a short harangue I explained how trade was increasing and what a mighty loss it would be to them to have all the white traders leave the river after they had become nicely settled, and the tremendous loss to them of the year's trade or more. Furthermore, the Bimvool were willing to meet them halfway and would take an everlasting peace, a thing they had never enjoyed. I sat down. The old chief smiled broadly and called on the next counselor, who failed to rise. Then he called on the next and the next, nobody rose to reply. He then rose and said, You have listened to good counsel and the white man has spoken well. He then lifted up the bowl of sticks and poured them out at my feet saying, You are right (*Ow embami*). He then ordered his chiefs to counsel the people and bring in the reply, telling them only what had been said in council and to bring in their wishes to him so that he could settle the matter, which he had left entirely to his people for good or for bad.

They all immediately retired, leaving only me and their king in the lodge. We both took a drink and he shared supper with me, which was brought in on a tray which he greatly admired. This I gave him immediately and he was greatly pleased. Supper over, his son entered and never spoke but took two spears, one was painted red and the other was a well-made M'pangwe spear. They will soon settle all, he said. I asked him the meaning of the spears. The red one was war, the other peace with *honor*. The men all passed by the spears and placed a stick or counter by them. If the red one won then it would be war, if the other they would do the best to settle things as I had promised to help them.

I thanked the old chief for his explanation and after about one hour's wait, in came his son with the spears and sticks. They had taken two votes and each time the spear of peace had won. I gave the chief a few presents and made ready to leave as I had to see the other side again, that is the Bimvool, before the meeting which was to take place next day. He understood the situation quite well and after having taken a tot of liquor, he called for his eldest son. I retired to my canoe and left them in council and had an hour's sleep. All the boys were snoozing, as they were tired.

It was nearly daybreak when a young warrior came to me and told me the chief wanted to see me. He then introduced me to a few of his men who were ready to accompany. These men, he said, were to meet the Bimvool and whatever they did would be sanctioned by all his people and himself also. We exchanged a few presents and I departed with five counselors onboard and, through the strenuous efforts of the canoe boys, I reached home before midday, and after having introduced the deputation to Mr. Sinclair immediately proceeded to the Bimvool village and came back with a load of counselors, the head of whom was my friend Matam.

To this man, who was my blood brother, I spoke freely and he agreed with me that peace could easily be arranged, and he told me that he would do his best to get the business settled as soon as possible. I left them together, as I knew Matam and his people perfectly. They were a proud and warlike race and wanted submission only (Top Dog). The son of the chief, father of the dead boy, rose first and made a speech of about fifteen minutes' duration, and then Matam rose. His delivery was perfect and he spoke for full half an hour. In his discourse he dilated urgingly on the premier rights of the white man. It was not fair to put them to trouble and the Bimvool would receive nothing in settlement of the troubles of the M'pangwes; he left this to their own manhood and as he had had many a battle with them he knew they were too proud a race to allow such a thing. They could well afford to pay one ivory and they (his father the chief) would supply the other. That, he said, was the utmost limit they were prepared to go and he knew they would agree to this. Think and reply as soon as you are able, but let us not keep the white men waiting, especially as they have gone to much trouble for the sake of peace and trade (Okita). I will now retire with my people and await your reply.

He withdrew to the pier and I followed them, as I had been sitting smoking under a tree a little distance from them. What was said by the speakers I did not know, nor did the party I was with utter a word. In less than ten minutes Matam was called, and in a few minutes he beckoned me to join him. It is settled, he said, and send me now a piece of sugar cane. I could find none but told him the white man's bread would do (as a pledge of brotherhood), and I handed him a piece of bread. The blood-brother ceremony was quickly over. This was between Matam and the chief's son, whilst both parties formed a circle. All was over and I went in and reported to Sinclair, who said he had been watching operations and had had the speech reported to him as the council proceeded.

My friend Matam, he said, was an orator of the first water and a man whose acquaintance it would pay us to cultivate. A peace dance followed this meeting of these two warlike tribes and they kept their mood as long as I remained amongst them. This meeting put aside, all contentions on the overland route to Gaboon and everyone who wanted to travel to and fro could do so without any protection. Word was sent to the mission doctor and his wife at Kangwe and they came down and made friends with these savages. And thus ended the tribal wars and murders which were frequent before this, and trade went along steadily and unhampered and, as Herr Schiff said, was a boon to all.

"Aye, Sinclair. That feller was always more than agreeable to see me off on any little expedition'd save his skin a bit longer for the Orkneys. Or make a bit for the firm that'd sound well in a letter. Agreeable as such outings were to a lad like myself, I couldn't but see that it gave Sinclair a comfortable sensation in the pit of the stomach. 'Twas that photo. It turned him to cowardice and his veins to milk.

"Grand opportunities there were in those days for a bit of natural diplomacy. 'Twas a man's life. I often wonder what all the old traders felt like when they saw a so-called *bonne entente* between France and Britain. Giving the Ivory Coast away to France for some dirty little rights in Newfoundland. Canning stinking fish in exchange for ivory and elephants. That's what *bonne entente* means. Swapping life, swapping *my rivers*, for the pleasure of extracting the guts of a cod in a filthy factory on a freezing coast. That's the sort of thing's make a Frenchman laugh. Aye, he'd snigger a bit at that.

"Come to that, what would the missionaries either say to a bad bargain like that? Livingstone? He was no different at heart from us traders. 'Get on!' was the cry always in his ears. 'Let us march,' was oftener on his lips than 'Let us pray,' if the truth of all hearts were known. Dragging that poor girl, Mary Moffat, along until she was forced to a long rest in her grave. A fine feller but he should 'a' been a trader out and out. He should 'a' kept his wife in Scotland same as Sinclair did. He'd 'a' been better for Hatton and Cookson's than that strict Presbyterian Sinclair. Livingstone was never one to get the sentiments over a photo.

"[When his wife died he faced the fact that he needed a woman and married a black one. One o' these morganatic marriages same as Rhodes made with one of Lobengula's daughters.]

"Aye, he'd 'a' made a fine trader. The custom of the country was an easy alphabet to such as him. He was ahead of most missionaries in common sensibility.

"That *bonne entente* did not take much account of us traders who'd pushed their country's interests ahead. Haven't I worked for the honor of my country same as the missionaries? The Good Book'd not go far without the Day Book. What I've always said is, one's dependent on the other. Haven't I explored unknown country same as de Brazza? A thorough gentleman, de Brazza, though. Silent as a duke. Working for French interests but more for the taste of adventure it gave him. France has no adventurers unless she can coax some foreigner to risk himself for the country. Same as they do in the Legion of Honor. If it's courage you're looking for—if it's honor you're looking for, you'll be more likely to spot it in the Legion than in any other regiment.

"Some o' those American missionaries from Cincinnati were above par. Good fellers, brave as lions. Same as that sweet lady at heart. But looked at from all angles I've always arrived at the notion that nature's a great big unknown god we've got to make terms with without the humiliation of prayer. This constant nudging of the Almighty is a mistake. *Homo sapiens* with a spear or a gun'll go as far, and with less trouble to the great Onlooker.

"Not but what I always felt like saying me prayers when I first got there. One doesn't easy drop a natural habit, especially when you're away from your home and it's the one familiar sound. And Renchoro, my boy'd watch me and kneel down and murmur before he went to sleep. No harm in that. I'd always been used to see other lads at it in the dormitory.

"That bad boy, Horn...Farest in the wilds of any of 'em. Explorer with any of 'em....

"I'll be going Ma'am. I must twist a bit of wire up before I go out tomorrow."*

---

*In response to letters on the subject of the first paragraph on page 118 to my publishers since the appearance of *Trader Horn* it is necessary to explain that by a series of accidents, delays or errors, due partly to my long distance from New York and partly also to the fact that letters and manuscripts go through two or three offices, this sentence, which in my typescript had been blocked out by me in square brackets for deletion, unfortunately in the haste of a lightning production of the book (which was printed within five or six weeks) was left by the compositor exactly as it stood, private bracket marks and all. At this distance from New York I naturally never saw the proofs, which was a calamity to me in many respects and most of all in this particular does not appear in the English edition at all.

I should like, however, in connection with this subject, to quote a letter from an American minister of the First Congregational Church, written to my publishers in New York, which is of extreme interest and value. His letter is dated 12th January, 1928:

"May I draw attention to one fact in Horn's book which may be misconstrued. It is that having to do with the 'marriage' of Livingstone with a native woman. There are relationships of honor and dishonor in this respect… Some, I find, think this 'marriage' of Livingstone's was a thing of dishonor. I find from Finger's recent biography of Livingstone that it was a thing of 'honor.'

"If this aspect had been clarified by Horn I think it would have saved a good deal of needless suspicion."

EDITOR

‿ Chapter XV. ‿

*I*LEFT the old trading station after being thanked by all and was glad to be once more free as a bird and away from troubles of all descriptions. I had full instructions from Mr. Sinclair as well as from Gaboon, our headquarters, as to the vital importance of the use of the rivers for steam navigation, which had proved to be the real economy in trading, so that I spared no pains in charting the various channels in the big rivers as far as navigation was possible. As no white man had ever been entrusted with a task of this description and had not even visited the interior, I felt proud as I could say, without fear of contradiction, I was the first white man who had ever set foot in many of the places I visited and was generally welcomed by the chiefs as a good omen of the future. Then again, as Mr. Sinclair explained to me, if I could only follow de Brazza and be the first to open up trade routes, this explorer might be of good service to us in opening up the commerce of the country, which would not only benefit our firm but would mean the beginning of a tremendous trade with a large portion of Africa which had practically no outlet but the Ogowe and its tributaries.

As there were many difficulties to be overcome before this was an accomplished fact, I was well supplied in every way with food and necessaries, as well as with rifles and ammunition. I carried 27 men in all; all old seasoned fighters and boys you would rely on to death. I had always treated them well and, unlike most white men, had never struck a boy under any circumstances and was well loved by them. A lad that I found who did not do his best I paid off at once, generally giving him a present and always found him another job without saying anything to him except an excuse that I could not keep him. I also carried an old poet and doctor who was considered good at his business, and as he was a beautiful harper and singer who composed his own songs, he was looked upon with great favor by the crew. This man was the most beautiful storyteller and had a repertoire of such a length, he always delighted his audience, young or old, by something new in the folklore of their country.

I first visited John Earmy from Salem, Massachusetts, an American half-breed who was one of our principal traders and lived on an island in the middle of the Ogowe River with the M'pangwes on one bank and the Okelleys on the opposite side. Here I learned that trouble had sprung up between these people and three or four days after I left John Earmy, hostilities were in full swing and continued for several weeks. I called on Apaque, the paramount chief of the Okelleys, but he laughingly declared it was still too soon to interfere with his people, and as they had no war on anywhere else at the present time, it was not only a good pastime for his men but was necessary for the education of the young adults in the true art of war and there was only one way to learn this art and that was to be in a few battles and get used to the game, which he said was a necessity for all men. Apaque had the name of being a great general, he was crafty and invariably won, often with less numbers. As the news of the war arrived by his runners several times a day, the old chief was kept quite busy.

I slept that night at Apaque's and although the roll of the firing lasted all night and was continued that following day and lasted through the dry season, the old man was never disturbed, but as we would take a wet from my best brandy, Apaque would dole out to me one of his fighting stories. How he managed to outwit his enemies. And it was later, before I closed my eyes. Apaque was indeed amusing and as I often visited him in later years, I often slept in Apaque's town, if possible, the grizzled old man was always pleased to see me. Whilst my canoe boys called him *bal mo,* which means your uncle Apaque, he was a powerful chief and although Apaque's territory joined him, he was enjoying quiet. Although the M'pangwes were inhabiting the bank across the river, he had always lived in peace with them.

Here I had the pleasure of meeting one of our traders. His name was Yousoff and as he was an old Senegalese soldier and wore the red button of the French Legion of Honor, we thought quite a lot of him and always treated the old soldier as one of our own. At Samquite I saw the native blacksmith make the largest spears and the best made I had ever seen. They were real works of art. Their heavy swords, which they handle with two hands, are also beautiful specimens of workmanship. I bought quite a lot of them and, as these natives sell them first-handed, the prices were very low. They all had copper handles whilst some of them were very short and heavy. They were a splendid weapon at close quarters.

After leaving Samquite where the river is very wide, we came on a whole troop of elephants about a half mile up the river. They were having great fun whilst two bulls, nearly full grown, were having a fight on a sandbank. We slowed up and watched the fun with the glasses. Whilst the two battled, the females stood around. Leaving the canoe, we stalked our way to the bank where we found a small path along the river well hidden by trees. There were four of us. On arriving I let no one fire. I was within 200 yards of the contending bulls. One of them was slightly larger than the other whilst a full-grown bull with ears erect was enjoying a toilet from the *ziczic* birds. Some were perched on his upraised ears and some were picking low down on the loose skin away in the cracks of the skin They were removing ticks. There were a dozen of them around the tail end, which was opposite to us. And 10 or 20 cow elephants a little distance away were also being manicured in the cool of the early morning.

The two fighters did not charge each other but with head to head pressed each other's back. There were great gaps in the sand caused by the weight and pressure of the fighters. They moved slowly in a circle. Now the younger one was forced head to ground and seemed fagged out, and was bleeding from tusk wounds, and the larger elephant, taking advantage of his position, now forced his head up and jabbed him fiercely several times with his tusks. The fight was about up, I thought, and giving the motion to aim and pointing the animals out with my finger. I fired dead at the old bull behind the ear and he fell limp with his trunk stretched. The larger of the younger bulls was also down but the smaller one got clear to the other side of the river along with the rest, followed by Renchoro and the other boys. I would have willingly followed but as I had slept very little for the past week, I went home to my canoe, and taking a stiff wet and giving my poet-general and doctor a good one and a ration of rum to my hardworked boys, I told the general to cut out the ivories and make all ready for a good rest. The old man agreed with me. I handed out a rifle each and told them to eat drink and be merry.

I had my *odo* (bed) transferred to the sandbank and turned in after a dive and a rub, which was my wont. But being a youngster with too much business in my mind I could not sleep, and so I told Iwolo just what was the matter. He said he would fix that, and giving me about enough dry dust medicine from his wallet which I washed down with another tot, the old songbird sat on the sands and sang his sleep song in a low voice whilst his harp kept wonderful tune with his wild native ryhthm and I closed my eyes in a deep baby sleep with the sweet music still in my dreams.

I slept soundly till sunrise and when I woke the sandbanks were responsible for a din of contention. On rising, Renchoro and Iwolo and two repulsive tall natives who had been waiting for my awakening, came forward. I waved them off with a smile and dropping my nightgown as nimble as a cricket, I executed an armspring and somersault as I dived from the sandbank. There was a rush amidst loud laughter to the water's edge, and when I came up from a long fetch (dive) and swam towards the bank, there was a quick retreat of the two strange natives who had never seen a white man before. They had settled all their arguments and contentions and when I commenced to take my drying spin round the long sandbank and ran around them, they hurried away laughing and shouting *O tangani* (the white man). I had a clear course and was soon enjoying a hearty breakfast, whilst the natives were surprised to see the well-cleaned trays and cutlery laid out on a dining rug with woster sauce, French sardines, roast and toast, etc. They kept shouting *Va Bue* which means anything from "Bully for him" to "get along with it." In fact it was marvelous how they eyed every item, and on finishing I let go a cork of Herr Schiff's best lager beer, which went off with a loud report. They all scampered off shouting he is drinking medicine made of gunpowder. (*Impira*, native name for gunpowder. M'pangwe name for gunpowder is *fitta*.)

The trouble took place over who owned this elephant and, as Renchoro had sold four carcasses, one female he came up with, and the smaller of the two bulls, the M'pangwes should have been satisfied as these two animals were lying on their side of the river. I explained this to them and took over the ball rubber they had brought and bought it from my hunting boys. A good explanation and the gift of a few plates of salt, which is highly esteemed in this country, settled all argument.

The Okelleys were the last of these people, for after leaving I met no inhabitants on their side of the river. This seemed strange as the country abounded in elephants and game. The Okelleys told me that the wild Osheba tribes hunted this country yearly, and they were a fierce tribe of man eaters. The M'pangwes had chased out the original inhabitants, the Okatas who had taken possession of the river islands further up the river. I was anxious to see this country, as its valleys between the mountain ranges looked beautiful when viewed from the hilltops. The Okelleys offered to accompany me from their village but did not care to hunt alone. They said I would have no difficulty in killing elephants as they were plentiful this year, as two new large herds had crossed the river and also one big rogue elephant and this animal had done great damage to their plantations. The gorillas also were numerous and destructive, so that in some places they had to clear new ground and make new *impondis*, as the animals were increasing yearly since the Okatas had left the country. Next day before sunrise found myself and Renchoro, along with the hunters from the village, about four miles inland from the village on the banks of a river.

———

"Aye, a boy adores life where music and birds are. If it's not at Gillmoss with the gulls in your ear it's up my rivers with the harps o' the cannibals and the humming of the singers in the canoes. A deep sound, that. Aye, when you've heard the canoes coming along and the harp rippling over the water—

Umbrela n'oye mi koka inglea
O me Engalinga mazan chua—

O those sweet sounds from the sea! A song about a *seamew*. Bells from the sea it's called. Quite a pretty fancy to conjure up.

"I used to sing them to my sister, the one that played the harp and became a sister of charity. I'd walk about the drawing-room putting in the pretty action of the paddles and so forth and she'd try and catch the air as I sang. Only the harp can give those sonorous sounds that seem to rise from the breast of Nature. Deep, yet trembling, is what I'd say, with the pulse of life. A piano's always been a bit *stultus* to me. Aye, it doesn't breathe, same as a harp.

"I can draw you a M'pangwe harp, Ma'am. A little different in shape from the harp of those bushmen I told you of that's the very moral of those used in ancient Egypt. With all their learning there's few people that rightly understand the strange origins of some of these barbarous. The old feller I knew that was official troubadour always taught the children the tribal history. He said they belonged to the Five Tribes that used to dwell near the Mountain of Three Fires. And now there were only two. The burning mountain had pursued and swallowed up three of the tribes. And the great chief and founder of the five tribes, when he divided them for diplomatic reasons connected with the mountain, said: 'Go your ways separately for the preservation of our race. And remember—always hunt on one bank of the river. Trust no man. Keep your women pure. Have no slaves.' And 'tis true the cannibals are the most moral race on earth. They said he was the chief who stilled the Mountain of Three Fires so that it flamed and smoked no more.

"Aye, the little children are taught history same as we were. It was from the same feller they got the first tobacco plant. The M'pangwe tobacco's the finest in the world. They say this chief was born with the first plant of it sprouting from his forehead. I've no wish to rob Sir Walter of his reputation but I think he made a gross error in supposing that tobacco first came from America. That poor feller was treated something cruelly by the stay-at-homes of his day. Aye, they've always been the stumbling block of the roamers. 'Tis not savagery but the so-called civilized that's the danger to the man with a fret for wandering.

"Besides, talk about tobacco coming from the States, what about the pipe I found near my long-haired Malagash in the old workings up in Rhodesia? How did that get there since the days of Walter Raleigh? Very like a M'pangwe pipe it was. That feller'd been a smoker and a prospector like myself. Nothing unusual in *his* makeup. More of a brother to me than some of the fellers they put in my room nowadays.

"These voters or whatever they call themselves. They sure have a meager conception of life when they make a man pay for living in a city. Aye! My old animal nature says stay and eat in the sty but my human nature says walk out into the blue and have faith. The filthiest city in the world, this, and not fit for any man's deathbed that's been where I've been…. Birds—that's something a lad understands! No need for language when the eye and the ear is so pleased.

"They can't lay the foundation of morals on a pint of disinfectant a week. Not in a lodging house. It can't be done. The ladies that come nosing around for garbage've got to go deeper than a sprinkle o' disinfectant. They'll have to be fierce as this so-called John Knox to get it clean. A nasty feller that, but no reformation is going to spring up without unpleasantness. It'll not come just because you've said 'Good Morning' to a few schooner-rigged females in a lodging house, and left a cake of soap and a tract on Fly Week or other religious subject.

"I shall be telling you a bit more about Nina T—— next week. A story that's founded more on fact than on fiction has a natural meagerness here and there. But it's been in my mind to tell you, Ma'am, that if you care to do so, you can add something to the contents of that parcel I unpacked from L——. I'm not using his name. Better stick to Little Peru. Naturally there were undergarments—all that a lady'd need. No need to enlarge upon them but you, being a lady, 'll know just how much to say about it. You'll know what a girl's requirements would be that's been brought up in a Josh House. Aye, not but what it was all strictly moral in the Isorga place. She was watched—better than if we'd sent her to a convent school. She never moved without an escort, or somebody with his eye on her from behind the stockade."

↜ Chapter XVI. ↝

O N ARRIVING at the *impondis* of the Okelleys, I could soon see that great havoc had occurred on account of marauding elephants and gorillas, besides other animals. One rascal paid them nocturnal visits and was supposed to be the most dangerous of all the animal visitors. The native hunters then told me that the next unwelcome customer was a very large old gorilla who was likewise greatly to be feared, as he had already charged a party of men who had followed him to his home about two hours distant and had been heard giving voice and truming* at dawn. He was somewhere in the vicinity of a grove at the foot of a small rocky rise on the opposite side of the creek, which ran through the grove. They thought there would be a good chance of getting him that morning and we wound our way along the creek to the place mentioned.

I was told to take a stand beside an old fallen tree as he generally passed that spot if disturbed. If he came their way they would surely have him for the damage he had done to their plantations. I

*Drumming.

took the stand with my faithful head boy and from where we were we could see the Okelley, four in number, lying prone in the bush at the edge of the clearing. We waited for some time but could see or hear no sound indicating his whereabouts. I was just about to give up the gorilla chase and try my luck at spooring the rascal elephant when the sound of a rolling stone reached us from over the creek. Once in a while we could get a glimpse of his head and shoulders, as he showed up above the round large boulders. Presently he rolled over one of these large stones and he was busily engaged breakfasting on the large insects which were under the rocks. Having satisfied himself with this kind of titbit he peered around and, thinking the coast was clear, he walked cautiously towards an old peanut clearing, and as he came up within about 20 yards of where the native hunters were concealed he seemed to suddenly hear something out of the way.

The Okelleys now fired on him, but instead of scampering away as he was only slightly wounded, he made a bound on them using his arms. One man and gun he sent fully ten feet high in the air and played havoc with the others, scattering them with a snap of his arms while one of them gaining his feet was knocked sideways again. He used his knuckles and long arms (I never saw him bite) so quickly that one could scarcely see which was gorilla and which was man in the mix up, as he played skittles with them, he seemed to knock them before him. Contrary to what I had expected he never used his teeth, although their bite is terrible and said by natives also to be poisonous. I never have seen a man brave enough to stand and let him seize a gun before firing, as I heard the hunters say was done by the Ivilis of the Angani. He then came bounding towards us and seemed to have sighted us. I fired low under the chin and Renchoro followed suit. He rolled over and over stretching and lay dead at the other side of the old fallen tree. He was very large, and although I have hunted them for years, he was by far the biggest I ever saw alive.

I now hastened to where the hunters lay stretched out. The first fellow we met was laid 20 yards from the others, and as we tried to rear him up so as to give him a brandy from my hunting flask, he came to, but must have been dazed as he broke away and began to run on all fours in fright; we shouted to him to stop and he took his tot like a good man, and when he had completely recovered from his shock, his memory returned. We examined him but only discovered a bruise on his right thigh, and he also had a few corners knocked off him, which must have been done when he was knocked amongst the small bushes. I commenced to pour brandy on these wounds but he resented this waste and laughingly said it would do him more good to drink it as it was fine medicine, so I gave him another wet. The next man was badly wounded by a hit upwards along the ribs and had also a long wound from above his knee cap, and he was bleeding profusely and was unconscious.

I sent the one who had now recovered back for help and he returned with a dozen men and women, and likewise the chief, native doctor, and old Iwolo also made his appearance with his medicine bag and two bottles of rum. They washed the wound, and during the medical operation the badly wounded one opened his eyes and was soon able to take a drink of brandy; the other two had already recovered and could stand erect, and although they were wounded and bruised badly, their native doctor laughingly declared them to be all right. We sat down in a ring while Renchoro explained the whole to-do amidst great laughter, and he gave a great description and mimicked the antics of both gorilla and men as the men went spinning one way and their guns the other and when he saw the first one spring above the ground he felt like running himself. We now looked at the dead gorilla who the chief said had grown so big and wide on the food he stole from his plantations, that he was the largest he had ever seen.

I returned to the village with the chief, who promised to have the animal brought in at once and buried over a large antheap so that I could call for his remains on my return from the upriver country. At the village I enjoyed a hearty meal and sat and talked away the time with the old *ogo* (native for chief). The gorilla arrived, but unfortunately was disemboweled and cut in two halves. As this was done it was useless to say anything. They had done this as he was too heavy to carry otherwise. He was duly buried and was a grand specimen and fetched a good price in England in spite of the fact that his spine had been badly hacked by an axe and several bones broken.

Late in the afternoon we received news of the rogue elephant who was heading towards us, as he had been frightened by a bank of Osheba hunters who had crossed over from the north bank of the Ogowe at a point about twelve miles north. He had been seen entering a grove about 5 miles away where they said he would spend the night and could easily be followed from there by his large tracks as he was very heavy. The evening was spent in spinning yarns about the Oshebas, who the old chief assured me were not like the M'pangwes and only eat men of their own tribe who are conquered in war, and he assured me they had killed and eaten many of the tribe. There are groves and places where these man-eaters generally eat their poor victims, and as I afterwards saw many of these and the crosses to which they tied their victims, I was forced to believe his statement, although I never saw this grue-some sight for myself. However I saw a M'pangwe being tried for murdering his father-in-law, whom he had eaten, and was found guilty and punished with death.

I was awakened before daylight and had trackers following the rascal elephant, which we found in the edge of a grove of *illundas* (trees bearing nuts). As still-hunting is the only method of hunting elephants attended by much success, we separated into three parties and advanced cautiously in file, following in the wake of the trackers. A couple of rifle shots by the party to the left of me rang out, followed by heavy rustle of underbrush. We had all lain low, and as he came along at express speed he charged past us at close range but gave us no chance of shooting, as the underbrush was high and we only had passing glimpses of his huge body.

After he had passed us, on came the trackers following the blood spoor, which was heavy. We followed him, although we had great difficulty in seeing him as we still kept file for speed's sake. Presently he circled, having sighted a crowd of men and women who were following us with their baskets ready for elephant meat, as he was considered a sure capture. On his return he rattled through the bush to the right of us still going strong but we had lost the tracker, who eventually appeared, telling us that the elephant was badly wounded as his strides were shortening and he would no doubt make for the river crossing. We followed on quickly and this time kept the tracker well in sight as he ran doubled up. He was an experienced tracker and hunter and could pick up the spoor like a hound.

As the underbrush became more open we could travel faster but my luck was out as I knocked down a small wood-hornets nest which was hanging from the branch of a tree. I was knocked clean out of the hunt as I was badly stung over the face, neck, and back and was forced to fight a battle royal with my hat. I was not alone in the battle and as I ran and hit them off I could see two of my boys fighting boldly as these flying pests took vengeance on their naked bodies. The rest of the hunters vanished laughing. The pain of these pests of the forest was intense. We left the hunt and made for a small stream, and after plastering up our stings with soft blue clay and mud, we sat down and drank copiously from my flask, waiting for our pains to pass.

"I've remembered the name of the feller that had the tobacco plant growing out of his forehead. Better than the Turkish plant, this tobacco. It was Talaqui. Came to me when I was waking up on Thursday morning. If only we could learn to make regular use of the powers of the memory when asleep, history wouldn't have so much nonsense about it. Old Dr. Lingard was a fine historian. Lived at Hornby in Lancashire, where my cousin lived in the same house after him. Documents and that, and some notable old pictures. That old chest of yours reminds me of that house. A good bit of Anglo-Saxon design on the chest. You'll not bear it. The Norman never lived that could twist a pattern as good as that.... From a Yorkshire farmhouse, you say, and sixty years ago. Most likely raided from a church in the olden days. I was a lad then with all me bright journeys just before me.

"Talk of history, those cannibal tribes were just as particular as we are. Oshebas, Fans, and all the rest of it, their genealogies are as honorably cared for as a duke's. Aye, and there'll be less blots on the scutcheon. Not so much of these Stuarts and Charles the Seconds. Come to that, the Georges were not so different, only a bit quieter.... Always the strictest rules against immorality with other tribes. Oganga—*that* was the feller's name! He was troubadour to the M'pangwes. There was a place where the stories were told and the children taken regularly to hear him sing the great doings of the tribe. Sing 'em to the harp. The Palace of History it was called—*N'kokoo Incoge.*

"Aye, a man that knows his family record'll always get on better with savages than he does with the sort of riff-raff you knock up with here in the Golden City. *Homo stultus* in big houses or the same make of man getting drunk in the—saloon.... Fellers like George T—— and Carlisle. They see a certain look in a man's eye that tells them, here is my brother, black though he may be. A gentleman always makes the best trader for that reason. Rubber and ivory, George T—— must have done well over that. Mangrove bark for tannin' he was interested in, too. Pity for a feller like that to die out in the male line. One of Nina's brothers died. I told you that. And the other one, Joseph T—— was taken by Carriala, an Arab pirate, when George died. Very good to him, it was believed. All down the west coast was his beat from Morocco downward. Yousoff Carriala. 'Twas better for the boy than being with his mother. 'Twas Carriala's sort that did for poor Tom Keating. Always a good living to be made down the Coast. I used to know the coast of Morocco quite well, one time. After my wife died I was over there.

"How'd you like my bits about gorillas? The Americans'll fancy that for the children. If you can write a book that knocks young and old, gives 'em a good laff and no harm to the susceptibilities— that's what goes in America. A moral people except when it comes to murder and so on. They kill very easy in some o' those places. I've been. When I was in the Diamond Detective Agency I was looking for a feller amongst the moonshiners along the Blaau River. The families take it in turn there to shoot. God's acre was full of 'em. Rival families had to lie divided by the path. 'Twas like the M'pangwes and Oshebas over again. Human nature's hard to kill wherever you find it.

"Aye. A gorilla's what a lad'll never stop watching. They say on the Ivory Coast that there's three things never stop growing. A croc, a gorilla, and an elephant. Add to that the fact that the gorilla isn't normal in the head. His brain is different from the brain of a man—and I've seen a few. I sent the biggest gorilla head in the world to Gerrard, Camden Town. The natives used to set store by gorilla brains for *muti*. No doubt they've destroyed many a valuable skeleton for that. Same power as human's it has.

"I could do very nicely with butterflies, too. Sent 'em over for quite a long time to Horniman. One of the tea nabobs. He was like a boy with the butterflies, in spite of the business. He gave me £12 for every one I caught of a certain species. And once I got £14 for a very big one. He lived at Dulwich when I knew him. Quaker family I believe.

"The Quakers, Ma'am, I've always held to be above par, whether in trade or in religion or in ordinary life. Young feller I knew in Madagascar was a Quaker, from Philadelphia. One of the ministers—if so he may be called that has a silent religion. Nice feller that, with goodness writ in capitals over his face. 'Tis a look one doesn't forget, in the ultimate end, whether on a Quaker gentleman or on that poor lady I took down the river for safe burial. 'Isn't God here?' she says, 'Just the same as in America?' Looking at her face you couldn't deny it. Giving the children sweets, when we walked through the village. 'Why, what's the matter, Mr Horn?' That woman, Ma'am, almost made me believe we'd reached this so-called millennium. Those great idols she kept stopping to stare at—as if they were in a museum. Her courage was bigger than Stanley's. And she died without a boastful word.

"When I heard of it I said, 'There goes one more victim to add to their great Josh House called Christianity.'"

↭ Chapter XVII. ↭

E WERE told that the elephant had been killed after a good chase and that the Oshebas who had been seen away to the east had been watching the hunt from ambush. We hurried up following our guide and found all of our strength and ten or twelve of our Okelley friends, all carrying guns in extended order in the rocky ground to protect the men who were cutting up the carcass and chopping out the ivories. Iwolo pointed the (Osheba) cannibals out and I put the glasses on a small hill covered with bush. They were moving round excitedly and were no doubt preparing to attack us. We took up a position about 200 yards south of where the dead animal lay and were about full strength and therefore well prepared for any emergency.

The tusks were now free whilst about ten large baskets were filled with elephant meat ready to carry off to the village. The women now excitedly shouldered their loads as well as the tusks, which were a fine pair, when the Oshebas, in an extended line, began to advance on us. Old Iwolo now ordered the ivories and meat to be brought into the bush at the foot of the hill where we were posted. Iwolo ordered no firing until the Oshebas came nearer. He handed me the field glasses. They were coming in extended order like skilled fighters, taking short runs in turns so as to avoid fatigue. They were now less than 80 yards away, were painted up, and armed with guns, crossbows, and spears. They made a fine show as they came forward. The Okelleys amongst the rocks began to fire, whilst the enemy came on firing but still kept formation, when Iwolo gave the order to open on them.

The effect of our rifle fire was instantaneous. I saw several fall through the glasses, but they now took a prone position and crawled near the Okelleys. They were brave men and I asked Iwolo, who was an old fighter, if he could not call the Okelleys off. But the old man only laughed, saying "their meat and their fight," and ordered the rifles to cease fire. Too many good cartridges wasted on the Oshebas, he said. As he spoke, a bank of young Okelley warriors appeared and advanced to the native firing line and the battle commenced now in earnest. The Okelleys are splendid fighters and after a short space of time the Oshebas cleared away with the Okelley following them up for some distance, but they were loath to leave the rocky ground and soon the Oshebas were well away, brandishing their spears in defiance.

The Okelleys plundered the dead and left the wounded naked but did not kill them, as they said it was foolish to kill out, as fair fighting was looked upon by the Oshebas as sport or fun, but on the other hand they knew their wounded and would revenge them but would be satisfied with their good beating and would most likely for a good time hunt further afield. We now left the hill and as the Okelleys were busily engaged cutting up meat and carrying their wounded to town, these numbering five, and one lay dead in the stone pile. Coming to the Osheba dead and wounded, we counted seven killed and twice as many wounded. The wounded men conversed freely and to those who wanted it I gave a good tot of good Red Heart Rum, which I found better than brandy on such occasions. One tall cannibal who was not able to walk, but was badly hit down in the stomach, smilingly said, *Ma Ke Wa Kirria*, I shall die tomorrow. Two or three of them walked towards their camp.

The Okelleys found very little plunder, a few knives, spears, and a crossbow or two. The Oshebas had carried away all guns and ammunition belonging to their dead and wounded. It was getting late in the evening when we retired and the Okelleys left with two large baskets of elephant meat and likewise two bottles of rum given them from my small stock. As we left, the enemy had already returned and they soon had fires going and seemed to be quite as lively and happy as ever. These Oshebas took their hardships and mishaps quite as a matter of course and were surely quite the most happy race I ever came in contact with under any circumstances.

On entering the Okelley town, the chief and his headmen who were all old, came to congratulate us and thank us for the assistance we had given them in drawing away their enemies. The night was spent in music and storytelling by Iwolo, and the town hall—a long grass roof supported by hardwood posts—was well filled whilst the women brought in plantain leaves full of cooked elephant meat and such, berries, and bonbons as the bounty afforded. We had a pleasant time amongst these children of wildest Africa and left next morning on our upriver expedition straight in the heart of wildest Africa.

The river now commenced to narrow and whilst the south bank was made up of stiff cliffs and hills, the north bank was inhabited by small tribes of M'pangwes, and the flats, or what the natives called *itovis,* were mostly inhabited by wandering Oshebas. The bush paths led to the bigger roads, which ran through the wild country and joined the big ivory track, which wound away through the elephant country. At times the distant mountains showed up in low sierras extending away in the blue to where no man knew. The river and its banks were full of water-fowl whilst the animals, aroused by early morning song from

Iwolo, would frighten them away from the banks into the bush. The animals could be seen peacefully grazing on the hilltops and, as there were no inhabitants, this peaceful country was hunted by the wild Oshebas who generally crossed the river on rafts, and we passed many of these.

After a few days the rapids became more frequent, whilst every day the sleeping snakes, aroused by the singing, would drop into the big canoe, but never during my many, many voyages had we a snakebite, but they made a quick getaway into the river. Some of these were very venomous and often a large boa would fall and make for the water. These large snakes were very long and were splendid swimmers. Early morning was invariably attended by all kinds of animal and bird sounds.

We now entered wild and very picturesque country. Whilst we passed many islands, and after again passing small M'pangwe towns, we came on the most beautiful portion of the Ogowe River which here widened. Numerous islands are inhabited by the Okowas, a superior race of Negroes and the best canoe men in rapid waters one could wish for. The villages nestled amongst the trees, whilst the large native huts composing them were well built and clean. Their plantations were well kept and were crowded with quite a variety of vegetable foodstuffs. They were also great fisher-men and hunters. But they were always at war with the Oshebas and often killed them at sight. They gave me quite a history of these people, who they said were never to be trusted, whilst with one or two of the M'pangwe villages they were friendly.

They told me of the paths which led to the great ivory track and also of a large M'pangwe town called Mogubakang, from which district the ivory came, but as it was a two weeks' journey and the roads were full of Oshebas who demanded toll or even plundered those who refused, it was useless for me to try to get there or think of sending traders out on the main road. The ivories nearly all come to the Ogowe from the different towns and was sent down to the M'pangwes for sale, whilst the hunters waited their return. They would like a trader posted amongst them who would buy their rubber, but would on no account allow an Osheba to set foot on their islands.

I took two days rest here. I had the pleasure of finding the nearest point of this greatest of ivory tracks which runs, so the Oshebas say, to the lands from which they all come, which I think must be somewhere towards Equatorial Africa and yet further towards the lakes, as the old natives have it in their fables that they were once living at the base of a chain of mountains which suddenly began to eject fire and ashes and deadly smoke and by the order of their grand chief were commanded to separate and flee at once, and pointing to the four great winds, North, South, East, and West, he bade them adieu, telling them never to return but conquer all they met. And he gave to them each a tobacco plant grown from the one which grew from his head when he was a boy.

Every M'pangwe is supposed to quote his ancestry before he is allowed to marry and the names of forebears are so many I had generally to beg them to keep quiet, so they were surely descended from a race who must have lived before the Egyptians. As I smoked M'pangwe tobacco for many years and I found it far preferable to any other. I have often wondered whether it was not indigenous to the soil like wild coffee, sugar, and many other plants. And then the question would grow in my mind: Was Sir Walter Raleigh the first introducer of the weed into Europe? He may have been. But as to the rest of the world, I have my doubts.

I left the Akota country and the next tribe to them on the south bank of the river are the Okandas. The Okanda country is full of *itovis* or plains on which roam great herds of wild cattle or *nyari*, whilst there are a few small buffalo but their horn or corona after leaving the temple plate are straight up and make them greatly feared by lone hunters, as they will often charge at sight and can waltz round like buck.

The Elima River turns south from the Ogowe and this was the one followed by Count de Brazza, who followed this river and then crossed over the Elima Desert where he was attacked by the inhabitants, who live mostly on ant rice, i.e., the ant eggs to be found in the small mounds or antheaps, which are numerous. As he was supplied with a small French machine gun and had some French and Senegalese soldiers armed with the Fusi Grass, he had no difficulty in driving them off. As he stayed with us at Adimango making ready for the expedition, we became very friendly.

———

"I've got a bit of fighting this time. In a book that's got truth at the bottom it can scarcely be avoided. But it doesn't do, Ma'am, to run too much bloodshed through a book. We must suppress some of that. Aye, too much of it becomes meaningless. Unliterary. When you've seen what I've seen as a lad you'll not be wanting to write it out with all the commas complete. Same as the lads as was in it won't talk about the War. I've no wish to emphasize what the eye and the brain will never forget. Leave that to the little fellers turning over the mythology of foreign spots they've never been to. Writing out their bloody scenes all within the sound of Bow Bells. Aye, 'tis man's natural instinct. If you don't see bloodshed you've got to dream about it.

"Winding up past those *itovis*, Ma'am. I could write a book on the animals I saw there, happy as nature planned for them to be. Never being shot for anything but the food necessary to natives.

"When I'm near to sleep or on the edge of waking up I see those creatures again, bright and moving as when we passed them. Africa, Ma'am, as nature molded it. And believe me, when man has destroyed nature, then it's his turn to go. Sure. The barren world will swallow him up. 'Tis a lucky thing the cannibal tribes have kept the elephants safe so long from these so-called big game hunters. An equatorial gang of cut-throats, wasting wildlife to make what they call a bag. While the cannibals are there, there'll be no lack of elephants. They never kill wanton. Only to eat. They'd never be so childish as these dukes and colonels who have to count the head they kill same as we counted our marbles in Lancashire. The cannibal lives as nature taught him—kill only to eat, keep your women moral, hold no man as slave, be content with your side o' the river, and cast no eyes across the water.

"'Tis when a tribe keeps slaves and marries 'em that it begins to go down. The cannibals know that clean morals make a strong fighting race. 'Tis no different with white men. Rome never went down till she was pulled down by slaves and fancy women. Marble baths and so on, 'stead of a good fetch in the river at dawn.

"Aye, I see them swinging along. Or having a quiet siesta, where nothing could startle 'em but a mouse on the trunk. As frightened of a mouse as any lady he is. I've seen a little fright like that amongst sleeping elephants startle a whole herd into disorder. Trumpeting and plunging. An elephant is wonderfully choosy how he disposes his trunk in sleep. Likes to have it curled up on something for safety from small things. His trunk's his living and he's got to be as careful as a fiddler of his fingers. Aye, he has the brain of a fair man in his intellectual make-up.

"Often I have a good laugh to myself when I see de Brazza's donkeys chasing a whole village before 'em. The white man's deer they used to call 'em. Yaw! Yaw! It sure was a comical apparition. He'd just landed 'em—a great meeting of jacks and jennies that he'd brought in two boat loads. Yaw! Yaw! they said and kicked up their heels like the best two year olds. Drove the whole village before them, faster and faster. Aye, those donkeys made more of a conquest than penetration by battle. They put flight into fellers a bevy of elephants couldn't have scared. 'Twas the voice that did it. Yaw! Yaw! Someone said they were lions and that made everyone run the faster.

"They knew nothing about lions in those parts beyond what slaves from afar had told 'em. Those donkeys, being no more than human, galloped for pleasure at finding old earth under their hoofs again. Seasoned fighters fled whimpering before 'em. Aye, it sure was the donkeys' hours.

"Showers of hawks after a bit of a set-to like that I had with the Oshebas. The sacred hawks of the M'pangwes. They picked the bones of the wounded. So choosy, they'll not wait for death. One poor feller came to and found a hawk had plucked his eye out. He jumped up and walked about holding his eye that was empty, and when he fell again I shot him out of his misery.

"Pity sure makes a man callous at times. The witch doctors are clever but there's some things're better not healed—no, not even by these so-called Harley Street experts—and 'tis then powder and shot are the best physician. Those witch doctors…I'm a humanitarian, and I like to give my knowledge to the world. There's things there that ought to be known. That Calabar bean that cures hydrophobia. Cures snake-bite, too, they say, and other forms of blood-poisoning. They cauterize very cleverly too, in cases of snake-bite. Fill a pipe up full of tobacco, get it red hot with hard blowing and clap it upside down on the wound and suck without stopping. Seems to draw the poison and cauterize at the same time. Then there's that chicken cure—if there's one handy. You pluck a bare patch on the chicken's breast and scratch a slight wound into the flesh. Apply this to the snake-bite pressing hard. The chicken'll soon die of the poison and then you take another. That may likely die too. But the third'll not die. It'll be somewhat wilted but should recover. And the patient'll be all right.

"Aye, nature sure has spread some of the ingenuity of a man over the wilder races. 'Tis not all reserved for Piccadilly."

ᴄ Chapter XVIII. ᴄ

I TOOK GREAT pains in charting and sounding, as I found after giving all routes due consideration that the only one of any use from a commercial point of view was the great ivory track, as I had found an island called Isange the key to this big road. This island was situated about twenty miles west of Akota and commanded the river as well as the high road to the interior of the most unknown portion of Equatorial Africa, and ran through the country inhabited by the Ashebas and the wild tribes further in the interior, and was the one most used at this time by the savage ivory hunters.

As the first thunder and rain of the season had now commenced, I turned down stream so as to be ready to pilot up from the river mouth any of our company's steamers which happened to come along. I had had a splendid trip and was now anxious to return and report my doings. The voyage down the river was easy going as we were helped greatly by the current being in our favor, and we soon found ourselves camped for evening opposite where we had our battle with the Oshebas. The night passed peacefully and we woke early intending to visit the first Okelley town which we hoped to reach about dinner time. As there was no driftwood for a fire along the sandbanks we pulled out early after taking our morning tot and dip, but as we all felt hungry about nine o'clock, we intended to pick out a shady spot on the riverbank near a large spreading tree where we could breakfast in the shade. The canoe was paddled inshore but before we could tie up we were fired upon by a band of Oshebas at short range, whilst I received a bad wound on the wrist from a spear thrown from ambush.

We were completely taken by surprise and several of my boys, rifle in hand, reached the bank and commenced firing. I followed suit but was pounced upon by two Oshebas. The first one I got with a revolver shot whilst the other one thrust his gun forward, which I grabbed as it went off but I had thrust it aside. I then jumped back and fired again but my trigger refused to move, being caught by a few grains of coarse sand I had picked up getting ashore with my unwounded hand holding my shooter. He was a tall, quick, lithe fellow and throwing my gun at him and hitting him squarely in the nose, which I badly split, he fell, but was up in an instant and made to draw his dagger which was barbed near the handle, and this I saw was caught by a small thong. I was now between him and the river and with one tremendous leap he jumped into the water. I dived after him with my drawn hunting knife and as the hole we were in was deep, I dived under him. While he was battling on top I got right under him and stabbed him repeatedly with my hunting knife until he settled. I then pulled him out on the sandbank but he was all in. I was weak as I had two bad wounds. The last one had gone through my left hand and was a bad shot wound and had nearly torn my thumb off.

I soon commenced to weaken through loss of blood. Presently Iwolo returned and seeing my predicament, came off with the small medicine chest and brandy revived me. And now the boys returned with several Osheba guns and trophies, as they had fol- lowed the Oshebas up and killed four outright whilst my long one and his mate on the bank made six, beside several they had wounded. There were six of my boys wounded by gunshot fire but no one had got as bad a dose as I had. The canoe was brought over and after another wet and being patched up by Iwolo's medicine or by Friars Balsam, we pulled downstream, having recovered my six-shooter and likewise the two Osheba guns. We now kept to the other bank of the river, as many a trader or poor canoe boy had been shot by these warlike cannibals.

We arrived that afternoon at the Okelley village where my gorilla lay buried and were well received by all, especially as we had again defeated their enemies, the Oshebas. The old chief could not do too much for me and I was soon being treated by Iwolo. I was still bleeding but he sewed up my long spear wound with nine stitches, whilst everyone was busy turning over old wood and catching black crickets, the white of which was squeezed from their bodies and was used for packing up bad wounds after being well washed with very hot water and piled over for heat with the *icundo* or cotton from the underbark of a tree. The process was repeated three or four times a day, and after a long time closed up and gradually grew together, but the thumb never grew and as I was young, I have one thumb shorter than the other.

I left the gorilla with the old chief as I was sure of returning and this greatly pleased him. We passed a pleasant evening and after dressing our wounds we again made off downstream and reached Samquite late that evening, as we did not hurry but watched the effects of the rising river. At Samquite I heard all the news of the Apaque war from old papa Yousoff, the Senegalese legionnaire. According to Yousoff neither Apaque nor the M'pangwes had suffered much, although they had wasted much powder which was good for trade. We told Yousoff of our two small battles with the Oshebas whom he said were a bad lot and would give the French government much trouble if not kept ruled by an iron hand, but that, he said, would be simply a matter of time. But I doubted him, and as nothing of any consequence was ever done to help out the trader in my time I question if the government did not think it would be money thrown away to bother with these wandering savages. We chatted till late in the evening and left Samquite for Apaque's country early next morning.

On arriving at Apaque's we were more than well received and we all had reached home sweet home. The chief laughed heartily when he cast eyes on the patched up lot, but was highly pleased when I told him of the beautiful country full of game which the Okatas had evacuated on account of the marauding Oshebas. This he said he would see became their property as he had a pull on the paramount chief at Ngilla and this would be a fine country for his people who were increasing rapidly. And it must be taken from these cannibals if he had to go there himself and drive them away. In any case, he said, these people must keep to their own side of the river and must never be allowed on his side, as they were a dangerous lot and they would surely cause trouble if they were allowed to get a strong foothold. And this he would see to at once and would send one of his sub-chiefs at once to Ngilla on that business.

———

"I shall be getting back to the love interest soon. If so it could be called—my old school fellow coming thousands of miles to have a look at an unfortunate English girl. Adventure. That's what he liked. 'Tis the one thing money can help you to.

"Excuse me if I bring forward my idea that this account of what happened to Nina T—— has to be drawn out and embellished a little with my experiences as a trader. The one'll help the other.

"I think I told you how I got the ruby away. I've often wondered what that white crystal was. Too big for any diamond. Fire and water, the priests told me. Blood and spirit. Aye, a poetic people.

'Tis only towns such as this where you'll not find poetry. Even a cannibal has it as a gift from nature. What is poetry but the leavings of superstition? If it's a cannibal we say he's superstitious to talk about blood and spirit. If it's a Christian same as you or me it's got to be poetry. Lord Tennyson was a poet but there's nothing very different in his make-up, come to fact, from those priests that were always pretending two stones were fire and water. Come another thousand years and Nina's savage guardians'll be tossing off odes. Panegyrics for old college chums and so on. I'm told they've already got visiting cads on the Ivory Coast. However that may be for truth, I'd rather go through the sugar-cane rite with a savage than be handed his visiting card printed in Oxford or London. Egbo sees you through, else how would I be here today? Look at my thumb. Egbo cured it. That feller nearly got me that time. 'Twas the only time I enjoyed watching a man die. We were watching him and passing remarks about his broken nose. On the edge of the water he was lying.

"Aye, I swam under him and tapped his claret enough to fetch a whole bevy of crocs for a meal. A crocodile won't eat unless he smells blood. He always needs some appetizer before he'll trouble to eat. But a croc's a thorough pig when he gets you. The smell of blood goes to his head, as they say. He gets a good grip through nature having provided that two of his teeth grow upward through the nose. He's fanciful too about his food. Never cares for it too fresh. His cave entrance is always a bit below the water level, but having dived in he then climbs up to dry ground above the river level. A wonderful instinct for safety from intruders. He leaves his meat until the processes of nature invite him to eat. A proper pig. And never stops growing, the natives say. Aye. Olive-green in hunting time. Yellow when the fish are breeding.

Cecil Rhodes once ran a fair chance of being put on the shelf in a croc's pantry. I'd been making some prickly-pear brandy at the back of my store in Rhodesia and Rhodes came along for a bit of fishing with one of his friends. Colonel ——— it was. They arrived in the forenoon and nothing would please them but they must take some of the new prickly-pear brandy. Said they wanted a novelty. They wouldn't listen to me when I said it'd treat 'em queer, not having matured. They took a good lot of it, and their lunch in a knapsack and my boy took 'em to the spot in the river where they'd find good fishing. 'Twas a place where a nice flat rock rose up about twenty feet from the bank. No more than a foot high and nice deep water all round. I thought no more about 'em until somewhere about half-past two, when my boy came rushing in and said if the Baases went on sleeping the crocodile would come. He'd taken a woman off that rock only a week before and she'd been wide awake, too, over her washing. I rode down to the spot to see what he meant, and there I saw Rhodes and the other feller fast asleep. Dead drunk they both were and very red in the face. They might 'a' got sunstroke lying out like that, let alone the crocodile. Full up 'a' raw prickly-pear spirit as they were. They'd both left their lines in the water and a fish was caught and splashing about on one of 'em. They knew nothing about it.

"We got 'em lifted into the boat and I had 'em carried over to the back of my store and spread out a forage bed for them to sleep it off. I lay they never approached prickly-pear brandy again. Heads like cannon balls when they woke up. Sick, too. Rhodes was properly astonished when he found where he was. He wasn't a man was often caught napping. But he was always a feller open to novelties. He could never keep his hands off a novelty, whether prickly-pear brandy or a lion with a wooden leg, same as he bought from Honest John. Like a lad in a toy shop, Rhodes.

"Honest John, the first Jew in Rhodesia. Him that was offered the half of Swaarbooi's kingdom if he'd sell him a wagon-load of rifles. Over on the German-West border that was. A good shot, too, for a Jew. Nature has deprived the Jew of the joy of life. He'd rather sell ivory than shoot it, and he'd rather shoot than be content to watch the fine apparition of nature. The first Jew in Rhodesia, same as Joseph was first in Egypt. Joseph was objectionable to his brethren and following the custom of the country he was sold as a slave. The first in Israel to settle in a foreign country and then send for his relations to come and set up for themselves.

"Aye, a brave feller, Honest John. Sets off on a long trek into Tanganyika and takes one boy with him. He was prospecting, of course, but he came to grief with the natives and only managed to get away with his life. Aye, he faced things, did John. And when he got back to Rhodesia he looked like Crusoe with man Friday. All in rags and no boots to his feet and terrible sores all over him from thirst and hunger. Turned up one day when Rhodes and Karl Peters were somewhere about. Karl Peters looked him all over and turned away without a good word. He was always a bit of a brute. And the natives thought he was mad, or a kind of witch doctor, always looking for bugs in the bark of trees or in cattle dung or in water from the drinking pools.

"But Cecil Rhodes was of a different stamina. He loved a struggle and he loved fellers that could battle-out for themselves. Aye, he and Honest John had a similar make-up from the hand of nature. Gave him fifty pounds out of his pocket to get a new rig out and started him with a store.

"Mind you, though, generous as he was, Rhodes was naught but a man. Susceptible to wine and women as they say, if you'll excuse me, Ma'am. Come to that, what is any hero but a man. Wasn't Nelson a man, obeying the dictates of nature even in the midst of fame? Napoleon, too, was choosy about women. And given a feller starts out to conquer a piece of Africa, he'll gather up what comes in his way, whether my prickly-pear brandy or a chief's daughter. Aye. Always on the battle-out was Rhodes.

"He'd 'a' liked my job. Quite a lad when he came out first. But older than I was when I got this thumb shortened by a feller with filed teeth and so on. High cheekbones.

"Took me by surprise. Deceit makes a lad angry. And when you're angry you're strong. There's some things you remember. And one's the first feller you've had to kill. Aye, I wake up sometimes and think we're struggling in the water....

"But looking back over the panorama of my life why, I think I've been merciful."

∽ Chapter XIX. ∾

M'BALWAMI, my uncle Apaque as he was called, was about the most intelligent savage I ever came in touch with, and as I was a lad who, ladlike always needed someone to really love him, I found Apaque to be really *it*. He was a king in his own right and that he really was fond of me and would have given his life for me at any time goes without saying, and being of a romantic nature I would have done the same for him. Nobody in the world ever feels this kind of love—only two men surrounded continually by danger night and day really can understand what it means when you meet. You are absolutely free from all worldly care for a time and feel doubly secure in your mutual strength.

Apaque's delight was to watch me muster my little army of twenty-nine rifles, these men I had togged up in old 17th Lancer jackets and caps. We had a great sale of the west coast for old army clothes which came packed in large puncheons and barrels, which were returned to England loaded with rubber. Of course, I picked out the best, and as I was well up in drill which I learnt at college, I took a great pride in making my little army efficient. Clean weapons I insisted on. The old chief would continually shout *Va bwe!* (well done) as I would give the orders in English form fours! Sections, right sections, left shoulder arms extend, file, marching, etc. Apaque would be in his glory and would even have his spearmen line up and would try to imitate the sounds of the English words of command. I gave him a fine military overcoat and sword and these he would don and give the most comical orders, which really meant nothing till he had his fun out and then would shout dismiss, which was always well understood. I found these parades were a good advertising medium for sale of these soldiers' coats. The natives, especially the Camma boys, were very fond of these parades after which each boy would fold up his coat and return it to the locker where they always remained clean.

After leaving Apaque's town the river widens and the rise of the water on the sandbanks gradually grew less. As evening drew near we had a good view of the natives who were fighting continually from the sandbanks, but they always suspended operations as we passed and both the Okelleys and the M'pangwes cheered us as we passed downstream.

We arrived all well at Adoninango early one morning and felt at home once more. The overland mail had just arrived so that I had the great pleasure of reading home news and the doings of my friend Little Peru. We were all busy reading when the news came that one of the missionary boys had been captured and was even now on his way to execution, as he had been preaching against the Izaga of a nearby village. The doctor in charge of the American mission heard of this happening just in time to save the poor boy. Gathering his lads together, the brave doctor rowed to the village where the boy had been imprisoned. He made one dash for the skull-house and, revolver in hand, he rescued the victim. The natives were so much taken aback by surprise that an old white man dare enter their temple that they did nothing but looked surprised. This gave the doctor time to pull his boat in midstream whilst the natives fired on him from the banks as he pulled away to the mission station, but he got away without any damage. This was a plucky deed and the old doctor of that Presbyterian mission station was always considered a hero after this deed. He had saved the boy from a terrible death and had risked his life for his mission boy.

∽∾

Count de Brazza, the explorer, would be with us in the spring and likewise several other visitors. The river had not risen enough to allow a steamboat to make the trip and as the river was still low no business was done. I made ready however for my trip to the sea and the lakes, and after discussing all matters concerning business to be done on the first rise of the river which might come at any time, and so it did. Quite unexpectedly the rain had fallen in both rivers and a steady rise took place. The sandbanks disappeared as if by magic. And all was hurry and scurry. I left for the sea that evening there to meet the first steamboat from Gaboon, which I was to pilot upriver as far as our trading state at Adoninango.

The S. S. *Pioneer* was the first boat due to arrive at Angola and this I was to pilot up to Adoninango and then to Samba Falls on the Angani River. Quite a long trip and I was anxious to have the chance to prove my maps and charts all correct. I must say that our future prosperity in the rivers all depended on those charts, etc. being correct, and Sinclair also was as anxious as I was to prove them. So by mutual consent I pulled downstream, quite confident that all would be well. I had a great send off from both Herr Schiff and Sinclair, and although my left hand was still in bad shape it was curing up nicely.

My first stop was at my old friend Efanginango's. where I had killed the rogue elephant. And he made us all feel quite at home, and leaving the old man I pulled out for Lake Azingo, which I reached in nice time and found all well. And after attending to what business was necessary and dispatching the overland mail I made for Nina's town. Here of course I had business of importance. The witch doctors and Nina came to the beach to meet and greet us. And of course I made myself as congenial as I could. The old chief doctor had quite a lot to tell me of things that had taken place and as we chatted I invited him and his companions to help themselves, and this they did in great style, soon being quite happy. Of course I told them to get ready for me at the Josh House as I wanted to make a big wish and was ready to pay for any favors I received from their ceremony and they were all more than pleased. It was not long before they announced themselves all ready. Now was an important time for me, as I intended to come away with a ruby at all hazards. I had the position of the masked fakirs at a glance. The goddess looked charming. She looked better than I had ever seen her before. I called the headman and had him lay down the presents and then palmed the ruby bending low and making it appear that I was receiving a little pain from my wounded left hand which I carried high enough to hide the actions of my busy right. The ruse acted splendidly. I had the ruby in my right pocket whilst I held the imitation in my hand. It all looked quite natural. The wand now moved down and my wish was granted amidst the weird sounds that came from the spirits, which the headman said were all pleased. And so was I.

The presents were removed and I walked away as usual to the music of the *ngombi*. I felt relieved when I reached the village and was soon joined by the fakirs from the Josh House. We all enjoyed ourselves and the headman and his folk chatted merrily. Nina now joined us and I gave her the dresses, shoes, etc. that had been sent her by Little Peru. This greatly pleased her and I chatted to her in both M'pangwe and English and we were soon the best of friends all round. The old man was especially thankful and so were all the assistants. I left them after making them a few more presents and they all agreed I was the best church member they had and they would do all they could to ward off many evil spirits which might try and harm me. I promised to call again as I would be often passing, and this I did.

I do not think they ever noticed the change I had made in the rubies. If they did they never showed it at any time and were always glad to see me when I called on them. I was always careful to hide the ruby in the locker till I had managed to ship it to Little Peru. It arrived all safe and was worth more than I ever imagined. It was sent to Tiffanys in New York for valuation and was also valued at Hatton Garden in London. The American valuation was by far the highest.

The trip to the sea was made without any trouble and as the water was continually rising I was quite sure of being able to run the steamer as far as Samba Falls anyway. All my triangulations and workings proved up to the mark and even eclipsed our expectations.

The first boat to show by smokestack was the paddle steamer *Pioneer*, a large river boat which could navigate in eight feet of water. As she crossed the bar and came in sight of T——'s grave I boarded her. The skipper was a new one and was a nervous man and as he insisted on throwing the lead. I told him I was in charge, being the company's pilot, and if he insisted on being bull-headed I would put him in his cabin and take all responsibilities on myself for my actions. At this he stood aghast and wanted to parley. I felt insulted and offered him his choice, either the boat *was* in my full charge or in his, if he wanted to take the boat up himself he could do so. At this he cowed and told me I looked so young he hated to give in, as we had a valuable cargo. I only laughed at him and showed my papers. Pilot in full charge. So the old paddles smashed away. She was a splendid boat. I took him in record time to Angola.

He now got quite chummy and as I was always at home with the native chiefs and in fact everybody else, he commenced to get confidential, told me of his old woman at home and showed me his daughter's photo. Like all Liverpoolers he became very communicative and before long grew quite chummy, especially on going ashore at various landings. I made it a strict practice of showing a military front, which he soon found was quite necessary in a land of piracy, slavery, and murder. As the old salt talked at me with my bandaged hand and many of my boys still patched, he began to think that this was surely a land where for a lad romance runs amuck.

I had always placed the wild Ogowe River second to none where human life was at stake and I soon had the old Captain thinking as I did. At Angola I took on a few tons of farina food for the boys and a supply of fine wood, and after a two-hour stay, the old *Pioneer* was thudding upstream (and all's well), and we battled up to Isorga town where I recommended a short stay and, of course, made another wish.

Here I found that the river was falling fast on account of the absence of rains in the interior and this I explained to the captain. We were in a land of chance, Chief Isogu on one side and Rengogu on the other, both notorious river pirates, and this I told him was a place where we could not afford to stick for long with a valuable cargo. If they saw us well-struck they would attack us in a minute. And then? he said. And then I answered, if they lick us we won't want any advice from anybody, we'll all be dead if we lose out. Lose what? he said. The fight through, I answered. Here they commenced to stack up and we were soon tipping the sandbanks, although we carried eighty pounds of steam. River still falling, we grounded fairly in midstream. It was evening, just after sundown. We worked her all ways, it was to no avail. We were stuck.

I called all my boys, with Iwolo my general, and we were soon putting the boat in shape to resist an attack, which would surely come. The old captain now got up all arms he carried for defense—about twenty old Snyders—and netting the stern we did all we could. Renchoro and Iwolo seemed to think we could lick any attackers and, of course, I thought so also. A clear case of Never Say Die. The ship's crew were all working boys, and although they would fight their best, we relied very little on them. The engineer, a half-breed called Davis, now coupled up two hoses which were to throw scalding water on anyone attempting to board, whilst Iwolo and myself with our rifles piled up Manchester goods in a ring, determined to hold our own from aft. The old captain armed with a six-shooter and cutlass seemed pensive but I soon had him in a good humor by spinning yarns.

We were about all ready for anything when a canoe came alongside. It was Nina, the headman, and a couple of his witch doctors, and Nina spoke to me first. She was nattily dressed in the European togs I had given her and spoke in a firm voice which I understood. Come and see us at once, you will receive protection. If not, you will be attacked and will surely die. She looked me steadily in the eye as she spoke and insisted on my following her at once. I thanked her at once but told her I had a surprise in store for anyone if they cared to come and try. At this she smiled and said, don't be foolish, they don't want to kill you, I will see to that, but your boat is fast. They are ready to attack you and I give you this chance. Come with me. I told her how thankful I was to her but I could not leave the ship. I had got it into trouble and would get it out. She said no more but I noticed a water blot you call a tear in her blue eye. I waved her goodbye. We said no more. She had risked her life to save me.

There was nothing could help me, only my rifles. I had confidence in them, so had my boys. In fact, I wanted a go-in with these river men. If I won, which I knew I would, I was as good as King of the River. I knew the native. If I licked him I had his friendship. We had not long to wait, as out from the Isorga Point shot two war canoes bearing straight down on us. Iwolo now proposed a drink and stood behind us as we mounted the poop, field glasses in hand. We took things easy and opened out at 800 yards on Isogu's fleet. As we potted them they began to hesitate, and then making a swift turn back we played skittles with them. The canoes showed signs of the wildest disorder. This tickled Iwolo, who started up a song, *Iduma enywary calis a mo sacka* (the cheek of a slave always comes to grief). We potted them till all agreed to leave them alone and leave some of them living. We felt like going ashore and taking the town and killing Isogu.

And now a fleet of twenty put out from Rengogu's, but shared a worse fate as we popped in a few shots at them at 1,000 yards, and the effect was plainly visible—they returned. They had a life's surprise. I had all shots and we drank and amused ourselves whilst beckoning them on shore to come out awhile. They had the easiest licking I ever saw, and from that time on I always commanded the river. With a loss of nothing but a couple of hundred cartridges I had quieted the river to stay quiet. And old General Iwolo always smiled when we spoke of the battle at Isogu's.

After another piece of luck, which was the sudden rising of the river a couple of feet, we felt quite independent so I turned the big paddles round and dropped anchor at Nina's sacred town. The inhabitants seemed afraid of us to begin with but I hailed the sacred chief who came off in his best canoe along with several of his witchmen. I received them well on board but let them see I was prepared for any eventualities that might arise. This was a good advertisement, as they had seen how well we had disposed of our enemies without a scratch. I noticed he had his weather eye on our rifles and took all in. I never even mentioned the battle, only to say that anyone who was foolish enough to bother us would regret it and furthermore I told him my wishes had all been granted and if he wished I would come on shore and make another wish. He said I could wait till they had composed themselves, as there had been quite a number of influential men on shore who had been shot. And of course I was sorry especially as Isogu's son had been killed.

Of course I expected, as I was a full member of the temple, to be treated like any other member of the faithful and to this he agreed, but as the doctors were fixing up the wounded they would prefer remaining quiet. In fact, he had been averse to one member of the temple fighting another. But I chimed in. This boat is mine and the goods were mine and they had attacked me. What had he to say about it? He could only tell me he was never in favor of the attack and said, in a whisper, we warned you as a brother, did we not? Of course you did, I answered. You offered me protection if I would leave the boat, and I shall always be thankful to you for the warning and furthermore, I have come here purposely to reward you all for your good action now that the battle is over, and I want you to make peace with everybody on my account.

These wise men now had a confab and said they understood me exactly and would be glad of any help I could give them so as to commence peacemaking. I asked them to state what they wanted, and they asked me for five cases of gin and two bottles of rum, and they would begin to move away every evil spirit in the river, after which there could be nothing but peace. I had the gin and rum placed in their canoe at once and they promised to return and tell me how they had gone on in spirit land, but begged me not to come on shore until they had returned. In about two hours, the sacred boat put off with Nina and the old chief at the bow standing. She looked radiant, and in the stern sat Chief Isogu, who seemed to be depressed. He disclaimed all blame for the attack and blamed the creek men who had acted without orders. I made them all welcome and treated them as if nothing had happened. Nina was dressed in European style and on parting shook hands with me, leaving a short note. (Trust no one) or (Beware). I noticed the chief's eyes cast on my rifle brigade and especially old Iwolo, who they all knew as the best fighter and general of the whole Cammas.

They all went off smiling but could not help seeing that we were alert. I had made a good impression on them, and as they had downed many a ship in this very spot and I knew they were treacherous to a man, I felt proud as they retired friendly with my ruse. All the same I had steam always ready and sudden death to any false move were my orders to my fighting Chief Old Iwolo.

The river rose quickly and the captain reported ten feet or more in the channel between the long sandbanks. So we hove anchor and with a full head of steam were soon thudding away up the Ogowe. We woke up Isorga town on parting with three shrill blasts of our whistle and several ominous toots of the foghorn and as she was a powerful boat, we were soon well away passing the most dangerous spot in the river with two feet of spare water under us. The natives along the bank cheered us lustily as we passed onward and eventually passing Herr Schiff's we were all safe and sound alongside the pier at Adoninango.

There was a great gathering of traders ashore and discharging cargo was the order of the day. Sinclair was glad to see us. As the river fell slightly after our arrival, I took a good two days' rest, which I badly needed. Now the reloading trader's purchases took place and early morning all being ready, we sailed for far-off Samba Falls. A young Presbyterian mission lady (Miss ———) came on board and to my surprise she was bound for Samba Falls and was the first white lady who ever visited there. I could not help but admire her courage.

———

"I can't be second-rate in literature, Ma'am. I must give facts and novelties too. Properly woven they are the basis of solid interest.

"That old *Pioneer* sure came up to the scratch. Livingstone's boat she used to be, carrying a load of bibles instead o' Manchester goods. A favorite of fashion he was, with all the luxuries obtainable by prayer in Piccadilly drawing-rooms. A stand of arms they gave him. Ladies'll always admire a romantic figure. Prowess. That's what tickles 'em.

"Aye, I've been saving up this river fight to put in a bit of prowess for a reviver. When you're cornered, battle out! Keep your self-respect between your teeth! A fight lost in Africa's the world lost. Other places'll give you a second chance. The Ivory Coast gives you only one.

"'Twould never 'a' done for me to listen to Nina T——. 'You'd better come,' she said. A strange look that girl had sometimes....

"No, Ma'am, you'd hardly say I was in love. My little ringletted lass of the lily ponds in a Lancashire lane kept my heart. But it was only in nature for a boy to have a good stare at those eyes of a goddess looking at him so strangely. Kind but piercing they were. She'd never seen a light-haired boy and perhaps it brought memories of her father.

"'Tis a good thing I knew her so intimately. Any book, to catch the fancy, needs some attachment like Nina. Something that continues in the background and provides color. Aye. Come to Nina's story, I would have crammed the whole narrative into three or four chapters. There was little enough of it. But come to a book you need some proper understanding of selection, George Bussey says. He'd never 'a' let me pour out all the best in one gulp. That's why I've had to weave it in somewhat meager. Get me contrast and me solidity with gorillas and river fights and so forth and etcetera.

Mind you, there's some'll read the book for that. Fellers who'd turn up their nose at a so-called love interest. It's in the make-up of the natural man that he keeps a soft corner for a bit of a battle. And if he's ever been a lad he'll sure enjoy my rivers. Aye! Come to rivers, Ma'am, my knowledge would be sure considered a novelty even in America.

"And that bit about Miss Hasken. They'll appreciate that in Cincinnati. They sure will. They think a lot of goodness in America and they can't fail to be attracted by that sweet lady stepping aboard to sail up a cannibal river. The first white woman they'd seen. Like an angel she sat there, with her back against the bales and staring out. All on board loved her. 'Twas the look in her eye. Aye! 'Twas a look could 'a' taken Stanley and his sort to the world's end and heaven as a wind-up. But they hadn't got it. They hadn't got it.

"Never cared for Stanley, us traders. 'Twas no love of humanity made him go after Livingstone. 'Twas nothing but newspaper ambition. Always wanted the spotlight turned on *him*. There was that poor feller Pocock was with him. Got carried over Samba Falls in a boat. Very likely. But 'twas an open suspicion among the traders that the boat was cut from its moorings.

"Natives? Oh, aye, natives if you like. Better say natives did it if you're making a note about it. I don't want to be crucified with those notes of yours, Ma'am. Aye, he couldn't bear for any other feller to get a bit of credit.

"But that mission lady. She never thought of anything but the schools and churches she was going to build. Saw 'em all as pretty as a picture at likely spots up that wild river. 'How beautiful to see one there, Mr. Horn!' she says.

"Wear? What did she wear? Well now, Ma'am, I shall have to think. Nothing fashionable. No feathers or these so-called porkpie hats. Just one o' these leghorn hats. Nice and shady for a lady's eyes. And a dress of brown Holland same as my sister Emily used to wear in the summer. Buttons and so on the bodice. Braid. And she had to keep lifting her long skirt, getting in and out of the boat and walking in the dust and the long grass.

"Aye, I've seen so-called women explorers since then. Helmets and so on. Riding boots and ties and everything else. But I've never seen that all this men's truck made 'em any braver than that poor lady who never thought of her get-up.

"I must thank you, Ma'am, for asking the ———— Society to look me up with a bit of help. There was one of 'em came yesterday. Stout body, used to the job. Talks pleasant and never listens to what you are telling her. Aye, they look through the wall. Left a candle and two pieces of soap. Tickets for milk and meat once a week. I appreciate the way she's doing her duty but I should sure have preferred to get the soap and candles by ticket. When you're feeling too hungry to walk to a shop you're apt to cavil at what is after all but a kindly deed. But I'm bearing philanthropy better since I began with the book. I can sure throw it off the chest. Aye, there's something in writing's like armor to the feelings."

ꙅ Chapter XX. ꙅ

NEXT to board us was Sinclair and we steamed towards Eninga where the blind king lived. Miss Hasken had a drawing pad on her knee, and as we steamed by the villages she would make rapid sketches of the various places whilst I would tell her their history as far as I could. This seemed to interest her greatly. We traveled up the Angani as long as we could see clearly and could make sure of the positions of the channels, and dropped anchor at old Injuni's town, the chief of the Okelleys of Angani. The chief came off accompanied by his headman and women, and as Miss Hasken could speak M'pangwe fairly well, which language they understood, the greatest curiosity they had ever seen, the White Lady, made their visit onboard a great event. They would ask her many questions about herself which she readily answered and this pleased them immensely, and on parting she presented the dusky ladies with bonbons. This shore was filled with the inhabitants of the town and after weighing anchor in the early dawn we passed upstream, after giving them several loud blasts of the steamboat's whistle, which greatly amused them. They must have thought the whistle was talking to them.

We made several short stops on our journey and arrived early in the morning at beautiful and picturesque Samba Falls, which as the river was nearly at flood height looked very imposing, nestling as it does amongst the mountains. Soon everything was bustle at the big Ivili town, which covers both sides of the river and mounts up on each side of you as if it were perched on rocks and dangerous looking crags. Miss Hasken took great pleasure in visiting the natives and soon made friends with them. In her visits to the various parts of this mountain town she was generally followed by an admiring throng of youngsters and women and she took great delight in knowing their reasons for having so many wooden idols, some of which are quite large and grotesque, whilst some of them are even hideous and specter-like. I would explain what they were and she would always smile when I told her they were there to ward off evil spirits, diseases, and ill luck of all kinds. In fact, these people are about the most superstitious race you could meet and were all advocates of voodooism in its worst forms. Once in a while a human skull would be placed near a house as a fend-off for witches, which were generally supposed to be women.

After she had visited the villages, she produced her drawing material and made some splendid sketches of the winding river and the lofty hills beyond, and she presented me with one which I sent to England. These were the first sketches of this most dangerous country and were highly valued by all who saw them. They were charcoal sketches in black and white. The witch doctors were very much disturbed, as they often asked me what was the white lady doing. This I explained to them, but I could see they were very dubious. Miss Hasken also made a short trip above the falls and told me that some day this would make a grand spot for a mission station, but in reality it was such a stronghold of witchcraft that it was then about the most dangerous spot she could have thought of in Africa. She was, being the first white lady ever seen in that part of the country, always looked upon by us traders as a great female explorer as well as a heroine to thrust herself into the heart of Isorga. And the natives often spoke of her as their white sister and such she was, as being a perfect lady she treated them all with such human equality and respect that she completely won them over by her kindly actions and words.

We took on board a record load of rubber and our downstream trip was one of the greatest pleasures I had as a youth, and I have often thought about her in her leghorn hat examining the idols of these strange people. She came from the city of Cincinnati, U.S.A., for the benefit of these natives and I could see by her words and actions she would have given her life for their sakes. This was humanity indeed, and as this lady, about twelve months after her visit to the falls, died of West Coast fever, I had the honor of conveying her by sea and river to Barraca, the chief mission station at Gaboon, where she was buried with silent regrets. We could not have thought of a burial of a white lady at Kangwe, as there is no doubt the Isorga worshippers would have stopped at nothing to get her remains for fetish, but would lie safely and undisturbed in her grave at Barraca.

On my return to Adoninango with Sinclair, we found Count de Brazza was on his way and we had orders to do all in our power to help him which was done. He eventually landed with his quartermaster and several French soldiers, both white and black. His native soldiers were all from Senegal and were fine fellows. In fact, we all got along splendidly. Count de Brazza was a tall gentleman of what seemed middle age, although not thirty, and was a pensive man who never joked or smiled. His men were armed with the Fusi Grass, which I found was a splendid rifle and a French machine gun completed his armory. He brought along a number of beautiful looking donkeys who surprised the natives, whenever turned loose, by their loud braying and kicking antics, and the whole inhabitants would scurry away when the white man's deer charged through their villages. And this had a more pacific action on these cannibals than the look of his soldiers and guns.

De Brazza had to stay with us till his large canoes came from Okanda away up the Ogowe River. I had many a long chat with him and as he spoke both French and English I soon formed a great friendship with him and he promised I should have his assistance if I followed him up to establish trading posts. He also told me he intended to put up the French flag at Stanley Pool, and there he made his town which is Brazzaville of today. He also sent the news that any of the natives who were slaves would be free on joining him but, strange to say, although there were many slaves in that part of Africa, there were very few who joined him, and these who did were men who had been mostly sold away from their wives and children. He wanted a gorilla, which he intended to ship whole, which was to be preserved in good white spirits, and as the natives always knew where these were, we made up a large puncheon. The gorilla arrived and was an old man who had given notice of dawn for many years by his fierce howlings and drummings. He was a fine big fellow, and it took six or seven large crew boys to get him into the puncheon, after his head had been sawn across with a light saw, as he was wanted for the purposes of craniotomy (study of the brain). The alcohol was then poured on the large brute and the large barrel was closed and firmly hooped. I heard afterwards that he arrived all safe in Europe.

And now this famous explorer made all ready for his trip. The large canoes were manned, the donkeys were last to be put on board. And as we fired him a rifle salute, he waved us *adieu* and went off on his expedition. His fleet of large canoes, which were all flat-bottomed, were well manned by Okandas and Okotas, and followed the north bank of the river and these people are great singers and kept beautiful time and melody and this sweet savage music we could hear till they disappeared, as it was carried seaward by the light river breeze. This expedition was the means of adding a very large country to France. And as we all knew was made to cut off any chance of Leopold's annexing both sides of the Congo, which we all thought was possible, till all our fears were set aside. No one seemed to be very much in love with the Belgians at that time, especially ivory hunters and traders. And as I have watched events which have happened on both sides of the Congo, I have reason to think that we would rather have seen our own flag go up than another. Both the French and Belgians are poor colonizers as will be seen by a visit to any of their colonies.

Sinclair and I now argued the feasibility of following him up and establishing trading outposts in the best localities. This I agreed to do. I made several more trips to the sea and always contrived to meet Nina. She was more than willing to be carried off, by force if necessary, as the poor lass longed for freedom and had begun to realize her position. She had studied English in her spare time and could write fairly well, but I was careful to put nothing in them which might disagree with her captors, should any letter miscarry and fall into their hands. But she always told me to watch myself as the black Nkomi would take any chance to kill me, as they were determined to get even with me for opening the river up and especially for the fight I had won, and although they might not dare to attack me openly, to always beware. If anything happened whilst I was away she would always let me know if possible. I asked her if there was any likelihood of my being attacked from the Josh House or in the village, but to this she answered no, she did not think so as I was always too well armed, and they feared me more than they loved me, and especially the witch doctors who always were glad of my enormous presents to them, and they all said I was not really a bad man but was naturally fond of fighting. She said they really had thought I would leave the ship to save myself and they even had agreed to let me go free if they captured me. My resistance was a great surprise to them and especially as they had so many killed.

On a future occasion she told me of a spring which she used for bathing and was situated across the creek opposite where the Josh House was. But I must be careful not to let myself be seen. She generally took one of her maids with her but could send her back for something whilst I could come there from the big river by a small path which would lead me to the spring, which was easily found by the grove of tall trees around it. After discussing many plans we agreed on this last one as best. She had a good head. She would take over her clothes and hide them in the rushes near the big river. I was to drop a stone in the water from the bank into the creek, where she would always watch, when I was ready to steal her. Furthermore I could call when I was ready for her and make my wish with plenty of liquor for the holy men. And wear on that occasion a scarf round my neck and drop a piece of string on the floor with a knot in it. At the time I smiled and thought surely the tricks of a woman are wonderful. Furthermore, she told me she would slowly shut one eye and at this I smiled but I told her I thought this was a sensible way of getting clear. Yes, she said, and after that I shall come away from the *enago* (house) just as I am dressed, as it must all be done quickly to make all sure. I shall dive in the water without sound and shall climb to the bank near the *icundo* tree (great cotton tree). Then, as I can run fast, you will pull for the middle of the stream. The darkness and speed will help us. The poor goddess was really in great earnest and of course any fumbling meant her death, if not mine also. I had well understood. And afterwards made a short hand note in shorthand, as nearly verbatim as possible, of what she had told me.

As future events will show she was quite right, and as things worked out well on the memorable night, the night I stole her, I always gave her credit for having a better head than I had, as all the plans I could think of were a swift attack on the holy men during a visit and carry her off old Scotch-boarder fashion or young Lochinvar in a boat whilst the fathers were drunk. And I found her plan work out so plainly that Nina must have seen lots more happenings round the Josh House than what she liked me to know. Anyway she had saved my life by her timely warnings and I was determined on taking her away from those ungodly surroundings.

Strange to say, although I liked Nina and it would not have taken much to have balanced my loving in her favor then, I could never keep my head about a little blue-eyed lass I had known up in North Lancashire in the country we used to call the Clog and Shawl; we used to pluck posies together and she used to gather cowslips and primroses and garden pinks and tulips and make such pretty buttonholes, which always seemed to smell better when she had plucked them and pinned them on. She lived close to my grandfather's, who was freehold landlord of Frea, the family of the old Fist-and-Spear. The country, especially there, was supposed to grow fairies, which she told me used to grow from the pond lilies and would stand on the lilies to hear thrushes and skylarks, and I believed her as she was my great playmate in those days of ringlets, which I wore as well as she did, No wonder I could not get her out of my mind, and I just couldn't. Of course she would always crop up in my mind when I was admiring Nina, who never seemed to notice there was something, ah, a Lancashire fairy between, so there it was.

I wrote to Little Peru of course and explained how Nina herself had planned the getaway, and do you know to my great surprise in his next letter he declared he was going to be in at the stealing with me, and as he was shortly coming of age, he was going to see me out of that godforsaken land, the West Coast. Money, he said, was no object. I must come and sojourn with him where he would build a place in healthy and romantic Peru, where we could love and enjoy life as it should be, with my stolen goddess of high degree, and where they would both admire my wife and my ruby. I could only laugh heartily, as I knew his nature so well—British and Inca—it was just as I expected. But I wondered if I should tell of my fairy, but I never did. In fact he admired my sketch of Nina, which he declared was A-1. Somehow I felt that if he once saw my *belle sauvage* he would succumb—heart, silver mines, and all. And Nina had such simple winning ways, I thought it would be wise to warn him but I didn't. Anyway, come eventually he did but not before I advised him, and whether he succumbed or not we shall see later on in the story.

I piloted several steamers up without mishap or trouble of any kind, and as trade was booming these always came down with full cargoes. The *Pioneer* I conducted up the River Ogowe as far as John Earmy's, who did quite a large trade and had his store—a large one in the Bimvool country. On my return I made ready for following de Brazza and posting traders upcountry. I had quite a big flotilla with me and, selecting a few good ivory and rubber traders, we bade goodbye to Adoninango and Herr Schiff and started upstream, great salute firings from the stations and flag-dropping. I had good trading cargo and good men, and we were well-armed and provisioned for a long trip to anywhere. Before I left, both Herr Schiff and Sinclair told me I should make good and so it proved out.

"Aye, when I saw de Brazza's canoes disappearing to make new country for the French.... And the singing came back to us....

"Commissioned by his country to enlarge her territory. I could 'a' done it for England a dozen times and over. Charlie Thompson says they still talk of that river fight I had. They speak of me still, I'm told.

"Aye, if a roc could drop me there now I'd made headway still, on my river. Who's to know it better than I that charted it? And if the bottom's altered I'd not be too old to chart it again. To be continually taking your soundings is a course of nature whether with man or with water.

"If I'd been Sinclair I'd have owned the country. In Britain's name, of course. I'd have put up me flag even if only to Clog and Shawl. When it's for a savage's vision Clog and Shawl's as good as lion rampant. A totem he'll not understand. I could 'a' pulled big power from Lancashire in those days. The old Fist-and-Spear were always open to adventure whether of trade or battle. Strong and ambitious—that's Lancashire.

"Frenchmen are go-easy folks, like Italians. They'll not cut much ice when it comes to annexing foreign parts. I thought myself as big as de Brazza. I was better armed and I had the instinct for top-dog lacking in one of his make-up. A proper nobleman, though. Full of high thought and proud reserve with all his bravery. He could be as silent as a duke. Aye, it seemed like Africa kept him quiet. Always walking up and down with his eyes on the ground. He'd 'a' done better at poetry, perhaps. But a man, for all that. Aye, he stepped as if earth was his heritage.

"If I'd sent home for proper backing I'd have got clear of Sinclair's timidity and photo-worship. Rhodes knew the power of home backing. He knew that when his ambitions became *un fait accompli* he'd succeed. Nothing succeeds like success—with the stay-at-homes. But pioneers're built like that. It's not gaudy success that Rhodes was after. Leave that to Stanley. It was to make something to grow in the breast of tamed nature, when it's yourself that's done the taming.

"I'm glad to be able to save a brave woman from forgetfulness. Aye, the second day she went out and she sat on a rock above the falls. And there was a tree grew out over the water and she was sketching it. The Angani mountains, and so on. The natives thought she was trying to break the *ambwini*—putting the white god against the black. They were uneasy. They'd never seen a lady sketching. I couldn't help but keep an eye on her. Didn't do to let her see me, though. And I had to let the natives understand I thought it was the usual thing for ladies to do.

"My sister Emily was the sketch she gave me. I used to send her curios from the West Coast. Nay, I could never say what became of it. You know people at home will sit like magpies on a thimble over all the what-nots of a home. And then comes the old auctioneer we call Death and puts the lot up to a stranger before life's even been lived. Aye, it they'd run out o' doors a bit oftener, nature'd teach 'em to forget the gewgaws!

"I've collected curios for a good many people in my time. Speaking of gorillas in spirits, there was that feller I packed for President Grant when he came to the West Coast. He was naturally looking for souvenirs and I sold him a gorilla for thirty pounds. I put him in a puncheon of spirits same as the big chap de Brazza sent to his medical society. Aye. But by some misfortune the wrong puncheon got put aboard the *Alaska. Alaska*, was it? It's so long ago I can't trust me memory too well over names. Howbeit, I'd got a poor feller, a goldsmith from Accra, sleeping his last sleep in a vat of spirits in my store-shed, and only waiting for a ship to take him home to his own people. Mind you, 'twas a burial which, even as a temporary measure, would have suited many. That feller the Duke of Clarence would never have turned up his nose at such a purgatory.

"From Ashanti, that goldsmith. Josiah of Accra he was well known as. Made gold and silver ornaments from metal mined by himself on the spot. A regular artist at twisting metal into shapes of beauty. Like that wild feller in the Bible you hear of—Jubal Cain or some such resounding name. All up and down the coast he'd been looking for metals and working at what he found in the mountains. Nice little furnace for smelting. Bellow made of monkey skins. Got swept over Samba Falls when he was prospecting for copper. 'Twas treachery of one of the tribes did it. They were for burying the body there, but you know what that means. *Muti* for your enemy. Nothing more valuable than a dead enemy. So I took him down the river with me and put him in spirits till a ship should come along'd take the feller home. Every man has a right to burial on the spot we call home. He wants his own at such a moment, if ever. Aye, I'd like to think someone'd do as much for me when I'm beckoned. Ship me over to Frea. Or in sound of the sea at Gillmoss. But don't let the spirits leak. No sailor'll stand it and remain human. If they can't resist Nelson they'd think nothing of Aloysius Horn.

"Aye, I labeled him 'Accra' and I'd already written to the British consul at Accra to look out for him. But after the *Alaska* had sailed I found they'd put the wrong one on board. So he went to America as a gorilla.

"No, I never heard any complaints, I meant to write but— 'twould 'a' been a long business. And I was a gorilla to the good. I was doing a lot with the museums just then."

ᕀ **Chapter XXI.** ᕀ

I KEPT THE south bank of the river as far as Apaque's place, making only three short stops. I spent the night making plans for our mutual defense against the M'pangwes and Oshebas. As Apaque had a perfect right to the south bank of the river as far as Okota, he claimed also the interland. As he explained, if Oshebas and M'pangwes ever gained a strong foothold on the southern bank of the river, the Okelleys might as well move back. At one time his grandfather owned both banks up to the Okotas from Eninga, but the M'pangwes came down in hordes till at last, for safety's sake, they were forced to flee from their lands on the north bank of this great river, and had still to watch this cruel race of maneaters, who would always be the enemies of the more peaceable tribes. We finally agreed that if he was molested on the south bank I would give him all the help I could in reason, as I needed a safe passage at all times for my canoes coming and going from our chief station. And this agreement we kept faithfully. I also promised to make my headquarters on Isange Island just south of the Acotas, and as he claimed this island as his property and he was quite right I gave him a bottle of gin for it, and he signed a paper making Isange Island my property for all time.

After this was over he persuaded me to stay a full day with him as he had much to tell me, and we all agreed to take another day's rest with Uncle Apaque, the Napoleon of the Ogowe. He then changed the conversation to de Brazza who had put in a night with him, and had also offered to take away any of his slaves who wished to go with him, and although he was quite willing and called many of his slaves around him, none of them left him. He knew that a slave who wished to run away could always do so, so he would never hinder them in any way. He had lost but few during a long life, whilst many fled from other countries and *Boliaed Imanda* (begged him to accept them as their master). He knew how to get along with them and they were just as free as a free man as long as they were willing to serve him in wartime. He had always found them the best of fighting material and good workers as long as they were left to enjoy the fruits of their labor. He had no Josh House or voodoo in his country and in case of trouble they were tried by their own headmen whom he held responsible for those under them. Thus he had lots of time to study the doings of both free men and slaves, and under his rule they had increased and multiplied enormously, so much that he needed a new country, especially land on which his people could cut rubber, which he found was gradually fetching better prices and supplied them with all the white man's goods they needed.

What Apaque could not understand was the meaning of a French flag, and of course it was not my business to explain to him. The very idea of a man spending so much money carrying kicking donkeys and machine guns with him greatly puzzled him and he said, What won't a Frenchman do? He had visited Gaboon many times going overland, had seen the big mission station and had come to the conclusion that they were a race of people who were fond of wasting their time or were a race of white fools. At this solution of the whole affair we were all forced to laugh and this pleased Apaque.

We all enjoyed our visit and it was late when I went to sleep in his apartment, as he was fond of telling me the various episodes of his life when he had been Generalissimo of his father, the Paramount Chief of the country. He had also hunted ivory for many years and would take a large regiment of men with him and hunt the country, and not only did they rely on what they killed for food but always brought sufficient dried game back with them to supply their wants during the rainy season. This he said was the grand secret of creating a good army and he surely had one. In all his battles with the tribes both near and far he had always made them fear him. This he said had made them secure in the land they lived in. And no tribe had ever over run them.

We parted the following morning and were at Samquite long before sundown. We made a fond goodbye to old Samquite and in a few days we pulled up at Isange Island, where I made a fortified post at the east end of the island. This being finished I laid out my large stock of goods for trade and I had not long to wait before the M'pangwes and Oshebas commenced to flock in. I made it a strict custom that they all gave up their arms and allowed no one in the stockade carrying them. They did not like this for a while, but they got quite used to it in a short while, as I allowed no trouble of any kind to take place on the island. The M'pangwes and Oshebas came in their canoes to the north side of the island and the Okelleys and Oketas who were their enemies used the south side. Thus I made a free trade island and I had a better trade than I expected both in ivory and rubber. I made frequent shipments to Adoninango and my goods always arrived safely. Apaque's people arrived and established a small town nearby in the country vacated by the Oshebas. I dispatched traders upcountry and all did well. I had news of de Brazza from the Okandas, and he had opposition from the fighting tribes of the Ilige district, but his machine guns and rifles had proved too much for these savages and he eventually arrived with his donkey troop and his liberated slaves at Brazzaville.

Thus all went well for a few months till a large consignment of goods coming up the river to my depot had the misfortune to come up the side of the river inhabited by the Bimvool. All went well till they reached Ngogudema's town, the head chief of these cannibals. Here they were attacked and the whole of the valuable consignment was captured by this chief. I heard the news a few days after this event and immediately dispatched news of the occurrence to Sinclair, who sent me an answer that the chief had promised to send back the goods intact, as well as the prisoners if he, Sinclair, would agree to send me no more supplies and recall me. If not, he would not do this. He threatened to do his worst against him and if necessary he would raise his tribe and attack the chief depot. Sinclair consented to his demands and sent me instructions to come down the river at once and save myself as my accounts were already largely in my favor, and for my sake he would like me to return without delay.

There I was stuck. My pet project for which I had labored hard was smashed and I was obliged to acknowledge defeat. As I had little or nothing left in my store, I made a resolution to ship the balance down the river and thus obey orders, but abandon the post I would not, making the excuse to Sinclair that I had outstanding debts which I would collect in spite of his agreement. And if I had a chance, which I surely would have, I would pay the cannibal chief for his insolence.

I had not long to wait. I collected my outstanding debts and called in my traders who all came down the river in due time and I explained everything to them. All those who wished to go down the river to Adoninango I let go, reserving only such men and canoe boys as were necessary to man my four largest canoes. I then formed hunting parties and we hunted elephants and other animals on Apaque's side of the river. I sent a dispatch to Apaque explaining all and told him to advise me of any move, either on our chief trading station or in event of Ngogudema making a move upstream to attack me, to let him come as I was sure to give him a beating and was ready for any move he made. This he promised to do.

I had a large quantity of ammunition and my general Iwolo and I planned our mode of battle. One day whilst I was maneuvering my canoes near the island I was surprised to see quite a number of canoes coming downstream, some of them flying the French flag. I gave them a royal salute, and pulling back to the island, the soldier in charge of the party told me graphically of the doings of the expedition under Count de Brazza, which except for the battle with the savages of the Ilige district had been a complete success. The country, he said, was quite a good one to live in and all was going well. He had been sent down for supplies and would return when he had them. I now explained what had happened to me and my expedition, he knew I was following de Brazza as quickly as I could, and to be cut in such a shape reflected little credit on Sinclair. At this he smiled and said as we were speaking French, *Il manque l'audace* or some words of this kind but to me the words he had, a yellow streak would have sounded much better and given a truer picture of Sinclair. After he had dined, he said, he wished he could help me but promised to do all that he could, that to him it seemed impossible that a savage like Ngogudema could do what he liked on the Ogowe. We shook hands after having a parting drink and the young soldier whom I admired went off with his little flotilla rejoicing.

I received a dispatch from Apaque a few days later saying Ngogudema had started upstream with a large number of canoes in two sections and he also heard that he had also dispatched quite a large regiment of his warriors by land but did not hear what his intentions were. He would keep me advised however, as he was keenly watching from his side of the river. Two days after this an Eninga salt trader was fired on from ambush on the M'pangwe side of the river about twenty miles below Isange Island and had four of his men killed and several wounded and was forced to return to Eninga. The ball had well started and I kept well out of sight in the mouth of a creek on the south bank. I had left the island. Here the river was wide and had a big curve to the south and this we had picked out as an ideal place for our battle.

Early in the morning a messenger arrived by land telling me that the hostile chief and his canoes were travelling leisurely and would be due to arrive about midday. We kept strict watch and passed our time spinning yarns and enjoying ourselves when our lookout announced the coming of the cannibal fleet. In a little while we had a view of it from our hiding place. On they came, three deep, keeping near the bank. My boys were already in the canoes and we had with us two native women, the wives of traders. I thought it was best for them to go to the Okelley village which was not far away and wait till things were over. But they flatly refused. They would stay with their menfolk. The enemy canoes were now nearly opposite to us. And with the glass from the bush we could see men wearing red feather toppings. One of these was the chief. A few words to all to obey Iwolo, my general, were all the instructions and swiftly making for midriver we turned slightly and stopped still within 200 yards range and the battle commenced.

Although the shooting of the M'pangwes was too far to do us any harm still potlegs, etc., once in a while hit our canoes, which were a perfect protection, as we all knelt on one side throwing the canoe side next to the enemy high out of the water; we kept broadside on and a canoe length apart. One of the cannibal canoes contained several warriors who had red feather topknots and these we thought were the chief's bodyguard. A fighting chief wears one of these [headdresses] which opens up and closes and is made of red parrot feathers. They were all painted in the colors of the Bimvool red and yellow and looked formidable. We opened up our fire slowly and old Iwolo, who had the glasses, gave us orders from the bow of my canoe. Our fire soon began to have a telling effect but they were no cowards and two large canoes even made a break for us. This was just what we wanted. Iwolo tendered cease fire, and we made off keeping our distance. Three other large canoes now came out followed by others in quite a long line.

We had them nearly in the middle of the river before we turned and opened a brisk rifle fire on them. No. 1 canoe taking the nearest, No. 2 the next, and so on. My boat being the last and nearest I had more than a good chance of using my two big Colts two-handed. They suffered terribly but held on. These were men. A signal was given from the bank and they all turned tail, making for shore and dropped like skittles. Many of them jumped into the water and swam for shore or were drowned. Iwolo now pointed to a tree where he said a man was sniping with a rifle. I took the glasses and found him and dropped him with the long Colt. The rifle fell in the water and he hung head down from a fork in the tree away out over the water. I took the glasses again. There were many who had climbed ashore and were firing from the bush but were doing no damage. There were two canoes adrift. Their crews who were not killed must have been hiding on the canoe bottoms. I told old Iwolo to cease firing, but he laughed saying, you want an open river these men you are fighting are stopping it. What do you say? I consented and many of them who were climbing the banks, which was a difficult job, were spotted and fell back in the water, whilst now and then Iwolo gave the order to fire on the men shooting from the bush. They were a hard lot and I admired their pluck. But after a while a loud voice was heard from the bank calling on us to parley. At this we ceased fire and Iwolo, who had a loud voice called, I have heard you, now speak quickly. The voice answered saying, White man, you have beaten us. What do you want of us? I had previously instructed Iwolo and told him I wanted legal rights with Ngogudema and the Bimvool. Give us time to speak, they said. Iwolo consented. We could hear them arguing and after a while he cried in a loud voice, Answer now, or continue the battle, we are not children. Now they answered that they had not understood. I then told him equal rights for everyone to come and go by water where he likes, without your interference. The question came, And what of the Bimvool? Shall we also go unmolested? We answered, Yes, on your own side of the river. I have nothing to say about the other bank, that is Apaque's. Then give us time. We agreed. After a while the words came. We are willing. We answered, we have heard you. Now we will leave you to do as you please.

We commenced to pull up stream when loud voices called. Stay yet and listen, the chief wishes to speak. We slowed up again and Ngogudema, the paramount chief of the M'pangwes of the Ogowe, spoke. We listened. The words came slowly and were barely audible. He said he had listened and hoped he had understood what we said. To what we said he agreed and he spoke for his people, but he had one request to make. He must of course go back to his people and tell them all what he had said. This day I suffer. I have listened to evil counsel. Now all I have to say is you are a young man, white man, and had you come to me and made the same agreement you have done today I myself would have agreed. I told my people of this before, they would not listen. I followed their counsel which was not wise. You cannot make a young man speak like an old man. No, my counsel was, peace with the white man. But today, though you are young, I know you speak words of wisdom, a free river for the white man and his people, is that not so. We all answered, that is so. Then I have understood, it shall be so.

He finished; we were sorry for the old chief, and Iwolo answered *Ow Embeme erre aso* (You are right, father of us all), and we cheered him as we departed. We pulled up silently until all out of hearing and then the conversation on our canoes commenced in real earnest. The Nkomis thought he was talking through his hat. He was king of his country, why should he listen to the young men. No, he had received a good licking and now of course he wanted to throw the blame on someone else. He had done it all himself and would be blamed by all his people. In fact they knew him too well, others said. If he had beaten us we should have been eaten. But such a licking. And the men in the second canoes in the leopard skins and those with the red topknots were all chief's sons. And so the conversation went on.

When we were all well away we pulled up on the south bank. And we all drank to our luck, which had been truly great and would be talked of for all time. We now made merry and cooked a good meal. We had nothing else to do. After this we went back to Isange Island. As we neared this we could see many canoes pulling from it going shoreward. A little nearer we could see smoke rising from the point, our camp was on fire. We hurried up and were just in time to save it. Dried brushwood had been placed around the palisade and this was easily pulled out. Whilst all we lost was the powder house which was small. These were the men sent by the M'pangwe chief to attack us on land, but having heard of their defeat had taken a mean revenge.

———

"What with Leopold and de Brazza putting their flag up…But to gain respect of a cannibal you'll find a flag is no good. Not half so good as your enemy's head on a pole or a river fight won.

"Well, we saw the lovelight begin to glimmer in the last chapter. Now I've been filling me lungs with a bit of prowess again for a change. There was never a Fist-and-Spear from Lancashire didn't know how to dispose his vessels, come to water fighting. Aye. That half-moon formation of the old Vikings comes in again wherever you are. They say nature abhors a straight line, and never more so than in water fighting. Keep to the crescent curve of nature and you'll battle out of any difficulty. Plus a little common sense. If those fellows'd tilted one side of their canoes as a barricade same as we did they'd 'a' saved some useful lives.

"That French lad I saw was the best Frenchman I ever saw. They say the Normans are the same as ourselves in their origins, and he must 'a' been one. Aye, if he and I could 'a' worked together… 'Stead of Sinclair…

"There never was anything got by this submission business. At best it's but a fanciful idea. Pretty, but beyond the scope of nature. Look at Rhodes's expansion cry. Exeter Hall was against it. Until he began to succeed. Aggression is what pays. Look at America. Aye, aggression. The French call it *élan* or *l'audace*, but what they really mean is that kind of intellectual make-up that helps a man to be top-dog. Sinclair never had it. He had a yellow streak that let him down in the ultimate. A man that lets down a colleague is preparing a bigger slump for himself. A shaky conscience'll never stand against fever, even if you get properly drunk on quinine.

"Aye, the power that used to be called Nemesis by the ancients tapped him on the shoulder in the streets o' Liverpool. Just landed and getting his ticket for the Orkneys after he'd wired to her. That poor lass never knew what a curse he'd been to a man out for a living in Africa. Betrayed his colleague so as to keep on smiling terms with a man-eating savage.

"He lost caste after that fight, old Ngogudema. Whenever you lose a fight in Africa you're lost. There's no softness about nature. When you're driven from the herd it's for good. I've seen a beaten old chief weep. Cover his eyes like a child. No wounds, mind you. But his heart broken. Aye, he knows there's no redress, in a state of nature. No newspaper talk to prop him up again. None of this so-called diplomacy. He sees *finis* written all over the sunlight, same as an old elephant.

Aye, pity's a fancy article Nature in her wisdom can't afford to handle. Pity versus preservation of the race. That's all it is. And it turned out a good system till man thought he knew better than the powers that made him. In nature, as in international comfort, it's the balance of power that must be kept delicate as a hair spring. Big issues from small adjustments, like the big weight o' steam I could get out of the engine if I respected its mechanism and remembered that its inventor knew more about it than myself. Handling any engine keeps a man off the wild-goose track, whether its politics or a new river in darkest Africa as they call it. 'Tis a newspaper word, that. There's no spot in savage Africa as dark as the end o' ———— street where I live. The demimonde and that, drunk with methylated. Fellers that are hungry and then foolish enough to sell a bottle of wine to a native. 'Tis a first step they always take. Next thing is to steal. Darkest Africa. And what do I see from my window against my bed? Not much, for the brown paper that's pasted over the broken panes. But what I do see is not calculated to bring light on the subject. Little sluts hanging out their pink stockings ready for the cinema at night. Decent native lads staring in and smiling. Lads living in filthy yards kept by Jews, that'd be as good as my Renchoro in a state of nature. Their fine bodies rotting to pieces in the Golden City.

"Ma'am, it sure is a consolation to turn my eyes back. I could write all day if you wish it. This pencil and paper's good as a whiff of opium…. They had a raid two nights ago just near our place. They caught a couple of silly Englishmen but the Chinks that run the place were gone. They've had about five thousand years start of these young Dutch policemen you see gaping about. They must have many a good laugh about it.

"Well, I shall be getting along with Nina T—— and Peru. Nothing shows up in a narrative better than a college lad, or a lad of high society. And that's what Little Peru was. His mother had good Inca blood. The pure Indian breeds forward. Never back, like the Negro. Republican tastes, that feller. Funny thing, all Peruvians are republican at heart. They hate the Spaniard. A natural contempt for the conquered.

"Silver mines. That's where he inherited his wealth. He and I nearly got away from St. Edward's once. We made arrangements to go as stowaways on a fruit boat for the West Indies. They caught us. That feller Horn again. The Fathers were always sorry for my people to be so worried with a worthless lad. I could paint a bit. Took prizes for that. And I was the best swimmer and wrestler. I could fetch (plunge) further than any of 'em…

"Aye, we must pack in as much originality as we can. But the correctful thing in all literary books is to remember that even the truth may need suppressing if it appears out of tangent with the common man's notion of reality.

"Do I believe in realism? It's a thing I've never had anything to do with, Ma'am. Reality's good enough for me. In plain words, facts. And that's what I've built on in this book.

"Well, I'll be getting on to adieu. What's that, Ma'am? I thought I'd just been telling you he died in the streets of Liverpool. Within a few hours of landing. That poor lass waiting for him—'twas her doing he was a coward. But she never knew it.

Where was it he used to be always talking about, now…. It came jumping about in my head one night when I woke in the dark. Kittle—Kittle Burn was it? Some little spot he could smell the smoke of. It's gone again. I've not got it right.

"Aye, 'twas hard, but he drew it on himself with his antics. Always hiding and ducking and peering out to see if you're being observed is not exactly the way to put a wild beast off the scent. He'll come the closer, out of natural curiosity. And Death's like any other untamed creature. He respects a scornful eye same as a sailor'll respect a man cutlass-armed. 'Twas the only way to enjoy yourself on the old Ivory Coast in the earlies."

ꙮ Chapter XXII. ꙮ

THE CELEBRATIONS of their victory I had no control over. Even old Iwolo slipped off. I had only one line-eyed man in the crowd perfectly sober and that was Renchoro who, although greatly amused, kept a keen eye on me. Iwolo's harp pretty nearly talked as each Encomi took his part in the dance to the tunes and words of prowess of bygone days, and the way they made imaginary feints and stabs would have tickled even an audience of the best of our modern warriors. As each spear thrust was made and parried by these best of the wildest of nature they were received by the hearers by such words as *Va bue* (Bully for you), and the next one would jump into the arena with his own mode of fighting and was received by such encouragement as: Hit red, Give it to him, Now for a kill. And this went on till the sun rose. In fact I fell asleep amongst it all and in my dreams I had hundreds of rifles and Encomi warriors, and had even married Nina (silly dream). Also the little blue-eyed fairy of the ponds far away popped in on me and actually scraped my face with her ringlets and pinned me a sweet bunch of wildflowers on, and when I awoke finding all well and as it should be, I felt relieved. Great things these dreams, when you come to look back, and I had often thought as a lad—Do they ever come true—but that dream did, strange to say and she pinned many a posy right in old Lancashire near the old lilly pond where the old stony brook sang its song for us amidst the song birds. That was surely heaven on earth to me, at that time a simple child of nature after all.

On awakening I was surprised to find the island was visited by many natives, some Okelleys and some M'pangwes, who were quietly waiting for my awaking. Of course I gave audience to the Okelley chief who was a younger brother of Apaque's. He had heard of my doings and had come to see if I intended starting business again and this I assured him would be done. I pointed out to him that the delay in trade had not been caused by any fault of mine and at this he laughed (I found him very sensible), and said I was quite right and he knew the reason of the delay. As he said this he pointed downstream to a large number of vultures which were circling high in the air above the old battle place. That was the cause, he said, and I smiled but was careful to make no allusion to the fight. He told me that he had many cutting rubber and many more were coming from Ngilla who intended to settle on the land, and declared the rubber was not only good but there was a life's supply. It was to be found in larger quantities than they had ever expected to see and, of course, they were anxious to have a trading station again on the island. I assured the good chief that I would send him two traders as soon as possible to Apaque's and I knew that all would be well.

After this he left fully satisfied with his retinue and next came the M'pangwe chief who explained his wants, and he also withdrew promising his loyal support against anyone who would at any time disturb the trade of his country. I now called on all boys, traders, etc., and counseled them to say nothing about what had happened and they all agreed with me that this was our best policy. As Iwolo put it, was all in the game.

We now dipped paddles and went our way rejoicing, not forgetting a few loving cups which strengthened us after our celebrations. Passing the point where the cannibals had made such a stout resistance, we saw many black vultures who were evidently having high times onshore, and the most ghastly sight of all was the torn body of the man who shot the rifle. He was still hanging from the tree, head down, having been firmly caught by both feet in a fork. I mentioned the advisability of diving under him for the rifle he had let drop in the river but this they would not do as they were afraid of the *imburus* or spirits of the dead, which they declared would forever haunt that spot. Of course there was nothing to be done but to wait for some other chance, and eventually this came. I recovered the rifle without much trouble and it proved to be an old Snider which had been stolen from the firm I was representing.

We left the land of ghosts and were soon racing for who should lead at Apaque's first. As my canoe was always manned by White Nkomis, supposed to be the best canoe men in the world, we were soon flying downstream at a terrific speed. My canoe of course carried the rum, which was always a big incentive, as the ones following had always to catch us at tot time, and the ones left missed their rum. At times the race was very close and we reached Samquite by sundown and, after a short rest, made for my uncle's, arriving at midnight. And were received by a shower of welcomes. This was surely a home sweet home for me, and I turned in near old Apaque's, who of course received all the news from me just as it was. The battle especially excited him as they had seen the passing homeward of the defeated chief at nighttime. But as he had received my message he had given the order to his people not to attack him. But he could not understand why I had not sent him word as the two of us could have wiped him out. I explained that one licked man was a better man to deal with than one unbeaten one. And considering the innings I had given him and the promises he had made, I thought I had taken enough out of him for the time being. Oh yes, my uncle said, for the time being, but why not finish your enemies once and for all? That was his belief. However, in my position he could quite understand my feelings.

The old warrior was a happy-go-lucky sort and during the conversation would help himself after which he would laugh loudly and say, Well, what a beating old Rengogu got from a young white lad. And although I would tell him again, he would keep me talking while he laughed heartily, so much so that one of his wives, who always sat by him, would also raise a laugh. She would then go to the door and clap her hands, still laughing, and the rest of his wives would clap hands and laugh so loudly that it seemed like a universal clapping, and without doubt it was a universal laughing as I could hear it being repeated from afar.

Tired out at last, I fell fast asleep and it must have been at sunup that I woke. Apaque was still snoring and I made all arrangements for departing. When he awoke, he commenced laughing again, saying, Tell me that speech of Ngogudema's about bad counsel. Here he would laugh whilst I too was forced to do the same. He put everybody in good humor with his jokes.

My boys were now ready. I always had a gun inspection to see if the count was there, and I likewise kept the guns as clean as possible. Apaque liked this and jokingly said as I lined up for inspection, Oh yes? And these were bad counselors he listened to. Boys, did he cough when he spoke? The whole company laughed at this. If I had these guns just now I would make all men cough, he said. These are something that I have always wanted but they are no good if you cannot buy the cartridges. At this I smiled.

But he was not willing that I should go at once. Wait, he said, these two traders are coming back to Isange. How long will they be before they return here? I told him I would send them back as soon as possible. I might send N'dama with five canoes of merchandise at once and Iweke Wilson would follow on at once with five more, and so on. These two men were ivory buyers. Oh no, he said, there is quite a lot of rubber waiting up here for you and I will send you as many canoes as you wish and these will cost you nothing. I will help you. How many do you want? A hundred? N'dama and Iweke Wilson both agreed that twenty large ones would be quite sufficient. The old chief got busy and in one hour, whilst we waited and laughed and he took nips at the expense of the defeated cannibal king, his neighbor, twenty well-armed, manned, and provisioned canoes arrived. We bade fond adieus. Apaque, who was a big man, gave me a squeeze under the arm. The old man was fond of me and I surely liked him. And we all left smiling and loudly swearing allegiance to Apaque, who smilingly acknowledged the compliment.

Before starting, the chief had called me apart and said, Young man, you are white and I am Apaque. You have won the river for me. I have waited for chances like this. Now let no one tell you differently, you will never fail, trusting Apaque. My people shall never owe you. I know where the Frenchman is, many of my slaves come from there. Now you want rubber and ivory. On your account I will agree to make peace even with my enemies. I can see the power of trade.

I was astonished. I only answered, I shall do all you wish that a good son can, but trade and war go hand in hand and here I shall always be with you. Have I ever deceived you? he said. No. Son, listen, you shall have all the two rivers to yourself, no one shall ever disturb you. I am Apaque. He was always my bosom friend in whom I could confide and he never betrayed me, this savage Napoleon of the Equator.

I reached Adoninango in due time, my mail was at our new station. The last steamer load of gunpowder and sundries were being put aboard. Matam came at me with a jump and put my hand on his head saying, *Wa Ka wa Ball Ngogudema*. You defeated the big elephant of the M'pangwes. You are our chief. I laughed and told him nothing of the sort. No but listen, he said, some of our people were there and some are still there. How could this be, was there no fight? I told him the fight was nothing. He looked at me strangely.[1] Have you got any ivory? I said. Fetch it along to me, I will give you a good price for it. Oh yes, they had much to sell me and would be at the new place tomorrow. We both parted laughing, but I called him back and writing out an order for a pot of jam for his father, I parted with my blood brother. Strange people these. He was actually proud that I had beaten his paramount chief and that some of his mates, probably his relatives, were lying at death's corner away up in the high Ogowe. The children of wildest Africa are surely difficult to understand.

I told Iwolo to sound all aboard, and with a quick pull out we left the nearly deserted place. My cannibal friends and in fact everyone cheered me as I left with my little fleet and we were soon passing Herr Schiff's and as I was in the van, he hailed me. He had two letters in his hand from Little Peru and one of them, as per usual, contained funds for the stealing of the goddess. I had to laugh, he was still juvenile. Herr Schiff noticed in my pocket the wad of notes which was the largest he had ever seen. The next missive said he would soon be coming of age, etc., etc., and I was forced to laugh. Was he really in love without sight? No, my last sketch, he said, was superb and then the broadminded manner in which she had laid the plan for her own getaway simply overcame him. There were also useful presents if it would not be an insult for her to accept them, shipped at the same time as the letters went onboard the mail. I read the finale after I left Herr Schiff, who was all smiles, as likewise was Herr Boome, who said in English, which he was picking up fast, You are now a hero. I said, of course, why

---

1. The savage was at a loss to understand the conventional false humility of the white man. (Ed.)

not. It's just as cheap to be that as anything else, when you travel in new worlds with a full ticket, you can be anything you wish.

Schiff now got serious and in answer to a few questions, I opened up. Look here, Herr Schiff, I have one piece of news that might interest you and your company. You remember our agreement? He answered yes. Has it been satisfactory to you so far? He answered, saying just so. Well, Herr Schiff, are you willing to shake with me on behalf of my company that we shall not interfere with each other's posts on the big river? He answered yes and shook on it. Then I said, you have a free river as far as you like to go and there is enough trade for five or six more firms. I explained and told him my center was Isange Island. Not one of their men should go near it, he said. I then told him quite sufficient about the high river. That he said is quite sufficient, I shall see to it at once. Free trade for all but no cutting or crowding and mutual protection by arm if necessary. It was done and that agreement was always kept.

I had to go, as Mr. Sinclair might think something had happened. But I went away with my private locker full of Hamburg's best and that is what I call fair trade. And it all proved out in after years to be so. For these two firms[2] in spite of wars, etc., are not only strong in their various branches and companies but have opened the trade of Africa and of other lands. Wherever you meet any of these genuine giants of commerce, you will always find they are run by gentlemen who are even at the present day bound by sound reasons to accept each other's burdens for the sake of commerce which cannot exist without unity.

So long for the present Herr Schiff, I said, and the good old man gave me a great handshake. He had been a daddy to me and knew me better than I knew myself.

I soon arrived at our new place and had a great talk with Sinclair. It was a charming trading station, well built and commodious,

---

2. Carl Woerman and Hatton and Cookson. (Ed.)

with large verandahs, and was well fitted in every way for what it was intended to be. My canoes he agreed should be dispatched at once, as I was responsible for their cargo. I paid good attention to the assortment and this being done, my outfit traders, etc., swung clear of the wharf and I wished them godspeed. I made a trader out of old general Iwolo and dividing my rifles and men, the outfit pulled out beautifully and I watched them till they were well away.

I took care to say nothing to the agent Sinclair of the fight, although he tried hard to sound me. I knew the cause of my troubles hung against the wall in his sanctorum. He was not a timid man, but this was a fine specimen of an Orkney Island girl, his wife at Kittle Toft, of which he often spoke. Poor man, he left the river after I did, intending to return to his native home and enjoy his earnings, but as was the case with many others, he died after landing at Liverpool. And so did Mr. Carlisle, our chief agent at Gaboon, one of the finest samples of a gentleman I ever met. I knew the lady he intended to marry, she was the only daughter of an old whaling captain who had made a fortune round Greenland. And I could mention many more. All the West Coasters have passed away that I knew when I was a lad, and most of them met untimely ends either being killed by natives or succumbed to the Coast fever. Verily this is what it is called, the White Man's Grave.

After dispatching my outfit to the interior I journied to the coast to meet the new tug, *Iowatha*, which had been specially built for both sea and river. I had a good talk with Nina on my way down and also studied the boat with its engineer, old Peter Nolan, who handed over to me at Angola. She was all one could wish. Was swift and powerful and would tow twenty canoes or more anywhere. Old Peter and I soon became great friends.

"Aye, I was always tickled to death to have a fight of me own to study out. I could 'a' wiped out the lot, as old Apaque said, but there's a certain portion of mercy in human nature. Although, mind you, it's sometimes got to be roused up to killing pitch, like when I got the feller did this thumb for me. Feller like that's got any amount of ladies on their knees for him in London, but they didn't stop his intention to kill by treachery. Treachery's always a startling thing and that's why you'll never forgive it.

"Aye, I've been fighting all the time and building Empire— so-called. Me first fight was up my rivers and me last one was when I was with Kitchener's cattle thieves in the Boer War. Unless you count being on a mine-sweeper when the big scrap was on. My cousin H—— D——, that's a Fish Commissioner, he got me into it. Depth Charge No. 3, I was. And before that there was General Villa's turn-up in Mexico, but I'm not counting that. But after all this, and we'll throw in the old Matabele War long ago. I'm to find my confirmation certificate before I can ask for a pension. Confirmation? Why, I've not even got my marriage lines or me Scotland Yard papers when I left the force of my accord. Come to that, there's lots of bigger things of mine than confirmation certificates knocking up and down the east coast here. Zanzibar and so on. Guardafui.... You'll find an old portmanteau of mine in most of the places round Africa and a good few in America. That's why I've got no more than I stand up in—barring me prayer book. There's always one function when that might be needed. Aye, I've sure left a lot o' stuff knocking about. You see, you always think you're going back. Or I might 'a' been in a hurry at the moment.

"'Tis a good time to push a book like mine forward. There's been nothing novel lately since Rider Haggard. One of the biggest mythologists in the world, that feller. But mine'll be facts. You can weave a lot out o' that.

"The Germans'll like my book. I'm not asking any Frenchman to tackle it. Even Shakespeare won't suit a Frenchman—they'll not mention him if they can help it. And Dickens—you may's well ask a Frenchman to read the Greek Testament as get him to understand Dickens. He'll not understand the soft heart and the smile with it. Whether in trade or literary matter he's hard.

"Aye, he prefers the Moulin Rouge. I've been in the Moulin Rouge. A poor show. Too much French tinsel about it for me. I'd rather relax the mind on a robin contest down at Greenwich. Or a bit of a cock fight. That's the sort of spectacle makes you want to go home to your wife and fireside. Cradle. Muffins and so on.

"We had a house on the corner, one time. Plenty going on, if you felt like looking down through the window on a Saturday night.

"Aye! London…. Whenever I've turned up at home I've got to go first and see if Lancashire was still there. I had to get me fill of it for a few days before I took London at leisure. Have a look at Gillmoss and so on. Here the chuets[3] and the gulls. Sit on the edge on the old marl pond at Frea for old time's sake. A good setting for fishes, marl. Some of those old bullnoses were as old as myself. I knew the marks on 'em. We'd poked 'em out from under the rocks often enough, as lads. Aye, the place welcomed me, if not always the people. Places—*they* know you. Which is what people don't always do. An old tree, or a bend of the river'll hang out a flag for you even if you find a few doors inclined to be shut. Aye! In the ultimate we'll not turn to flesh and blood but to soil and running water. It bred our fathers. And that's as near as we can get to 'em.

"A good many of those traders were less fortunate than I was. Same as Sinclair and Carlisle. They'd either die soon after getting home or they'd be buried where poor George T—— was. And

---

3. Chuets = plovers.

Tom Keating, who was done down by pirates. But the sea's washed away many a good chap from that island. Same as if it knew they'd not want to be trapped there all their lives. Washing up against Liverpool is what they'd prefer.

"Aye, there was some great old firms in Liverpool at that time. Look at my own firm. Hatton and Cookson. Used to be Hatton and Jackson. Sold more powder to natives than any firm known to man. Before the steamer came, *they were.* Swooping round Africa and elsewhere in their fine sailing ships. First traders to take ore out from Port Nolloth. Established whaling at Port Elizabeth. First over at Tierra del Fuego. Old-time sea captains, educated by Hatton and Cookson, and ships going from father to son. Aye! It sure was a notable firm until it was sold to the Nigerian Company and got mixed up with Port Sunlight. 'Twas a pity it couldn't battle on without that sort of regalia.

"Liverpool men! They'll not let their ships down nor their firms neither. A sure thing, Ma'am. Taken one with another they were a grand lot for duty. There was only one I knew was a bit inclined to overdo it. Captain Holt was a man to be feared at all times. The natives feared him, and the white men feared his effect on the native. 'You'll never quieten 'em that way, John,' I used to say to him. 'My way's better, that's based on our human make-up. Follow nature. She'll never let you down, nor the firm you're working for.'

"Aye, John would flog a boy for not pulling his weight, or a bit of impudence. All wrong. The boy that needs castigation is not one to punish but to get rid of quietly. No words. Pay him and let him go. If ever he comes back, he'll behave. You've got to watch savages, same as a politician's got to study his opponents in the House. Matter of insight, so-called instinct. *Dum vivo sper's* as good for the cannibal as for ourselves. The trader who'll not allow the element of hope amongst his boys is no student of human nature. More than that, he's doing his firm a bad turn.

"Come to think of it properly, by Holt's severity and Sinclair's timidity, those two were robbing their firms as surely as if they'd robbed the office till. Aye! When I think what I could 'a' done up my rivers—"

ꙮ Chapter XXIII. ꙮ

THE *HIAWATHA* was wide and roomy and had a high forecastle of a kind where I and old Peter had plenty of room and light, fresh air, etc. I quickly made so that all on board were snugly housed. She towed with very little sound and we always kept her up, filling the brass steps and kept her always new. The man who had designed that boat was a sailor engineer and an old equatorial sea dog. She burnt little fuel, got upsteam in no time, and had no tricks and would ride a rough sea like a gull, so that under sail and steam (the sail I filled her up with myself) she looked like an old Viking ship. And still wearing my youth well, I made many a rough trip to Gaboon. When everything was howling, the little *Hiawatha* was at her best. Something that would lull you to sleep in the whitest squall, if you like rocking.

We born in Lancahsire are always rocked to sleep, and in fact I have often seen a sailor's wife, often with many children, pull a laughing lad from his milk and say, Nay tha waint, thart foxing. She would then slap him in the cradle, which was cocked so as to give the cradle a jerk, and he was soon fast asleep under the influence of the bob rocking, like we in our ships fo'csle. Too much coaxing makes a small lad, so that the good old sailor type found real pleasure in hardships, he invariably had a hard rearing but enjoyed life. One of the happiest race of humans in existence, the Western Ocean Seaman, and he could always find rocking enough at sea. Well, such was the Liverpool-built tug and I was proud of her. Whilst I was running her she never had a leak or a mishap to her machinery. She was a good home anywhere.

I received several boxes containing apparel for the goddess and also a box of things I knew nothing about, or Little Peru either in fact, I was right, as a gentleman of his caliber would not go into Bond Street and order anything for a lady. I know I wouldn't have done it at the time for anything. But there they were, stays and cosmetics and other things I never understood. And as he told me afterwards, he had done all this through his agents. I was right. I had also received several boxes for de Brazza.

So bidding goodbye to Angola I swung clear with my first tow and stopping only once at Nina's and delivering the presents and also a few welcome bottles for the voodoo fakirs, I held on upstream night and day, making a record voyage. The little steamer caused quite a commotion as we steamed by the many villages on the banks. Whilst the boys on the steamer answered the shouting of these simple natives, Where did it come from? They laughingly answered, *O wamuti impolo agani* (The high steamboat has given birth to this little one), and this many of them believed. We had many visitors after our arrival at our headquarters and Sinclair was especially pleased with our new acquisition, which could bring supplies from the coast at any time.

The next trip I made was to Samba Falls, as the rivers were now falling and it was dangerous to risk a trip in large craft. I made many trips up the Angani, and even in the dry season, I very seldom had any trouble, as she drew very little water when not overloaded. On these trips to Samba Falls I was always asked when the White Lady was coming to visit them. They never seemed to forget her and they would prefer to see her than the new boat, she had made such a kindly and lasting impression on them. I always brought large tows of canoes down with loads of rubber, etc., so that my boat soon saved her cost and proved the worth of cheap water transport. I soon made a floating fortress of her and settled many difficulties with which the navigation of the rivers had been dangerously full.

I arrived at Sinclair's with my tow but was always held up by Herr Schiff, who greatly admired the *Hiawatha* and was very fond of Peter Nolan. I had brought down many of our traders, who were always anxious to square accounts, but the stores were always full of goods and they generally took a siesta of a few days, giving me plenty of time to visit other trading districts. When returning I would always tow them back, but I must say those frequent changes and a snug home onboard made things delightful.

I had many a shooting experience, both with elephants and hippos and other animals, and once ran on to the largest herd of elephants I ever saw crossing the Angani River by moonlight. They separated however and some of the bulls, tired by running top speed on a long sand bank, turned to charge, but we soon put them to flight tail straight out with a few varied blasts of the whistle blown by old Peter, who was very fond of making stampedes. There was always some excitement by day and night and in no place in the world does the moon shine so brightly as the high rivers, which are healthy to live on. I have shot many animals by moonlight and have often amused myself reading if I did not feel sleepy. The nights are deliciously cool.

Arriving at our trading station, I was kept busy on the big river. Although the waters of the Angani River were now low, the main river the Ogowe had such a big watershed and was so long, it took its rise far away in the interior from where nobody knew at that time and I doubt very much whether they know today. However it had a rise and fall for a month or more after the other river had fallen. Although the French claimed a tremendous territory they were rather premature in annexing such a large hinterland which stretches practically to the headwaters of the Nile, and through this country no white man has ever trod. Not at least in the country inhabited by the same race and speaking the same language as the Oshebas and M'pangwes, who are all cannibals, so that there are still many portions of the African continent offering good chances of making a world-famed name to a daring explorer.

From the minerals I have seen carried in the bullet pouches of the Oshebas for slugs, I am sure the country is rich in precious minerals of all kinds. And the only reason I can attribute for the ancients not having invaded these lands, which I visited myself nearer to the coast, is that the inhabitants are such a hardy and fearless race that it paid the old ancient prospector and gold seeker to give it a wide berth. Which they did, as I never saw any old workings except the copper holes of the Angani mountains and these were the work of the Ashiwas of the higher Angani. These Ashiwas are the best workers both in copper and in steel I have ever met with during my travels among the savages of many lands.

On my way up the river I always called at Apaque's. He took a passage with me. On arriving at Assangi I found more ivory and rubber, etc. than would square my accounts and give handsome profits. Even the Oshebas had their small houses, which were rudely constructed of great sheets of thick bark tied together by bush rope, and had settled down to rubber cutting, whilst the ivory, always escorted, came down from the interior and was sold either to N'dama or old Iweke Wilson, the buyers. On the opposite bank, Apaque's men had built temporary homes and were all busy cutting rubber or hunting elephants, and the chief was well pleased with his newly acquired domain and here Old General Iwolo, helped by his wife who had joined him from the coast, held sway as chief trader for Apaque. He was doing a good business in salt and powder and no doubt was on the right road to wealth. He kept all his accounts on notched sticks and it was really marvelous to see how well he could balance up, and in fact knew how he stood in his trade relations to the firm, far better than many of the Gaboon-born traders who knew how to write.

It took a few trips to get down the produce and I felt quite sorry when I had to bid a fond goodbye to these good people, as I had at last made up my mind to take a trip home to the old country, as my folks in the old home in Lancashire were continually writing for me. There was quite a gathering at Apaque's when I finally left for good, and all which expressed heartfelt sorrow as I departed, especially old Apaque who declared I was the only real friend ever he had had in his life, but of course understood perfectly well my reasons for visiting my old home far away. As I departed they lined the shore and the cries of Come back to us we shall always be thinking of your return, could be loudly heard. I felt sorry to depart from such friends. But a good lasting upriver trade had now been firmly established, so I parted without a single regret excepting at the loss of true friends which is a high loss at all times.

On my return to our supply stores I met many new friends. The little French soldier who had served me so well when I was in need of help at Isange Island, had received his final order for his up country journey to join de Brazza, and we spent the night enjoying ourselves and I saw him off with his fleet of canoes next morning. He was a Breton from Brittany and was fine company. We quit the best of friends and he carried my respects to his chief, de Brazza. I next paid my attentions to Mons La Glesse, a famous French naturalist who was especially sent out to study the gorilla, stuff him a la nature, and learn what he could about him. I helped him to do this by procuring boys for him and in less than a month he had secured all the specimens he wanted. These were shot by shotguns so that they had practically no bullet marks and I have no doubt as he was a first-class taxidermist he put them in their natural poise somewhere in France.

I now proceeded up the Angani on my last trip, carrying as well as a large tow, the traders who were following their calling in that part of the country. We had a great trip, as I told them it was my last trip and I was homesick, I bid fond goodbyes to the old king of the Ivilis and his chiefs and they gave me a royal send-off, telling me to be sure and return after my trip and bring back the White Lady (the Presbetyrian missionary). Old Njuki expressed great reluctance at my parting but this had to be.

I arrived at our new station without mishap, only old Peter Nolan was down with slight fever chills. I was next ordered to Gaboon for a small tow and also some passengers who were anxiously waiting. All my accounts I had made out. I had a fine balance and I took the news of my intending departure to Sinclair. I had a fine record and I was satisfied and this I carried with me. We had a fine trip down the river and I called only for a couple of hours at Nina's and told her what I had done. And that as soon as I was able I would see to her escape and would see she was free as any *engelangi* (white bird from the sea). I could see the emotions I had produced in the inmost soul of Nina. She looked superb under the effect of my little whispered speech. And all she answered was, I am ready any time. And as I parted she gave me a most thankful smile. The rest of the attendants at the Josh House I left either drunk or half drunk and was soon well on my journey to Gaboon.

Poor Peter now got much worse in spite of the attention I could bestow on him and as we had a rough passage by sea it seemed to make him worse. On landing he was sent immediately to the French hospital but only lived a few days after I left Gaboon on my return journey. I gave in my resignation to Mr. Carlisle, our chief agent, handed over my accounts, etc., and we spent the night in his sanctorum as he had very little time for conversation during the day. He meant to retire himself as soon as he had made all arrangements and, of course, as I knew his intended we had no secrets. Of course he would meet me in Liverpool and no doubt we should often meet at our Lancashire house, as his intended was a great friend of our family as was also her father the old retired whaler. I also told him I might have a visit from a college friend of mine who contemplated visiting the coast for a couple of months shortly and when I told him who he was he laughed and said, Birds of a feather. The young gentleman would visit the coast as Mr. Graham, botanist from Liverpool, so that he knew exactly what to do when he came. Of course he would forward him on, and he would see that he came incognito. Any time I wished to go I was at liberty, he would see to everything for me.

So I bade him goodbye for the present and taking my tow and three clergymen passengers (one American missionary and two French priests), I was soon on my way back to the rivers. The two French clergymen were bound for the M'pangwe country, and as they both spoke the native language well as they had been missionaries on the higher rivers of the Gaboon amongst the M'pangwes, they were quite at home anywhere. The American gentleman was on his way to Kangwe, the Presbetyrian mission station. We all got on splendidly as I was interpreter for him when he wanted to speak to the two Fathers. They all enjoyed their trip immensely and I landed them all safe at their various destinations, none the worse for their journey.

I now had time to re-read my mail, most of it being from Little Peru who had received my letter telling him exactly how things were with me and that I had made up my mind to steal the goddess, as per her own plan which I had detailed. He was coming at once he said, and as he was nearly of age there would be no lacking of funds, etc. As I was now a free man I often visited Herr Schiff and he told me that if I wished to return to the Coast he would supply me with any goods I wished cheaper than I could buy them in Europe, and would back me to any amount. Of course I told him if I returned I meant to do business on my own but I made no promises. Sinclair himself was anxious to hold his trade and I had brought him a mulatto from the River Niger district who proved first class and could manage the tug anywhere, and the boys I left with him knew the river channels as well as I did, so all went well. I passed most of my time hunting and was able to ship home quite a large collection of the denizens of the African forests and glades, besides curios of all kinds. During these trips I often visited Azingo always calling at Nina's.

———

"Of all my memories of the rivers that White Lady shines the clearest. White she was, Ma'am, right through to her heart and with no more fear than Stanley on a cannibal river. Aye, it was my sad pleasure before I left the coast to take her body from the Falls to Gaboon. When I heard she was dead I said 'Another victim of that old Isorga the Church.' I had to take her quietly from her last resting place. Not wishing to offend the natives. They naturally would consider such a fine woman to be above par as *muti*. They'd not long have been able to keep their hands off her. But her power after death could not have excelled the influence of the living woman.

"Aye. Churches…. Man, as we know, is the flower of all creation. But he's only a flower when he ceases to be animal. That's what that lady was. I'm Catholic, but I'm not so Catholic as to think we're the only ones can raise a saint. I'm not grudging her to the Presbyterians. They've got fellers like Sinclair to contend with, who're not doing 'em much credit.

"This Christianity. When you've sifted it 'n' analyzed it, Ma'am, what is there left in the sifting of all the churches together but a little bit o' gold dust. And that's humanity, the essence of life. I've found more of that essence on the Coast there than ever I noticed in London. Sundays *or* weekdays. It doesn't take the metropolis of the known world to make a Christian. 'Twas on my rivers I found that fine lady. Two voyages she had with me. All eyes she was, that first time. But the second—it seemed that all eyes was looking at what I carried. Boggarts and voodoos.... Every mile of that river is haunted. The most sacred river in Africa. And kingfishers, Ma'am, with their bright toppings. And some of 'em jewels no bigger than a bee. But they must have their fish like the biggest and finest....

"And hadn't my Renchoro a heart of gold? I know humanity, Ma'am. Scotland Yard I was, and knowing London for what it was. I found as good as the best in Africa.

"'How beautiful is that sunset! How beautiful a mission station would be on that hill, Mr. Horn!' Aye, she went where du Chaillu dare not go. Great big idols and painted skulls.... Giving the kids sweets, she was, and smiling.... Putting religion aside she was a good woman.

"The surf was bad but we got her safe on to the vessel. One more spot of holy ground, where she lies. Aye!

"No, Ma'am, there's nothing special the matter with me. Only, every year I get more tired. I count the steps now, you may say. If they were leading me back over some of my old tracks I'd be content to count them.

"Just a little home backing same as Rhodes had, and de Brazza, and I'd 'a' battled through to those headwaters. Got in before the French. Open up the Lake Chad road for trading purposes. Ivory and skins and copper....

"That's fine adventurous country where Mahomet meets the cannibals. Aye! Rivers without names and countries without maps....

"When the French became a public nuisance on the West Coast a lot of us old-timers there went up to Nigeria to get away from them. A good many Mahommedan brigands inbetween. And once I found my little outfit of armed natives being watched by these fellers. They were interested in watching the French troops trying to pot us off across a deep ravine. Aye, for anyone with a bit of imagination, plus rifles, it's a grand bit of country.

"'Tis somewhere up there that George T——'s son disappeared, Nina's brother. After Yousoff Carriala was killed—the pirate that adopted him when the father died—a good feller to him too—he's supposed to have left the sea and gone into Mahommedan country with the brigands. A lad like George T——'s son when turned back by Providence back to the lap of nature would naturally turn to arms. 'Tis a gentleman's profession. Aye, it depends on no man's favors.

"'The Brigands of Lake Chad.' 'Twould be a grand title. They used to catch the women going to Fez to the harems. 'The Brigands of Lake Chad'.... I sure could have woven some good books if I'd always had the leisure I have now. 'Caravans and Camels' would be snappy. But when you're young you want to be always turning the next cover. Books don't grow when you're following the trail.

"Aye, and behind the Cameroons there's things living we know nothing about. I could 'a' made books about many things. The *jago-nini* they say is still in the swamps and rivers. Giant diver it means. Comes out of the water and devours people. Old men'll tell you what their grandfathers saw, but they still believe it's there. Same as the *amali* I've always taken it to be. I've seen the *amali's* footprint. About the size of a good frying pan in circumference and three claws instead o' five. There are some very big lakes behind the Cameroons. Used to be full of nice seal at one time. *Manga*, they call it. But the *jago-nini's* wiped 'em almost out, the old natives say. Pigmy elephants there too, and crocodiles that never kill humans. The natives up there talk of some Big Water. And what I say is they must have come from the Nile.

"What but some great creature like the *amali* could account for the broken ivories we used to come across in the so-called elephant cemeteries? Fine old green ivory that's valuable for inlaying wood.

Snapped right across in the thickest part and left in splinters. Aye! There's places in Africa where you get visions of primeval force. And not so distant either, as when you picture the prehistorics in Europe and America. I was prospecting one time in Florida at the river mouths for mastodon bones. Nothing handier for phosphates. But 'tis a thing of the dead past there. In Africa the past has hardly stopped breathing. You get fancies there if you're any sort of a man that's not *Homo stultus*.... What with the talk of the natives and the sounds you hear at night. And every swamp and mountain cave calling you a bit further. There are times when only a river seems safe. No menace in a river. Never still and never silent. Human as a man, and that's why we trust 'em. Aye, the savage'll sing on a river when he'd be trembling on land with the fear of something touching him. Nature's idea for a street—rivers.

"That *amali*. I told you I've seen a drawing of him in those Bushman caves. I chiseled one out whole once and gave it to President Grant for a souvenir. He naturally took a great curiosity in the West Coast, seeing that the Civil War he'd been so busy over had ruined an old trade there.

"Aye, the little fellers that drew those creatures, and manacled slaves and so on I told you about, were not ordinary savages. They sure were Paleolithic men from the north. They were remembering things, on those walls. Processions and so on. I bought a nice ivory from them once, carved with leopards and elephants. Nice little fellers, round about four feet and a little over. Shy as buck, until they'd had a good look at you. A living example of the survival of the fittest. Most gifted conjurors in the world. Use flint for weapons. Most harmless race, but they've had to flee from the French rule same as others. They've gone into the Cameroons for safety. Even the Arabs don't know the back of the Cameroons.

"Well, Ma'am, I'll have to finish up what happened to Nina and my friend Peru. It's sure been a bit of refreshment to tell about Africa. I could 'a' told what happened to Nina in two chapters, but it wouldn't be literature. Coordinate your material, George Bussey said, till there's neither waste nor paucity of interest.

"Came from Lima, that feller. The only feller I couldn't lick at school. 'Twas silver mines made him rich. I could lick Johnny Greeley, though….

"Aye, we must get our love interest in. Supposing something happened to me and I hadn't finished it. 'Twould sure be a disappointment to those who look forward to the love-light. If I'd been in love with her myself 'twould 'a' come easier. But there was always little Annie K—— at the back of my mind. Peru having Inca blood, he'd naturally understand a girl like Nina. Lancashire held me, where love was concerned."

❧ Chapter XXIV. ❧

I HAD AMPLE time during my frequent visits to the Josh House to make all arrangements with Nina for her final release from the terrible place she was in. I also told her of Graham, my friend who would come and help me to take her away. He would be here in a little while so I warned her to be patient, and above all to be as calm as usual for fear that the men who were continually around the temple should become suspicious and never commence speaking to me in real earnest before she was sure they were half drunk, as when the liquor was in the wits were out.

I noticed she wore a stiletto with a beautifully carved handle in her belt and asked her the reason she wore it. She replied that it had belonged to her mother and she intended to keep it by her, as if we failed in taking her away she intended to use it. I asked her how she meant to do so. Oh, she said, I should kill the first person who interfered with me before I have dived in the water. Should she be captured, she said, she would never let them take her alive, whilst she said this a gleam of vengeance shot into her eyes, but she quickly recovered and hummed a wild tune. I was surprised but smiled, and she noticed this and smiled also. It will all end well, I told her, if you only keep calm. My friend will be with me and I will bring enough force to wipe out the town if necessary. That I shall take you to a better place than this where you will be perfectly free, goes without mentioning. If I can do it by stealth without anyone here seeing or knowing, so much the better. If it comes to the worse I shall use force and act quickly. She was greatly pleased with what I told her and gave me a kindly smile of pleasure. I could not miss interpreting it. This lady, I could see more than ever before, was a fearless and most grateful piece of human structure and was highly intelligent.

Whilst the men folk forgot themselves in their cups I could have walked away with her often at these times, but there was no certainty of this at any time. Her own plan was the best and I determined to follow it as soon as possible. I had left word if news came overland, for the messenger to follow me quickly, as I would always leave my whereabouts at the small ebony station at the mouth of the creek. I waited for a week or more after the mail steamer carrying my friend was due, and decided to return to Sinclair and put in my time in patience with Herr Schiff and his assistant. I had not long to wait however before the messenger came with orders to send round the tug to Gaboon with the remaining ivory he might have on hand, as this was to complete a consignment now awaiting shipment by the S.S. *Angola* on her return from Gabenda at the mouth of the Congo. I also received my mail and also a letter from Little Peru (Mr. Graham): Come at once if possible, I am anxious to see you. In a short while the tug was ready and giving a fond goodbye to all, we steamed west with my boat towed behind. We only made one stop at Angola for firewood, and the little tug *Hiawatha* gave a splendid account of herself.

As I neared our main store at Coco Beach, I could see the schooner *Ruby Queen* and could see standing aft through my glasses a tall, well-built fellow dressed in white duck. He was waving his handkerchief and gesticulating frantically. It was my college chum Little Peru, now grown to a young man of splendid physique, and alongside of him also waving his arms stood Captain King, master of the *Ruby Queen*. I altered the course of the tug at once and was soon alongside the *Ruby Queen*. With one spring and vault I was alongside my old mate and we more than hugged so that even old Captain King wondered why such a meeting. My best friend in the world, and he had grown a perfect man, a kindly intelligent face, he was over six feet high, and had a mustache. I could not realize that the little lad I had left at college was the same, but when he commenced to joke and open up it was certainly he. He too wondered that a little lad that had been his playmate and had left him had grown so much and looked, as he said, a bronze picture of health in this deadly climate of the West Coast, and was now standing by his side.

The tug I sent on her way with the dispatches for Mr. Carlisle and also excused myself to him in a short missive for calling on the *Ruby Queen,* as I had found Mr. Graham onboard the schooner and of course we were having a *tete á tete* meeting. We drank a Moet et Chandon to Captain King and his schooner and slept onboard that night. The *Ruby Queen* had been built as a yacht for an old seadog who had made wealth in the good old sea days. She was fitted up and built regardless of cost, was a splendid sailor, and had been around the world more than once, and had been bought by the firm on the death of her owner who had succumbed to fever at Gaboon.

We were up early next morning as the *Hiawatha* was due to sail in the afternoon. We dined with our chief agent and I bade him a fond goodbye, as also did my friend Mr. Graham. I sailed at two o'clock, carrying Graham's luggage and never saw the good soul Mr. Carlisle again. He died of fever in Liverpool shortly before the day set for his wedding. We had a glorious trip to the Ogowe and as Graham had brought a beautiful Spanish guitar with him and was an expert player, having been taught to play the instrument in his early childhood, he could nearly make it talk, and I was never tired of hearing him play and sing, especially the true version of the old Spanish fandango with variations. He could soon tune his instrument to accompany the native *ngombi* or harp, and the two instruments played together sounded heavenly as the sounds were much better on calm water than on land.

We entered the river and had some fine shooting. He was a good shot with either rifle or six-shooter, in fact surprised me. He had lots of practice in England, but had also private tuition on the use of the shooter and he gave me quite a few good tips especially shooting right and left using each weapon consecutively. I soon caught the dodge and with a little practice I could use left and right without losing any time in false motion. Good weapons were of course essential and I was soon taught as I was always fond of the use of the gun. We now neared Nina's place and I told him so, furthermore he must be ready for an agreeable surprise. Why? he said. I said nothing but noticed he commenced to pay a little attention to his looks, arranged his hair, and asked me if it was usual to go without a coat, as I was in negligee. For myself, yes, but you are a first visitor so it would be well for you to be *comme il faut*.

Before we had arrived off the beach he had obeyed orders. Nina, I saw, was hurrying towards the temple so I led him to the large spacious visitor's hut which was always mine only when I arrived. It was a perfect model of African savagery, animal skins were thrown over the seats in a rough and ready style, but the floor and walls were strewn with native mats of rare pattern, and spears of various kinds hanging around ever-ready for use, completed a most charming decorative effect. Above all, everything was clean and tidy and was used principally by Nina, who superintended personally the sanctorum of this voodoo town.

As Renchoro knew the run of the place, he had brought up a few bottles of strong liquor for the use of visitors, the first of whom to put in an appearance was the old man, who had instructed me when I had been initiated. He invited us to be seated and to my friend Graham, whom he eyed largely he said, You are my *ogenda* (stranger). You are welcome and rest contented as you are under my roof. I translated what he had said and Graham thanked him and as the bottles were on the table I said, These are yours Father, and he smilingly helped himself and friends who were never more than six or eight men and were employed in and around the house of Isoga. I sent Renchoro for the boy who played the *ngombi* so well. I told Graham to kindly accompany the boy with the guitar and take all with an air of don't care and quite usual. This he knew of course would help us in our future moves for the liberation. He was a good actor and even yawned at times making passing events seem quite common.

The music was delightful and impressed the audience, especially as the *ngombi* player was a good singer and poet. Our audience now commenced laughing at the witty ready-made songs of the poet, and at this stage of the performance in swept Nina. I had never seen her look better and as she bowed to Mr. Graham, who continued playing, I noticed a slight blush enter his cheeks but he soon recovered and the song being over, he returned his guitar without seemingly being impressed by the gazelle-eyed goddess. He now sent Renchoro for a box of cigars, and placing the box on the table invited all to smoke. He was a perfect actor. Nina also seemed pleased with the new visitor, but also acted her part perfectly.

I asked Graham what he thought of her as I lit my cigar. The prettiest woman I ever saw in my life and I am glad I made this trip, he said, and I closed the conversation. I next sent for Mr. Graham's musical box and commenced by giving the "Carnival of Venice." Nina was curious and Graham explained by motions how the instrument worked. Several tunes were played in succession. Nina asked him in her best English where the sounds came from. Her voice was angelic so I tapped him with my foot whilst I explained to her in M'pangwe the inner parts of the little machine as best I could. I was afraid her looks and voice might be too strong for him to resist. He tapped me back with his finger and went to the door and seemed to be gazing out over the river. The beauty of Nina was such that she unconsciously bewitched everybody who saw her and her natural grace of motion and her speaking gazelle-like eyes were never forgotten once seen, and the grace of her presence I can picture out now in my imagination, although it is over fifty years since I first met her, on the day of my initiation in the Voodoo Temple.

After resting up for a couple of hours, during which we had succeeded in making all the assistants of the Josh House quite happy, we left without ceremony, leaving no present for the fairy as I had told her it was no use doing so as when she was taken away by me the utmost speed was necessary and, as we could always supply her with the garments she needed, it was better to leave them all behind so as to avoid suspicion. The old chief of the sacred town accompanied us to the tug and was quite anxious for us to call again soon as he wanted to hear the musical box. In fact he said he would like to own it or one like it, as it surely contained wonderful medicine and perhaps the happy ghosts of many musical spirits. He could tell this by the beautiful sounds that came from it. Graham told him he might give it to him before he left the country. The old man inquired then how long that would be, as he was eager for the box and answering I told him, Before the big rains come. He thanked us and wished us much happiness and told me to tell Graham he would ward off all evil spirits from him whilst he was on the river.

We now steamed away to Azingo where there was a cargo of ebony waiting to be moved. We entered the green-arched water-way and Graham expressed his surprise by saying, Land of Wonders, the most beautiful lady I have met living in fairy land. I had made it a strict custom during my many trips through this stretch of waterway not to shoot so the birds and monkeys, etc., were getting used to me and, as they were an essential part of this grand scenery, I left them undisturbed for the benefit of future visitors. We now entered Azingo and Graham was more than surprised at its singular beauty, especially the clearness of the water which was so transparent that it gave one the impression of sailing through mid-air.

We dropped anchor close in shore and Graham had his first introduction to the Bimvool, the true cannibals of Equatorial Africa. Graham had not talked much during our trip from Nina's to Azingo, only commenting now and then at the lovely changes of scenery, but now being composed, he became entirely himself during our stay. I pointed out the direction of Nina's as we landed and also told him the distance as the crow flies. I had intended, before he came, to take the armed cannibals to the creek and, after stealing the goddess, to make overland to Gaboon, having the cannibals who are splendid fighters as a rear guard to prevent any hostile native who might follow me from coming up until I was safely in Gaboon. But now I had changed my plan and would take her at dead of night to the coast, near Renchoro's place amongst the white Encomis of the coast, as these people would fight for me, Renchoro being their next chief. The white Encomis have never been defeated and are the finest race of natives in Africa, being fearless and straightforward in every way. Graham agreed with me that this was the quickest and safest plan. I told him of a parallel case where one of the guards of the temple had attempted to run away with an Amazon, who are all virgins, and make his way to Gaboon, but had been captured and put to death in a most cruel manner. The punishment for this kind of offense consisting of being tied to two stakes driven firmly in a giant antheap and being slowly eaten up by the insects.... Of course, I said, after we have stolen the goddess we shall have been guilty of the same crime and if caught we shall be treated to the same kind of death, the three of us. At this he smiled and said, If ever this came to pass I wonder what the boys we left at St. Edwards would say, when they heard that you and I had been done to death alongside a goddess we had stolen on the west coast of Africa. What a finale. That we shall have no trouble in carrying her off I am more than certain and if we play the game to its best tune, we shall do it as easily as falling off a log. By the by, said Graham, how did I act my first part in this little act? Splendidly, old boy, I said. Only you were love smitten, I could see by the color of your cheeks and so, for that matter, perhaps was she. You cannot blame me for losing perfect control of myself for a moment, he answered, and is there a man in the world who would not before such a beautiful apparition. I was not prepared for such a surprise and for that sweet voice I shall never forget it if I live a thousand years.

———

"Excuse me, Ma'am, but while waiting for you I've picked up this book of yours lying here. (It was William McFee's *Swallowing the Anchor.*)

"Just cast your eye over this and you'll see what I mean by a proper ending to a book. George Bussey always said the same. 'Tis my own ideas too, woven differently."

I took the book and read the paragraph while Mr. Horn watched me in ferment of excitement at having met a kindred soul—

"For in the meantime the story had grown, had got itself a name; but for lack of a clear perception of that high note upon which we believe a piece of literature should end, it had lain more or less inert. You must get that note or your labor will be drudgery and all your skill of no avail."

I felt once more that pang of regret, grown familiar in the last six months, that a mind so apt in the recognition of the literary instinct should have been wasted: should only at the end of life, and as a means of keeping that flickering flame still alight, be struggling to pour out its long buried repression in an indigestible mass as varied as the romantic conglomerate from under one of our old African wrecks.

"Now, Ma'am, hasn't that feller said just what I've always told you George Bussey used to say? 'Tis a matter of pure selection! You've got hold of the high light all the time or you'd never have the heart to begin a book. But if you let it shine out too early and too strong in the narrative, you're ruining your picture. Keep it subdued until the end, and keep your illumination for that. That's what he means. Aye! That feller knows what he's talking about. 'Tis like listening to George himself. One o' the best ever walked London was George.

"A marriage onboard amongst the seabirds. I've seen it all along. As far as I remember the facts were less romantic. I think they got married on shore at Madeira, though one's memory does take liberties so long ago. But 'twill be near enough to say they were tied in holy matrimony, so-called, by the ship's captain. And no less liable to be holy. A sacred calling, ship's captain. He takes life a bit more seriously—wedding *or* funeral—than one of these professional holy men that'll stare through either a bride or a coffin and not see the human in 'em. There's nothing of the parrot in a good sea captain…. His thoughts have to keep pace with every change of wind.

"A marriage amongst the seabirds. A fresh wind and a sparkling sea, though not rough, and the seabirds mewing all around. That'll take. It's truth plus a bit of seasonable imagination. Aye.

"Peru's ship was taking a deckload of fruit to Johns at Covent Garden. No interest in that but we'll keep it for truth's sake. The

Ruby Queen was classed A-1, for many a year. But Captain King died off the Muni River when his time came.

"I shall have to make somebody give them the loan of a ring. They'd not be able to buy one onboard and we'd no opportunity of getting one on shore, under the circumstances.

'I'll buy thee a Guinea-gold ring——.'

"My voice is a bit shaky today, Ma'am, but I used to be good at ballads when I was young. 'I'll buy thee a Guinea-gold ring.' Gold from Guinea it means. A winning ballad'd make any lad dream of foreign parts.

"'Twas a happy fancy of Peru's to bring his guitar. But poor stuff besides the natural music of those rivers. The harp can speak, when it's all the savage has to let loose the inner man. Aye! The only music in the world that catches the soul of any man that's got one. Speaks with a throb and it's like a weeping in the air.

"A man's charmed as a snake is. His muscles lie still under music and he looks beyond him. If not he's no child of nature. Many's the time I've been played to sleep by my boys on those river banks of mine.

'O those sweet sounds from the sea!'

"That was one of 'em. Bells from the sea. They meant the seamew. Pretty fancy it was.

'*Umbela n'oye me koka ingela*
O me engalingi magan chua.

"Excuse me, my voice is getting thin....

"The beautiful talking of the harps across the water. Coming along with the wind, on the waters of the big Ogowe. Yes, Ma'am....

"Rivers! 'Tis rivers are the friends of the hunter as well as a safe spot for the savage when he's afraid of rocks and shadows. Aye the river's the only safe frontier, if you can't have the sea. A dry frontier's no good unless you've got to deal with gentlemen.

"'Put a ban on the Englishman Horn!' All the cry at onetime on the Belgian border there. Why! That elephant was religiously mine! How was I to know when she went stepping over the border carrying a few of my bullets in her carcass. Do they lay down a tape measure for a boundary line? And if they did is a wounded elephant to respect it?"

ꙅ Chapter XXV. ꙅ

*A*FTER this short conversation, our meal being over, I turned in while Graham took a boy and spent the night fishing. On waking at sun up I found he had gone hunting, and had left a short not for me saying I was sleeping so soundly he did not wish to disturb me. He did not return till nearly sundown. He was accompanied by three of my boys, all hunters, and had seen three gorillas at good shooting distance but did not care to kill any of them as they were having such a royal time turning up stones and playing high jinks. On his return the boys showed him some elephant tracks but it was too late to follow them up. There were quite a host of monkeys and birds of beautiful variegated plumage, all these were strangers to him, nevertheless he had enjoyed himself immensely.

We left Azingo with our tow and were soon through the waterway. We next visited the big lake where he also took my boys and went hunting, but although he saw game galore and a few small gorillas, he refrained from shooting. He was full of compassion and would rather let them live than hurt them.

From here we went to my old friend Efanginango where, after visiting the chief in his town, we slept on the sandbank and so did the old chief. The most delightful place to sleep in is the sandbanks of the Ogowe River. It is cooling and refreshing after the heat of the day, you have a beautiful swim waiting you in the morning, and a good run round the sandbanks to warm you up. A few arm springs and sommersaults thrown in put you fit for a good breakfast and keeps you in the best of health and good humor. Graham was very fond of listening to the stories doled out by the old chiefs and interpreted by me and we usually wound up before sailing with a few songs accompanied by the Spanish guitar. As Graham put it, this was the best amusement to be had in the world and many people who journeyed to the Riviera and passed their time in forming classical mutual admiration societies, etc. would do far better to return to the wilds of primitive man, where all worries were forgotten and man himself felt rejuvenated by becoming a little bit primitive and getting back to nature.

We left Efanginango's place after bidding fond goodbye to the old man and were soon at our chief depot where we delivered the mails and were more than well received by the agent Sinclair. Herr Schiff, of course, had a good share of our visits. The M'pangwe villages were a favorite haunt of Graham, who was always amused by the sayings and doings of the wildest of men, the cannibals of the Ogowe.

Being fully satisfied and happy to continue our trip I now provisioned my boat after having a promise from Sinclair that he would establish a trading post under my boys and old servant Renchoro at his father's town on the sea coast, and I settled up with Renchoro myself, but he still accompanied us along with the rest of my boys and paraphernalia. My curios, etc. had all been shipped to Europe and we bade a fond adieu to the people at Adoninango. We were now on our own, of course, and more than well supplied with all we needed.

During the first night we spent at Efanginango 's we had lots of time to discuss the carrying off of the goddess. Graham was never tired of the theme. The first we did was to see what he had in his baggage. He had really forgotten and it was both laughable and amusing to see what a single man will actually buy for a lady, especially one he has never seen. We turned out all things in succession and had many a laugh. He had engaged his agent to buy these garments in Bond Street, Liverpool. I commended him for his forethought, as the lady they were intended for would have to swim and run to liberty, leaving all her belongings behind. To cap the climax he had some of them neatly marked Mrs. A. A. Horn, thinking of course that these valuable articles of the toilet he had marked would look better with the name of my wife engrained on them. Of course this raised an immediate argument which ran about as follows: What an idea, I said. Don't you think you were rather premature in conjuring up a wedding quite so soon? And to marry me right off the real, oh oh, let us talk it over, in fact let us argue things over as we did in our college days. Let us be boys again.

He rather liked that, he answered, and we would certainly be youngsters again. After all you must have seen some lady in England, who you really could have liked, I put to him. I possibly met many ladies, as regards beauty second to none, leaving out that goddess, whom I only saw once, was his honest reply. Then again, he said, I am a Peruvian and love my native land and all its old time history and am therefore a republican pure and simple. What difference would that make if you were really lovestruck, I said. Your status would have nothing to do with the matter and if the lady felt the same you could not help making a match. True love is as blind as a sand adder. To this he queried, And how are we to know when a lady is love smitten, as you wish to call it? Whoff! What a simple question I said. Why man, she cannot help showing it in some little way.

He laughed but did not venture any farther. I then remarked as regards the goddess, I plainly saw she was temporarily smitten when she first saw you and so were you old boy, so much so I had to give you a touch which brought you to your senses. Here he laughed heartily. Hunting has made you quick-witted, he said, but it was simply being popped face to face with such beauty I could not help it for the moment. Of course not, I said. Quite natural, we are all nature's children after all. By what you have said, he then replied, I am to understand you are not love-smitten as you choose to term it. If I am, I replied, I don't see my way clear to getting married yet awhile. As I have told you, my people are all living and my rambling nature forbids me to fall over head and ears in love at the present time.

If I was to take arms up the river I should merely leave behind me a host of enemies who might forgive me for defending myself against their hostile attacks with intent to pillage, but they could never forgive me for stealing their goddess, whom they firmly believe and trust with the present and future state of their souls. Even as things are it would be dangerous ever to visit this portion of the river again, so that if I succeed in carrying off the lady and giving her the freedom nature meant her to enjoy I shall undoubtedly have closed the river forever against myself.

With this he quite agreed, but if it was a simple matter of funds I could always be certain of his assistance to the end, and this had been his one idea. Without more ado I continued, You remember, Peru, that if we had any problems to settle in our younger days we always settled them by the toss of a coin. Let's leave it to damn fortune to decide who takes her. That is, of course, if she is agreeable to do so. If not, let the lady decide whom she likes best. He sprang to his feet with a loud laugh saying, Don't joke. This is, you probably know, the most important epoch of our lives, and yet you would gamble on an issue of this description. You have not changed one iota since you left me at college. I interrupted him here, Sit down man and be calm. He obeyed me, lighting a cigar and eyeing me intently. I had excited the Inca blood in him. He was thinking, but Indian-like he kept mum. I took a nip of brandy and also lit a cigar and kept mum and also pretended to have dropped the conversation.

This continuing for some time I again broke the monotony by saying, Are you game (this was our old school challenge)? He put out his hand without speaking. Lancashire broker's style. I took it saying, It's a deal, and for my part I think it a fair and square one. After a little thought he said he was forced to agree with me after all.

I now called my faithful boy Renchoro and walking out of hearing with him, I explained matters to him, Of course I said it would be better to get away before sundown as I wished to show him where I intended to land and how the stealing of the goddess was to be done. He smiled largely and said it was a little risky but he would always be with me and was ready at any time. I cautioned him to keep silence among the boys who were not to know anything of course, but they must be sober and if he would see to the cleaning of the guns and giving out of ammunition and get all ready for the journey I would be pleased, as I wanted to take advantage of the dark night, especially as the moon would not rise till early midnight by which time I would have done the deed and we would be far on our way to the sea. Of course Izoga might follow us but he would never come up with us before we entered the big river, that of course depended on how we got on with the job. If we had to fight I said I can give Isoga a better beating than I did when he charged down on my steamboat and he would be very foolish to follow us. He smiled and began to get all things ship shape. I left it all to him.

I now bade a fond adieu to Efanginango and left him well supplied with liquor and he expressed his gratitude. Peru and I had a drink on the success of our venture and telling Renchoro to give the boys a livener, we pulled down the river. I told them the time I expected to reach Nina's place and we were soon gliding downstream. The *ngombi* or native harp was kept going to drive dull care away and we were about the happiest gang of thieves, I said to Peru, as imagination could picture, considering our intent. He laughed and declared what I had said was quite true but he wondered what our old college chums would think if they could see this play being enacted. We passed our time on the trip discussing the future of Peru, which he declared was the richest country in the world in gold, silver, and precious and base metals, and was as healthy a country to live in as you could get. Any climate you could wish for all the year round. We halted at the inlet of Azingo before sundown, where we dined and rested, as we would surely have little or no chance of sleep between Nina's and the sea once we had the goddess onboard.

It was about 8 p.m. when we resumed our journey and we all felt fit for anything. I pulled up at the small island of reeds and landing with Renchoro I showed him the path and likewise where he could hide himself and see and not be seen. I had all these things studied out, the distance to the sacred spring was about half a mile or a little more from the main river. I ordered him to keep the boys from landing and let them know nothing of our intent till they found it all out for themselves. In case of accident of course we knew what to do. He understood what I had said and played his part well. I had explained all to Peru so that he understood exactly his part in this one important act of his life.

On landing we found the place very quiet as they had just had a great ceremony, the invoking of Renungo the rain god, who had finally after much supplication granted their request for early rainfall. Following the sacred chief one by one came the whole male portion of his attendants. They invited us to make ourselves at home and inquired if we had brought the musical box which they would very much like to hear. And Renchoro now appeared with a trayful of rum and Old Dom, about as stupefying a mixture as one could drink, thanks to the advice of my old friend Mr. Schiff. It acted splendidly, but of course he had no idea what I wanted the liquor for. All's fair in love and war, is an old true saying. The musical box was brought in by Renchoro and we were soon having a royal time.

The liquor had its effect, which was marvelous. The man who wore the big goggle-eyed mask and generally stood next to the Isoga was soon more than happy. We let them play away to their heart's content. The old sacred chief and master of ceremonies now asked when we were going to let him have it, as he was sure it contained the music of many friendly spirits. I told him we would leave it till we returned which would be in about twelve days, as we were going to Gaboon on business, and he could tell by that time if the spirits inside the box were to his liking. He felt overjoyed at our generosity and declared that I had already done much good by my visits to the temple as my presents had helped them out very much in their sacred work. I said I was quite willing to lend a helping hand at any time to such a good cause.

At this stage of the play Nina entered looking, if possible, more beautiful than before. I watched her eye the assemblage with a smile, we were all happy and smiling. I gave her the glad eye and then shut one without being noticed, also raised one hand above my head containing a small blue silk handkerchief. She threw me a look I could not mistake and she also touched one eye. She had understood, she was ready any time. I ordered more drinks for the faithful and bade them all a good *au revoir,* telling them I would be sure to call on my return. We now retired leaving the lot merry as sandboys.

Once clear of the place I lost no time. It was dark, only what light the stars gave, and our knowledge of the surroundings guided us as we pulled away without making a single sound, and entering the reeds I jumped ashore. Renchoro took his stand where I had told him, accompanied by ten riflemen. Peru remained in the boat with the remainder, all ready for action on the call of Renchoro. I now crept slowly and noiselessly to the place agreed upon by myself and the goddess. It was so dark I could just see her figure in white sitting on the bank. I threw some mud in the water and waited. I could hear her giving her female attendant orders to fetch something from the meeting house. I heard her maid walk away. Several moments after this the white object hit the water which was deep, making a beautiful dive scarcely audible. I waited quite a few seconds but could see no motion of any kind, but now a slight breathing struck my ear. Her head, which I could now see, quietly disappeared again. I crept to the point and waiting a few seconds out popped the head of the goddess. She held out her arm which I caught and, still crouching, she landed beside me. She took a few breaths for a second or two and quickly came to. She was a splendid diver.

We now crept noiselessly forward, keeping close to the ground and were soon out of danger of anyone seeing us from the other bank of the creek which widened here. I told her to rest a while but she was too excited to understand and was breathing heavily. Springing to her feet she ran for the boat at great speed, waving the stiletto she had drawn from her belt high above her head. I kept close to her. As she reached the rushes she fell heavily, unconscious, dropping the stiletto. I carried her to the boat and gently handed her to Peru, who placed her on the bunk in the small cabin forward. Renchoro and his men quickly boarded and we darted out into the river, heading for the opposite bank where the channel was wider and swifter.

Leaving Nina in the charge of my friend, I kept the night glasses on the mouth of the creek until we were well away past Izoga's town and had also passed into the wide channel of the river. I saw no moving object and heard no sound, and as we moved at great speed downstream which was continually widening I made sail and made sure that no dangerous craft could follow. I was, with sail and paddles working well, the swiftest boat on the river. I felt supremely happy. I had won so far against the terrible despot

Izoga, who I knew would not dare to follow me, and this he well knew even if his people had now been aroused. I told the crew to take things easy and Renchoro to give them each a tot of the best brandy we had, and took one myself on my good luck in having made such an easy capture.

I now went to see how Nina was doing and was surprised to see her asleep in her wet clothes. Do you think she can possibly be dead he said, she has never breathed or moved. What, I said, never? I watched her closely but the light was dim. Anyway I would do my best to restore her. I could not loosen the neck of her dress which was rather too tight round the lower part of her neck, so I pulled our my hunting knife and slit the neck and chest part open so as to give her fresh air, if she was still in a faint. I then gently placed my hand on her heart which was beating away splendidly. I then put my ear close to her head and could hear her breathing quite regularly. Well, I said, what a rumor. She is breathing away quite splendidly, just as you would expect an angel to do, and her heart also is moving splendidly. I am a poor doctor, I said, but you are worse. Her dress was now partially dry so I threw over her a light eider down quilt and we left her in her deep sleep, closed the curtains and joined the crew.

Can we speak now as loud as we like? the boys asked. Yes, but don't wake up all the river, just do as you wish as we shall not stop anywhere till we reach the sea. Renchoro now made up a good lunch for the boys and we all enjoyed it. And we followed this up by tots and smokes. I gave the crew a cigar each and told them to make merry and as long as they did not get drunk, could have all the good liquor they wanted. They had done their part of the carrying off of the goddess in great style and I was proud of them. This greatly pleased them and they commenced to sing in a low voice to the music of the *ngombi*, which sounded lovely on the water.

"I've written a double lot this week, Ma'am, I didn't want to lose my tangent by breaking off. George Bussey used to say the end of a book is the moment of delicacy. It'd never do now to roam away from the tangent.

"So—that'll be a double lot you'll be owing me today. But if next week will suit you better to settle—Excuse me. I know one's purse has moments of vacuum.

"Aye, the finale's the thing. But at all periods of composition you should be able to detract from the subject now and then, George Bussey says. Glance away from it and let the mind float free. Doesn't do just to say 'They were married onboard ship.' To leave out some pretty little vision of the weather and the sea-birds would be to miss out one of the greatest ingredients of life, which is—natural environment.

"Aye, environment. In plain Anglo-Saxon, the place where you live. George Bussey says keep off the long words if you call yourself an Englishman. Well, I'm not asking anything better in the way of environment than the old Ivory. And get your change of outlook in Lancashire. Wherever I've roamed I'll always be content with that.

"India? Do I know India? I've never set foot in it, Ma'am. I should have thought the world as I've seen it was big enough for one book, without India. Not one word can I tell you to increase the sum of human knowledge about India. I'm giving you facts, as they occurred to me. Rightly handled, that'll be enough without…. No, on the subject of India I must remain dumb."

Mr. Horn was hurt and rightly so.

"They tell me there are temples there. But hasn't Africa temples? Didn't I tell you about the one near Georgetown, somewhere opposite Parrot Island? Isn't there Zimbabwe, built by the

Malagassies, a race of close texture with the Hindus, and the Incas of Peru? There's some on the Lake Chad road, too, like that of Georgetown. Who says we've no temples? If the Malagassies didn't get round to build that one at Georgetown then I'd say it was Moorish. Of the time of Boabdil el Chico of Spain after he was chased out by this Ferdinand and Isabella. That feller Washington Irving knows a good bit about Moorish history. An American but a thorough gentleman.

"And if it's temples you're wanting, what about that one I told you is up the S—— river? A flight of steps right up from the river. An amphitheater at the top and big granite squares at the bottom, where you keep cool and look at the water or any sacrifice there may have been.

"Tom C—— and I used to go there for a bit of a rest from the gold. Take a bit of grub and our rifles—you had to be careful in those days when lions were jumping about in bunches up there. Aye, it was a beautiful spot for the imagination. Sure.

"Sheba's country I've heard it called. And some called it the Watch Walls of the Dead. Any amount of graves up there. We'd stumble on them in the thick grass and the bush. Made with a keystone so that no wild beast could rifle them. The contents always crumble when opened. Graves of the gold-seekers, that's what they are. There's always relics of gold-seekers somewhere about. Relics of their toil—old prospectors.

"Zimbabwe's a poor spot compared with that spot up the river where the *quaggas* cried from the walls and played up and down the stairway with their little hoofs echoing. Fierce creatures, but they like to sleep safe from the lions. They must 'a' been doing it for long enough—judging by the thickness of the dung at the top there. Funny echoes there—what with one thing and another. And nothing but the silence to listen to them and shout back at them.

"Only once I've heard sounds of reality there. I was coming up the river and couldn't make out what the cries and the shouting were from the river. 'Twas like the battle of Prestonpans, and I wasn't too well armed. I found out it was a circumcision taking place on the top there. They'd driven all the *quaggas* away. Hordes o' women and some priests or witch doctors making the noise to drown the shrieks of the little boys. A proper pandemonium.

"'Graves of the Gold-Seekers.' A snappy title that, if ever I'd thought to write about them. Look well in print. Oh, aye—don't you go giving out that Africa has no temples! If it's temples you're needing, just stay where you are. There's more than you think. Aye!

"Excuse me sounding somewhat harsh. I sometimes forget you're not my daughter. It's some time since I've had the privilege of pulling someone up a bit. My son's lying over in Mesopotamia there…. Yes, I've got a daughter but I'm not troubling her at present. Oh, aye, she's married. Got her own life to think of. In the States….

"Yes, Ma'am, wanderer though I've been, a wanderer has time when he seeks the common lot. Sailors too, they'll not be content without marriage. 'Tis an instinct universal to worship virginity. Same as they do in the Izoga house. You'd never think such innocence could dwell in a Josh House. But an Izoga goddess must be a maid, same as the Virgin was. It sure is a worldwide instinct to worship a maid.

"Aye, even a sailor knows that. And while he is apt to live according to the dictates of human nature in the exercise of his calling, yet he'll be choosy enough in the matter of a wife. Why? Because all men revere a virgin.

"There's traders too, who have their business in all lonely spots. They couldn't work with a sane mind if they didn't obey nature and accept what she provides. No, Ma'am. I hope I don't debase your mind by any utterance of the truth that's likely to occur to me as notable. The fact is that all men are subject to chance and it's not God, it's only some goll-darned girl that'll ever expect a sailor to have been something less than man in the exercise of his duty.

"Same with traders. I'm saying nothing about missionaries. They generally take a wife with them, by a wise provision of nature. But traders—you may take it from me, Ma'am, that a man who's spent his life in building up commerce and empire in secluded spots of land *or* sea is allowed by Providence a bit more tether than the chap that's living at home next to the Sunday school and doing nothing for his country beyond a bit of insurance agency or selling ladies' stockings. And when he's ready for it, the sacrament of holy marriage to some sensible virgin is going to wash out and purify all his wild doings in foreign parts. Which it might not rightly be expected to do if he'd given way to human nature in Piccadilly or Pimlico. Or Victoria Street, Westminster.

"'Tis not too refined a subject but it needs expression if you can see your way to doing it without offending the American public. They're somewhat more choosy than the English. The *Mayflower's* always been a genteel influence in the pages of History."

❧ Chapter XXVI. ❧

_T_HE WIND now freshened and the first dawn of morning was heralded by the twitter and moving of the birds. We passed Angola and were now heading for the open sea, carried along at top speed by the river breeze which carried us to the mouth of the Ogowe by sunrise. Here we were met by a host of seabirds and other welcome visitors. The change from the river to the sea was delightful and the boat seemed to catch the feeling of those who were aboard her and rode like a duck on the swell, which increased as we neared the ocean. I now peered into the cabin and Nina was still asleep. I pulled the curtain aside so as to give her fresh air. We passed the Vampire Island where we removed our hats, as this was a white man's burial ground. I explained to Peru, but he never knew the real truth, or the goddess either, as to who slept there. I looked at her as she slept. No sculptor could have added to her beauty. Next we were riding the big swells and in less than an hour's time we rode the breakers. Then after a spin through calm waters we entered the beautiful hidden cove near the Whale Rock. This woke her ladyship who, peering out, was surprised to see the beautiful grove on one hand and the ocean to the west.

The seabirds flocked around as I pitched my two camping tents in the shady grove near a beautiful clear spring, and we soon made a home sweet home to be proud of. We all had a good time for the first day and as the spot was charming, we decided to stay for one more day before we sailed for Fernandez Vez, where we were sure to meet passing vessels bound north. The evening was spent in merrymaking during which I thought I would settle once and for all with Nina the question of who she liked best, but to all my questions she insisted on refusing to make a choice. Of course, she said, she loved us both as much as a woman could, especially as we both had risked our lives for her. In fact, she had never dreamed any man would do so much for her and now she felt absolutely free, she would never leave us. I then explained to her that she could choose without choosing and showed her a sovereign. I then called Renchoro and we tossed for coins, sometimes he won, sometimes I won. I then invited her to toss the coin and after a while she managed it quite nicely, but insisted on laughing. But she understood what we were doing. I then told her that this was quite fair and asked her if she was willing to toss for myself and Peru, and of course she would be the wife of whoever won forever. She smiled and said if you two men are willing, so am I. I led her to the campfire and told all hands to form a ring. I also told Peru to come up. I explained to him what was going to happen, and Renchoro explained to the rest. The best eiderdown covers were brought, the lanterns were all lit and the fires replenished, making the old grove look more homelike. Take off your hat and lay it down brother and shake. We shook hands on the deal. I leveled out the sand and handed the gold piece to the smiling goddess of high degree. Your shout, I cried to Peru, are you ready.

Amongst the murmuring and now excited circle of men she tossed up the piece and strange to say it fell in the sand plum up as it could possibly be. No toss, I cried. Peru agreed and she laughed heartily while a murmur of appreciation went round the human ring. I leveled the ground off and this time I padded it well down. She held the coin ready. Your shout, said Peru. I called tails. This time she made a beautiful spin. It fell heads up. Great cheers wrent the air and re-echoed. I pretended to groan and again the noisy merriment went round whilst the lady, who was now leaning on the shoulder of her husband, was all laughter and smiles. Fate, the great master of men's destinies, had decided.

I now shook hands with my best mate on earth and complimented him on his luck. And I could see he felt both grateful and happy. All he said was luck was surely in and I thank dame fortune with all my heart. I ordered the best we had to be brought from the locker and we drank bumpers, one after another, to the success of the happy pair. Music was now king. Nina sang whilst the *ngombi* and harp rang out to the voices of the happiest crowd on earth. We kept going all night and the sun was high when we awoke. We now had a good hearty meal and took our usual swim, whilst Peru's lady took her usual dive higher up the beach with several of the Encomi women who had come in to enjoy the fun. We all dressed our best to celebrate this memorable occasion.

After dinner, Peru and his bride took a stroll, but they had not been long away when the man with the field glasses yelled ship's smoke to the south. I quickly climbed the tree, and there far away southward, I could surely see the smoke of a steamer, but I could not even see the smokestack. She was far away and we would have plenty of time to catch her if we got ready at once. I ordered Renchoro for the last time to make all speed and pack our goods securely and place them where they would be handy for removal should we be fortunate in boarding the steamer. I fired a rifle twice to hasten back Peru and his intended and they came running at top speed, wanting to know what had happened. I told him. He was now all excitement, packing up and leaving the tents standing, after telling Renchoro they were his to keep. We were soon all aboard. After jumping the breakers we quickly set sail, and using both paddles and sail, we were soon in sight of the big boat.

I fired a volley to call their attention and immediately the signal ran up. The vessel was now plainly visible. She had seen us and had changed her course to meet us. I told Renchoro I would leave him the boat and all onboard it, as he had been so faithful to me. I gave him a good hug. He said he would always help me if I ever returned. I thanked him. We were now alongside and all was ready for boarding her. The vessel had now slowed up. I explained who we were and what we needed—Come onboard. I have good accommodations and as I am bound direct for Funchal Maderia, you have just hit me in the right place.

Our luggage was soon aboard. Nina went first and her husband followed. I shouted best luck to my faithful boys who had been with me through many hard scenes. The boat swung clear. And the boys and Renchoro were still waving good luck as long as I could see them. I now joined my friends who were already in their cabin. Peru had engaged the small dining room, smoke room and two best cabins, which were delightfully situated and up-to-date in every way. I went down to make myself known to the captain, who was an old West Coaster. He had seen me before in Gaboon if he remembered rightly, with Captain Thomson of the *Angola*. That was so. He had a good memory and knew all my friends.

Who is that beautiful looking lady we have the pleasure of having as a passenger? he asked. Well, Captain, she will be that fellow's wife as soon as you can marry them. Here he laughed outright. You are surely a Lancashire lad out and out and come to the point at once. I like that, it saves time. We sat down and he was still smiling. I took a French brandy with him and he told me to get ready, it was a lucky event crossing the line, he said. I then saw Peru and Nina and told them. Oh, of course he said if the captain would be so good. I told the old navigator exactly what he had said, word for word. Be so good, why of course, glad to oblige the young gentle-man. A wedding on as soon as you can get ready. The handsome couple who have just arrived onboard. The mate laughed. A table was brought and placed just behind our cabin aft. I told Peru to get ready.

The captain and mate now appeared with the necessary books and pens. I hurried Peru up and he appeared with the bride, who looked her best. They both came up smiling. She wore a necklace of pearls with a beautiful diamond-and-emerald broach. After the necessary documents had been signed, the captain pronounced the words love, honor and obey. I translated for the bride, whose English was rusty, and they answered I will. I signed as witness, the smiling mate followed suit, and it was all over. A legal marriage under the British flag said the good captain. The mewing seabirds circled round and presently the brass bow gun boomed out we were crossing the line. The necessary marriage papers were made out (marriage certificates) and Peru and his lady shook hands with the officers.

I told Peru, who was wearing his best smile, not to forget the crew. Oh, of course not, he said, and handed me a roll of bank notes. You know all about these things so you must help me out. You have done splendidly. I called the captain and frankly told him what Peru had said. Oh, the captain said, it is not really necessary but give what you wish. I handed him a fifty for all hands. Oh no, he said, quite out of the way. Ten will be ample. I made him accept twenty pounds. He called the steward and told him to share it out and he thanked me on behalf of his crew.

We had the wedding breakfast and the good cook had not for-gotten the cake, which we really enjoyed. Peru spent much of his time teaching his wife how to improve her writing and reading and we had many a good laugh at the comical words she would scribble, whilst she thoroughly enjoyed the fun. We had a trip to Madeira, which was always full of enjoyable incidents. We all were sorry when the good ship dropped anchor in Funchal and we had to part with our sailor friends.

The tender came alongside and our luggage was handed out to the representative of Reed's, the principal hotel in those days at Madeira. Here we learnt that an American vessel bound for New Orleans would be due on the following day, and would coal and provision and sail as soon as possible for New Orleans. She was a steamer from Liberia. This was good news for the newly-wed and Peru booked berths for himself and lady. He still was anxious for me to go with him to Peru. This, I told him, was out of the question as I was answering a mother's call. The rest of our time we put in visiting Old Funchal. The American captain was an elderly man. He was a Virginian and came to see us at Reed's. He was a thorough gentleman and one of the most jovial men I ever came in contact with. He took a special delight in seeing his passengers were thoroughly happy, and for wit and humor he was hard to beat.

Peru was busy telegraphing to his guardian and agent and it took him quite a considerable time before he had finished his communications. He explained to me what he intended to do on his return to his home in Lima, and also told me that now he had come of age he had received a thorough statement as to how he stood financially. In fact, he was far richer than ever he had imagined, as since the death of his father his guardian had been very economical and had proved himself to be not only a father to him, but had speculated his interest in sound securities and his interests amounted to several millions. Of course I promised that I would visit him and his wife in Peru, but could not promise to stay with him for good, as I intended, if possible, to do all I could to satisfy my people in business and I had quite a lot to learn before I should feel satisfied that I could help him in any way. Especially in the help he needed, high finance.

Nina would have nothing to do with the ruby, which was very

valuable. In fact, she believed it would be the cause of bad luck if she wore it, as she wanted to forget the life of anxiety she had lived as a goddess. In fact, she begged me to accept the stone and keep it from her sight forever. She was as happy as a woman could be and wanted to forget the days she had spent a sacred prisoner. This, of course, she could forget and she was anxious to see her husband's native land, where she wished to live and die in thorough happiness. We enjoyed our stay in Reed's Hotel Funchal and were loath to part with our kind host. Peru and his wife made a fond good-bye. All the luggage had been removed to the American vessel and as the boat was due to sail in a couple of hours, we got ready for parting. The berths were beautiful and there were few passengers. I carried the private correspondence to be delivered to Peru's agent immediately as I arrive in L'pool.

And now came the time of our parting. The young people took their place aft, close to the American flag. The last whistle now sounded and Peru gave me a rib-breaking squeeze I shall never forget, whilst the lady, his wife, and who knows what her rightful title might be, had her father lived she might have become a duchess or other coroneted person, showered me with hugs and kisses and overcome with emotion she fell in her husband's arms, the silver tears falling as I hurriedly left. On reaching the tender they were cast loose and I waved them adieu as long as I could see them. I felt I had lost my best friends in the world and hoped from my heart that dame fortune, who had linked these two orphans together, would be with them to the end in their home in the valley of the Andes.

———

"Well, Ma'am, the finale at last. Take it inside and go through it. I should like to know what impression it leaves on the reader....

I'm afraid it's not too spotless for you. Feller came in three nights ago, litters the table between our beds all over with his jam tins and bottles, etcetera. Nice young feller, was pretending he was a machine gun one night after the light was off, and in the scrimmage something got turned over, as you see. You can't blame youth for eccentricities.

"That's all right, Ma'am. I'll be all right sitting here with me pipe. There's always thoughts to fall back upon, wherever I find myself. Aye...

"You think it up to the mark? You've been right through it, I suppose? Well, it's a *fait accompli* at last.

"I'm not denying it may differ somewhat from the actual truth of that getaway. But whatever would it have looked like to see 'my friend came over from South America and we managed to abduct George T——'s daughter from the Josh House, after which he married her at Madeira and they took the first available boat to Lima via New Orleans.'

"'Twould never 'a' done. All people like a little levity in literature. If you're going to write a book of the world as it is, you may as well leave levity out. But it'll not sell.

"I can't pretend to know just how much money Peru could lay his hands on. When I say millions I'm simply touching lightly on the fact that his father owned the famous C—— silver mine. Aye, a band of dark blood there is no disgrace. In fact, it's been the making of Peru. Where Spain made a mistake, putting religion aside, was in teaching the Catholic faith wherever she went. The Inca got a notion from the priests that he'd got a soul. Next thing is, he's using that notion to fight Spain with. Pop human equality in a man's mind and it'll work like yeast. It'll give him a faith that'll move mountains bigger than the priests bargained for. Aye, 'twoud 'a' been safer to treat them fairly in money matters and let the human equality go.

"That feller Peru was of good stock. So the marriage was suitable in every way. The way that girl looked at the world! Shops in Madeira and so on and Peru buying as fast as he can for her. Table d'hote at the hotel. Aye, she was all eyes. She hadn't wanted to leave the Coast, but when she did she was happy as a child at a flower show.

"When we first broached the idea of going abroad, she said she only wanted to live at Cape Lopez. 'Twas the only spot she'd ever known of home. 'Take me to Cape Lopes,' she says, 'I want to go to Cape Lopes.' 'Twas where her father had had his store and his rubber sheds.

"That girl had her failings and she must have had her memories. She'd not touch that ruby. It became mine and I made a good bit on it later at Tiffany's, when I heard Peru was to be there to sell it for me. But not so well as I might. It was big but had flaws in it spoilt its value. Still, it'd never do to put that in. Accuracy in money matters is as important in books as in financial circles. The Americans won't look at a book isn't accurate in details. So I've had to name a suitable price for the ruby—I forgot now just what it was I mentioned.

"Oh course I'm not denying I'm more at home on my rivers than chasing after romance. What's this, Ma'am? Let me get my glasses and I'll read it."

At the mention of rivers I had remembered a cutting I had saved for Mr. Horn. Quite early in our partnership I found that suggestive cuttings from the newspapers would often unlock little doors in his memory which otherwise might never have opened. I give the paragraph below.

Madrid: *Sunday*—An expedition headed by General Nuñez Deprado, and including two aviators and a group of engineers, doctors and writers, started from the island of Elobey, off the west coast of Africa for the Spanish territory of Muni on the mainland, to hunt elephants and wild game. They are now about to cross the region of the Benito cataracts, where there are stated to be many herds of gorillas.

It is common talk in the Spanish colony that these animals have a human captive, believed to be a woman, whom they keep in the mountains. The members of the expedition propose to beat the country and scale the hills if necessary in order to rescue the captive.

Natives state that they have heard human voices and signals made from a distance, evidently by some distressed person.

"Why—why, Ma'am—that's my Muni River! My Muni River! Now you see that it's true about my rivers!"

His hands shook and the tears rushed into his eyes.

"My Muni River! It means 'You shake as you dance! You shake as you dance!'

"Haven't I been telling you all this time about it? A river can't keep still, it's so full of falls and cataracts. Right down from the mountains it comes... The dancing river...

'*Mime J'ra Gogo*'....

"I know that far-off place! Excuse me, my voice is a bit thin today...

"They called me River-Hawk up there...

'*Mime J'ra Gogo*'....

"'A young man like me, I'm tired of seeking pleasures that are far, far away!' That's what it means.

"Aye, sometimes I think I'll walk straight out over the veld as the eagle flies and when my legs stop, lie down to a natural end. I'd sooner be picked clean by the vultures than by life in this so-called city. And there'd be no looking back. I'd know better than Lot's wife. No looking back across the plains for me, once safely with my eyes to the blue.

"I know that far-off place. I could take you there, Ma'am. It'd sure impress you. *Ingwe Yani* they used to call me on the Muni River....

"Excuse me laughing at this bit of newspaper rant. A herd of gorillas is what these gentlemen will never see unless they've been drinking somewhat. Families, no herds, is what a gorilla believes in. He's got a man's instinct for a home. He'll not live as if he were in a tenement. No, and he'll not intermarry too closely either. He's a few shades better than a poor white, that'll marry his aunt if she lives next door rather than give himself the trouble to go farther afield for a mate. A gorilla'll visit five colonies in rotation to avoid interbreeding. A regular scientist.

"All this fancy narrative about having a human being captive with them doesn't impress me. A gorilla's not feeling any enthusiasm for the human woman. He'll not look at her. Aye, I know what I'm talking about. When R—— caged up a slave girl with a big gorilla—we'll not mention names—think of his poor relations— there was no mating. Monsieur Jobay, the admiral's son, was a witness and will give evidence of what I say. The monkey sulked in a corner while the poor girl cried herself sick in another corner. Been all the same if she'd been a princess—he wasn't interested. Some of us traders caught R—— and shot him in the early morning. 'Tis such fellers make peaceful penetration a myth. He was no Lancashire man. Came from the south, somewhere near London. They get all sorts there, and more commoners than gentry.

"As for these camera gentry thinking they're going to rescue a human, what a rumor. I'm not denying that the gorilla can imitate the human voice something startling. Who's to say he doesn't forget himself now and again and let out some of his private knowledge all of a sudden? However that may be, 'tis only the old chiefs that make a sound of any importance, and that's the sound that throws all newcomers into a shiver. A yell that you'd never be prepared for in fifty years, and a growl that feels like a tremor you could touch, if you put your hand to the ground. The Dawn-Maker, the natives call him, same as we say chanticleer. They can tell one old chief from another by his voice at dawn and the note of his trooming (drumming).

"Aye, gorillas.... 'Tis Tarzan has set these dagos off. No doubt they'll bribe a native woman to say she'd been captured and rescued, and with a few photos of caged monkeys they'll arrive in Europe with some dandy cinema apparitions of pure unreality. But they'll not see the Muni River as I saw it. No doubt there'll be shocking changes there, same as they say there are even in Lancashire, since the war.

"Lancashire. Angels in heaven are no purer than a lad is when he thinks of his home...

"Aye, what the eye of a boy sees is without par in this life. Without par.... Full o' falls and cataracts dropping down clear from the mountains. A dancing river—you shake as you dance.

"And these fellers think they're first with one o' my rivers.

"I could sing you songs from Muni River still, Ma'am. What you've heard as a lad you don't forget too readily. There's that one that goes '*the voice of the bird has turned the lake to sunshine*—' Wait let me chase the tune of it...

"'*Silver shadows in a yellow moon.*' That was a pretty one on the water too. Twenty singers and harps in a canoe.

"Harps in the Isoga house too—

"The ghosts are listening and etcetera and so forth, and you catch the tinkle of the harps.

"That's how it goes when you're being initiated. Same as any other church. Touch the soul with music and they'll believe the words.

"But it's on the water that they pray the sweetest.

'Spirits inhabit your place in happiness and trouble us not;
'Listen to the words we sing to thee while passing————'

"Their pretty supplications'd sure fetch a god from anywhere, wherever he may be lurking.

"Aye, but they mean it so! Like children calling for someone to answer when the house is too quiet. They fear stillness like all primevals. Nature must 'a smiled when she heard the first harp—whether it might be Orpheus or a Pangwe warrior patrolling his river. How else could she express her pretty thoughts but by bird and man?

"Where they got that heavenly incentive from I don't know. It gets to the core, like Beethoven. And the harps waft the canoes along with the rhythm of it.

"When you see the poor make of white man'd call for benediction, 'tis no wonder if the Great Onlooker is prone to give the blacks an opportunity to make good. Who knows but what he looks to the Ethiopian to give the world another chance? Clever fellers, the West Coast native. Quicker than the Bantu. I've had many a good laugh to see them mimic a Frenchman. Not knowing the words but imitating the sounds and the fancy action of the hands. They could imitate an Englishman or a Norse either. Grunts and a few words. No hand action. They used to mimic de Brazza walking up and down the verandah, thinking and twisting his moustache. A white man's the only man that has to walk to think. It surely strikes a native as comical. Aye, clever—look at my Renchoro—

"Well, Ma'am, I mustn't keep you with my remembrances. There's some'd call me childish, but any writer knows how you've got to keep looking over your shoulder at yesterday. Same as an artist's eye roves over his subject to wring the meaning from it…

"Will it be very long now before the book is in view of the public? Excuse me mentioning it. It's when you're old there seems so little time to wait. Slips come easy when your grasp is gone.

"Well, Ma'am, I must be getting along to goodbye. Or shall I say ta-ta?

"Excuse my jocularity. It's often no more than a bit of armor over the feelings, naturally hidden by every man that knows the pangs of gratitude. Aye, even a dog that gets fierce with hunger and loneliness'll throw you a tender look if you're kind to him. Pariahs have their private feelings.

"You've saved my life this winter, but it's not a subject to dwell on without embarrassment. A warm coat and something to do'll go a long way towards sanity. The hope that comes from a literary horizon is a breed harder to kill than most. George Bussey taught me that when I was a young feller, and now I'm on the allotted age I have no reason to think him mistaken. You have sure spread a blazon of sunshine in an old man's path.

"Aye! And all from the gridiron I was twisting up one Sunday morning in my room, not knowing its peculiar properties. I knew you never wanted it."

FINIS

ABOUT THE AUTHOR

Alfred Aloysius Horn was born in 1854, and as a teenager sailed from the U.K. to Africa where he died in 1927. In between he lived a varied and colorful life. Amongst his many pursuits:

- Ivory trader in Central Africa, journeying into jungles teeming with buffalo, gorillas, and man-eating leopards
- Big game hunter—elephants, lions, and leopards
- Gold and copper prospector
- Scotland Yard detective
- Liberator of an Isorga princess
- Distiller of prickly pear brandy
- Admiral of a cannibal river fleet
- First white man initiated into the Egbo
- Mine-sweeper

He became acquainted with Ulysses S. Grant and Cecil Rhodes, founder of Rhodesia. Later in life, he turned to simpler things and became a gridiron peddler and dealer in literal novelties.

TRAVELERS' TALES
THE SOUL OF TRAVEL

Footsteps Series

THE FIRE NEVER DIES
One Man's Raucous Romp Down the Road of Food, Passion, and Adventure
By Richard Sterling
ISBN 1-885-211-70-8
$14.95

"Sterling's writing is like spit-fire, foursquare and jazzy with crackle...."
—*Kirkus Reviews*

LAST TROUT IN VENICE
The Far-Flung Escapades of an Accidental Adventurer
By Doug Lansky
ISBN 1-885-211-63-5
$14.95

"Traveling with Doug Lansky might result in a considerably shortened life expectancy...but what a way to go." —Tony Wheeler, Lonely Planet Publications

ONE YEAR OFF
Leaving It All Behind for a Round-the-World Journey with Our Children
By David Elliot Cohen
ISBN 1-885-211-65-1
$14.95

A once-in-a-lifetime adventure generously shared.

THE WAY OF THE WANDERER
Discover Your True Self Through Travel
By David Yeadon
ISBN 1-885-211-60-0
$14.95

Experience transformation through travel with this delightful, illustrated collection by award-winning author David Yeadon.

TAKE ME WITH YOU
A Round-the-World Journey to Invite a Stranger Home
By Brad Newsham
ISBN 1-885-211-51-1
$24.00 (cloth)

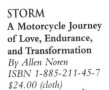

"Newsham is an ideal guide. His journey, at heart, is into humanity." —Pico Iyer, author of *Video Night in Kathmandu*

KITE STRINGS OF THE SOUTHERN CROSS
A Woman's Travel Odyssey
By Laurie Gough
ISBN 1-885-211-54-6
$14.95 —— ✦✦✦ ——

ForeWord Silver Medal Winner
— *Travel Book of the Year*

THE SWORD OF HEAVEN
A Five Continent Odyssey to Save the World
By Mikkel Aaland
ISBN 1-885-211-44-9
$24.00 (cloth)

"Few books capture the soul of the road like *The Sword of Heaven*, a sharp-edged, beautifully rendered memoir that will inspire anyone." —Phil Cousineau, author of *The Art of Pilgrimage*

STORM
A Motorcycle Journey of Love, Endurance, and Transformation
By Allen Noren
ISBN 1-885-211-45-7
$24.00 (cloth)

—— ✦✦✦ ——

ForeWord Gold Medal Winner
— *Travel Book of the Year*

Travelers' Tales Classics

COAST TO COAST
A Journey Across 1950s America
By Jan Morris
ISBN 1-885-211-79-1
$16.95

After reporting on the first Everest ascent in 1953, Morris spent a year journeying by car, train, ship, and aircraft across the United States. In her brilliant prose, Morris records with exuberance and curiosity a time of innocence in the U.S.

TRADER HORN
A Young Man's Astounding Adventures in 19th Century Equatorial Africa
By Alfred Aloysius Horn
ISBN 1-885-211-81-3
$16.95

Here is the stuff of legends —tale of thrills and danger, wild beasts, serpents, and savages. An unforgettable and vivid portrait of a vanished late-19th century Africa.

THE ROYAL ROAD TO ROMANCE
By Richard Halliburton
ISBN 1-885-211-53-8
$14.95

"Laughing at hardships, dreaming of beauty, ardent for adventure, Halliburton has managed to sing into the pages of this glorious book his own exultant spirit of youth and freedom."
— *Chicago Post*

UNBEATEN TRACKS IN JAPAN
By Isabella L. Bird
ISBN 1-885-211-57-0
$14.95

Isabella Bird was one of the most adventurous women travelers of the 19th century with journeys to Tibet, Canada, Korea, Turkey, Hawaii, and Japan. A fascinating read for anyone interested in women's travel, spirituality, and Asian culture.

THE RIVERS RAN EAST
By Leonard Clark
ISBN 1-885-211-66-X
$16.95

Clark is the original Indiana Jones, relaying a breathtaking account of his search for the legendary El Dorado gold in the Amazon.

Travel Humor

NOT SO FUNNY WHEN IT HAPPENED
The Best of Travel Humor and Misadventure
Edited by Tim Cahill
ISBN 1-885-211-55-4
$12.95

Laugh with Bill Bryson, Dave Barry, Anne Lamott, Adair Lara, and many more.

THERE'S NO TOILET PAPER...ON THE ROAD LESS TRAVELED
The Best of Travel Humor and Misadventure
Edited by Doug Lansky
ISBN 1-885-211-27-9
$12.95

★★★—

Humor Book of the Year
— Independent Publisher's Book Award

—★★★—

ForeWord Gold Medal Winner— Humor Book of the Year

LAST TROUT IN VENICE
The Far-Flung Escapades of an Accidental Adventurer
By Doug Lansky
ISBN 1-885-211-63-5
$14.95

"Traveling with Doug Lansky might result in a considerably shortened life expectancy...but what a way to go."
—Tony Wheeler, Lonely Planet Publications

Women's Travel

A WOMAN'S PASSION FOR TRAVEL
More True Stories from A Woman's World
Edited by Marybeth Bond & Pamela Michael
ISBN 1-885-211-36-8
$17.95

"A diverse and gripping series of stories!" —Arlene Blum, author of *Annapurna: A Woman's Place*

A WOMAN'S WORLD
True Stories of Life on the Road
Edited by Marybeth Bond
Introduction by Dervla Murphy
ISBN 1-885-211-06-6
$17.95

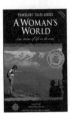

— ★ ★ ★ —

Winner of the Lowell Thomas Award for Best Travel Book— Society of American Travel Writers

WOMEN IN THE WILD
True Stories of Adventure and Connection
Edited by Lucy McCauley
ISBN 1-885-211-21-X
$17.95

"A spiritual, moving, and totally female book to take you around the world and back." —*Mademoiselle*

A MOTHER'S WORLD
Journeys of the Heart
Edited by Marybeth Bond & Pamela Michael
ISBN 1-885-211-26-0
$14.95

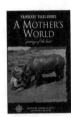

"These stories remind us that motherhood is one of the great unifying forces in the world" —*San Francisco Examiner*

Food

ADVENTURES IN WINE
True Stories of Vineyards and Vintages around the World
Edited by Thom Elkjer
ISBN 1-885-211-80-5
$17.95

Humanity, community, and brotherhood comprise the marvelous virtues of the wine world. This collection toasts the warmth and wonders of this large, extended family in stories by travelers who are wine novices and experts alike.

FOOD (Updated)
A Taste of the Road
Edited by Richard Sterling
Introduction by Margo True
ISBN 1-885-211-77-5
$18.95

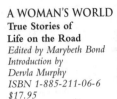

— ★ ★ ★ —

Silver Medal Winner of the Lowell Thomas Award for Best Travel Book— Society of American Travel Writers

HER FORK IN THE ROAD
Women Celebrate Food and Travel
Edited by Lisa Bach
ISBN 1-885-211-71-6
$16.95

A savory sampling of stories by some of the best writers in and out of the food and travel fields.

THE ADVENTURE OF FOOD
True Stories of Eating Everything
Edited by Richard Sterling
ISBN 1-885-211-37-6
$17.95

"These stories are bound to whet appetites for more than food."

—*Publishers Weekly*